The New Democracy

Library of Liberal Thought

Æsthetic
Benedetto Croce
with a new introduction by John McCormick

The Case for Modern Liberalism
Charles Frankel
with a new introduction by Thelma Z. Lavine

Changing Disciplines
John A. Ryle

Congressional Government
Woodrow Wilson
with a new introduction by William F. Connelly, Jr.

Constitutional Government in the United States
Woodrow Wilson
with a new introduction by Sidney A. Pearson, Jr.

The Correspondence of John Stuart Mill and Auguste Comte
Oscar A. Haac, editor

New Deal Days: 1933-1934
Eli Ginzberg

The New Democracy
Walter E. Weyl
with a new introduction by Sidney A. Pearson, Jr.

Party Government
E. E. Schattschneider
with a new introduction by Sidney A. Pearson, Jr.

Peace and War
Robert A. Rubinstein and Mary LeCron Foster, editors

Politics and Administration
Frank J. Goodnow
with a new introduction by John A. Rohr

Politics and Religious Consciousness in America
George Armstrong Kelly

Quest for Equality in Freedom
Francis M. Wilhoit

Tocqueville and American Civilization
Max Lerner

Toward a New Enlightenment
Paul Kurtz

The Transatlantic Persuasion
Robert Kelley

The New Democracy

An Essay on Certain Political and Economic Tendencies in the United States

Walter E. Weyl

With a new introduction by
Sidney A. Pearson, Jr.

Transaction Publishers
New Brunswick (U.S.A.) and London (U.K.)

Originally published in 1912 by The Macmillan Company.

This book is printed on acid-free paper that meets the American National Standard for Permanence of Paper for Printed Library Materials.

Library of Congress Catalog Number: 2004046056
ISBN: 0-7658-0835-8
Printed in the United States of America

Library of Congress Cataloging-in-Publication Data

Weyl, Walter E. (Walter Edward), 1873-1919.
The new democracy : an essay on certain political and economic tendencies in the United States / Walter E. Weyl ; with a new introduction by Sidney A. Pearson, Jr.
p. cm.—(Library of liberal thought)
Originally published: New York : Macmillan, 1912.
Includes bibliographical references and index.
ISBN 0-7658-0835-8 (pbk. : alk. paper)
1. United States—Politics and government. 2. United States—Economic conditions. 3. United States—Social conditions. 4. Democracy—United States—History. 5. Political science—United States—History. I. Title. II. Series.

JK271.W4 2005
320.973—dc22 2004046056

TO

B. P. W.

TABLE OF CONTENTS

TRANSACTION INTRODUCTION

WALTER WEYL: *THE NEW DEMOCRACY*, NATURAL RIGHT, AND THE TRANSFORMATION OF DEMOCRATIC THEORY IN AMERICA*

WHEN Walter Weyl's *The New Democracy* first appeared in 1912 it was widely regarded as one of the most influential works of the Progressive Era. In his memoirs written shortly after his unsuccessful bid for the presidency in 1912, Theodore Roosevelt ranked Weyl and Herbert Croly as the two writers who had most influenced his post-presidential thinking.[1] And Roosevelt's judgment on Weyl's influence was not an isolated opinion. Among contemporaneous reviewers, a critical comment on *The New Democracy* scarcely exists. Yet after his death from cancer in 1919 at age forty-six, Weyl slipped into an obscurity that is undeserved. The influence and political thought of Walter Weyl remain largely unknown and unexplored despite a renewed interest in the political thought of the Progressive Era generally.[2] This neglect is unfortunate. *The New Democracy* is one of the important links in the development of the liberal-progressive theory of democracy that needs to be better understood. Part of understanding the

---

* I would like to thank my friend and colleague Matt Franck for reading this manuscript more often and more carefully than anything other than friendship would merit. He saved me from countless grammatical errors and made helpful suggestions on the substance of my interpretation. Whatever shortcomings remain, however, are entirely my own.

roots of this tradition is to find out what it was about works such as *The New Democracy* that exerted such a powerful appeal at the time and why such works slipped so easily into neglect. Both sides of this question are important in the development of the modern liberal-progressive theory of democracy. For these reasons, Weyl deserves a rediscovery both for the light *The New Democracy* sheds on its own time and as a point of entry into the foundational arguments over twentieth-century American democratic theory.

A discussion of Weyl's work should begin with the observation that much of the revived interest in the political thought of the Progressive Era has its origins in a revived interest in the political science of the American founding. At issue is the apparent break in continuity between the political science of the founders and the very different political science that emerged over the course of the twentieth century. It is an issue that owes a great deal to the German émigré political philosopher Leo Strauss, from a work published in 1953. The unlikely linkage among these three periods, the founding, the Progressive Era, and the present, separated as they are by two hundred years of dramatic change, is itself curious. Strauss noted that whatever the opinions of the American people, American social science had broken decisively with the political science of the founders, especially as that thought was connected to the natural rights argument of the Declaration of Independence.[3] The rejection of natural rights carried with it the implicit rejection of republican government as the founders understood it. He attributed this to the influence of German historicism in the social sciences that made natural law unintelligible. German philosophy had created what Strauss called "the historical sense," or "historicism": the idea that all principles are relative in an evolutionary sense because they are products of a particular time, place, and circumstance. And it is in this context that Weyl emerges as one of the links in the breakdown of the natural rights understanding of the founders. The importance of Weyl is not merely in his rejection of the natural rights tradition, which is common enough in the liberal-progressive tradition, but also the basis of his rejection in a form of an economic methodology that deserves a closer scrutiny, particularly in progressive thought, than it has commonly received.

The Progressive Quarrel with the Founders and Natural Right

The rejection of a natural rights political science in the name of economic determinism was not unique to Weyl. Earlier, J. Allen Smith's *The Spirit of American Government* (1907) had advanced a similar thesis. The best-known Progressive critique of the founders based on an economic analysis was and remains Charles Beard's *An Economic Interpretation of the Constitution of the United States* (1913), which appeared a year after Weyl's work. Beard's work has overshadowed Weyl, but despite surface similarities there are subtle differences that make Weyl's work worth considering independent of Beard. What Weyl brought to the intellectual table was not merely an economic basis of politics, but the methodological tools of an academically trained economist that no other Progressive critic of the founders possessed. Beard, for example, had attacked the motives of the founders: the Constitution, as he interpreted it, was to be read as an anti-democratic document produced by a cabal of aristocrats seeking to protect their own economic interests in chaotic times. Beard read Marxist inspired class-consciousness into the founders' political science that saw natural rights as a smokescreen for the economic calculations of a small elite. This interpretation stands in sharp contrast with Madison who, during the Constitutional Convention debates, acknowledged the rivalry of social classes on economic matters, but denied that America in 1787 remotely resembled the class-based societies of Europe: "...we had not among us those hereditary distinctions of rank which were the great source of the contests in the ancient Government as well as the modern states of Europe, nor those extremes of wealth and poverty which characterize the latter."[4] If Madison was correct regarding the overwhelmingly agrarian nature of American society in 1787, it made Beard's class-consciousness interpretation of the founders' political science an anachronistic reading of *The Federalist*. But it did not necessarily invalidate the idea that American politics since the founders had become corrupted by the emergence of a class-based economic order that made economic inequality one of a hallmarks of the industrial age. Even if Beard was historically wrong, he might still be right in terms of a fundamental understanding of the basis of political action.

What Weyl argued was the notion that democracy itself was to be defined by economic rationality and not political rationality. His thesis was a moral reproach to the founders as well as the additional thesis that politics, or at least the founding principles of American politics, is ultimately driven by economic calculations.[5] History progresses and what was once a tolerably accurate picture of politics may be invalidated by the passage of time and inevitable change. Weyl was influential not merely because he posited economic rationality rather than Nature as a basis for virtually all behavior in politics, but because he was prepared to argue that what the founders regarded as rational in terms of political was superficial at best: that the classical typology of regime analysis in terms of who ruled and to what end was mistaken at the outset because it focused on political equality and not economic equality. In 1787 the distinction did not much matter, but by the twentieth century the distinction had become crucial. In either case, regime analysis was complete once the economic order of society was understood. Who ruled and to what end was a matter of economic calculus and not political theory. The distribution of wealth was *the* fundamental problem of politics and any other questions that might crop up were of secondary importance at best. Rights were not defined by Nature but by human institutions that distributed wealth.

In Weyl's science of democracy, political science was misunderstood economics. This meant, for example, that the entire edifice of the founders' science of politics built on natural right was mistaken in its most fundamental assumption that political equality was the starting point for defining popular government. The founders were not so much venal, as they were for Beard, as seriously mistaken in their science of politics and therefore an unreliable guide. By making economic rationality the basis of democracy, Weyl was led to the idea that political equality was meaningless unless economic equality was also present. In Weyl's analysis, economic equality became the prerequisite for democracy. And it was largely his economic methodology, combined with his critique of the founders' science of politics, that gave him his unique influence in the early liberal-progressive reformulation of American political science. We can see the significance of this change more clearly if we recall the political architecture of the natural rights argument as the founders understood it in contrast to both Beard and Weyl within the liberal-progressive tradition.

The founders' understanding of natural right specifically defended permanent moral principles anchored in a transcendent idea of purpose that could be known in part through reason. That is why the Declaration of Independence speaks of "self-evident Truths" and Hamilton says that republican government is founded on "reflection and choice" (Fed. 1). The founders thought that what they called the "new science of politics" was applicable to all peoples regardless of time, place, or circumstance; they did not, however, think it was adequately understood by all people at all times. Strauss thought that the abandonment of the founders' science of politics was significant because the historicist understanding of politics tended to relegate all traditional political science to obsolescence. And it did so in the name of "progress," which in the Progressive Era was inexorably linked to Darwin. Historicists in the social sciences made all principles, except evolution of course, products of the time, place, and circumstance of a particular historical period. But whereas Darwin struggled with the problem of *telos* or end, when the biological sense of evolution was used in a political sense, as for example in the writings of Woodrow Wilson, it did acquire an implicit *telos*. The liberal-progressive science of politics assumed liberal democracy was at the end of history and the social sciences would be handmaidens of this process. And, perhaps most important for Weyl, economic reasoning provided the tools with which this end could be calculated and achieved.

But economic calculation of the sort Weyl brought to bear on democratic theorizing carried with it a price: the relative certainty of economic calculation required that the relative uncertainty of natural right be excluded from the reasoning process. The objects of economic reasoning required that they be reduced to quantitative analysis that could be expressed in mathematical terms or the methodology would not work. Radical empiricism thus functioned as an intellectual gatekeeper that screened out any reasoning about the ends of political association, such as natural rights, that might not be affected by economic calculation. In this way modern social sciences cut themselves off from classical reasoning as a source for an authoritative interpretation of politics.[6] Thus did a science of politics emerge that was largely in conflict with the most fundamental assumptions of the American founders.

If Strauss is correct in his observation that this break in the social sciences marks a decisive break between the founders and later political thought, one question that naturally arises is, what difference does it make? A number of points might be raised in this context, but in the liberal-progressive tradition of political science the problem of authority as it is linked to purpose is especially affected. Neither the Declaration of Independence, with its natural right basis, nor the Constitution, which is dependent on the Declaration to give it purpose, can provide a source of authority to a science of politics that rejects both. Or to put it another way, when the Declaration or the Constitution are referred to as sources of authority in the liberal-progressive tradition it is with a changed meaning that has little in common with the political science of the authors of those documents. Authority emerges as a problem disguised by the use of similar words that have acquired vastly different meanings. And authority in this tradition is uniquoly dependent on the methodology of political analysis: the focus on means may, at times, overwhelm the importance of ends. It is certainly true that in Weyl's *The New Democracy* the question of political authority in a democracy is conspicuous by its absence. For the founders, authority was found in the political science of the Declaration. But its absence in the liberal-progressive tradition represented by Weyl does not mean that it goes away in reality, but merely that when it resurfaces later it is unlikely to be recognized for what it is.[7]

Weyl's collaborator in the journal *The New Republic*, Walter Lippmann, was quite clear in what was involved in the Progressive Era critique of the founders.[8] In a work that was almost a manifesto of the Progressive Movement, *Drift and Mastery* (1914), he wrote, "...men have to substitute purpose for tradition; and that is, I believe, the profoundest change that has ever taken place in human history."[9] The founders represented tradition and reactionary politics, while the liberal-progressives represented purpose divorced from those traditions. But the achievement of purpose required the exercise of political power and, for intellectuals, power required rationalization. The break meant, among other things, that new methodologies of social analysis would have to be devised since the older approaches ceased to shed light on the present. And the liberal-progressive tradition consciously embraced and promoted the methodologies, in writers such as Beard and Weyl who supported the critique of the founders.

The very language of the liberal-progressive tradition made it easy to define liberals as being in favor of change and conservatives as being opposed to change, and indeed there was some truth to that dichotomy even as the reasoning behind it was obscured. For example, Woodrow Wilson's *Constitutional Government in the United States* (1908) dismissed the founders' science of politics as based on an outmoded and static Newtonian model of science when the modern world was dynamic and answered to Darwinian science. Herbert Croly's *The Promise of American Life* (1909) proclaimed that "[t]he ideal or constructive relation between American nationality and American democracy is in truth equivalent to a new Declaration of Independence."[10] The break was clear and forcefully argued while much of the defense of the founders appeared to be a mere defense of the status quo, independent of the philosophical underpinnings of the founding.

In the case of Weyl, the connection between his break with the founders and his economic rationality can be understood at least in part by pointing out how it was linked to the emerging university system. The Progressive Era was a time when the social sciences took on their modern form in the university, where they were virtually created out of whole cloth.[11] The modern university, of which Weyl was a part during this formative period, fostered and encouraged specialization in the social sciences; what had been a more unified science of politics for the American founders was compartmentalized in the new university system. Scholars became specialists in history, economics, political science, sociology, and the like. Specialization, in turn, tended to produce specialized methodologies for each particular branch of the social sciences that did not easily lend themselves to other branches. One consequence was that it became increasingly difficult for scholars in one field to read the advanced works in another field and many stopped even trying to do so. Authority in such an environment tends to be conferred on elites who possess a specialized knowledge of specific subjects. And the authority is enhanced the less outsiders are able to understand its core assumptions inherent in the methodology. There seems to be little doubt that Weyl's influence among his contemporaries was a product of this newly minted academic authority.

With few exceptions, the pattern of post-Civil War American academic development followed the German model of a university system. Further, the method of inquiry into political-social subjects was heavily influenced by German historical and philosophical scholarship that rejected natural law as a basis for political inquiry. Congruence between these two developments is not causality, of course, but in this case the congruence helped to foster the intellectual climate and institutional base in which an academic elite converged on a "new" new science of politics to replace the founding American model of democracy. In the process of analysis and articulation, democracy came to be defined less and less by statesmen, or at least practicing politicians, and more and more by academics with little or no practical experience in politics. Abstract reasoning rather than prudential judgment became the basis for the emerging critique of the founders. And because the founders were practical men rather than philosophers, it was not difficult for academic rationalists to find holes in their practical arguments derived from natural right reasoning. Natural right political science was merely one school of thought among others and with less methodological precision than newer models. This was the intellectual milieu of the university system in which Weyl studied.

German scholarship decisively rejected natural right as a basis for political inquiry and American academics followed suit, although the rejection in the American context had different consequences than it did for German scholarship.[12] The American regime was founded on a specific, well-articulated natural rights science of politics reflected in a constitutional system that could not escape the focused attention of critics of that system. The rejection of natural rights in the American academy occurred across the newly formed academic disciplines: political science, history, sociology, and economics were all affected in various ways. Academic political science during this period is a case in point. John W. Burgess, one of the influential founders of American political science as a social science in this period, wrote in the inaugural edition of the *Political Science Quarterly*, a journal he helped to found in 1886, that reference to the Constitution and the founding principles of the regime was the "great fetish" of American politics: "every student of political and legal science should divest himself, at the outset, of this pernicious doctrine of natural rights."[13] The break as well as the strategic position in academia of the emerging social sciences altered the way subsequent generations have been taught to conceptualize the very nature of democracy. The prolific academic scholarship in the Progressive tradition has become the primary filter through which the American founders came to be understood and interpreted long after the roots of the methodological revolt had been forgotten. When seen in this way, there is a sense in which we may say that we want to understand the progressive-liberal tradition because writers such as Weyl seem to stand in the way of our understanding of the founders. The founders' science of politics has been lacquered over with successive coats of finely brushed arguments that had their American origins in Progressive Era.

The Progressives were well aware of a tension between the common perception of a natural rights grounding and their own more secular basis of the regime principles. What is significant for an understanding of Weyl's place in this emerging social science of democracy is his conscious rejection of both natural rights and religious foundations of American democracy. The new breed of scholars did not follow either a Jeffersonian grounding of rights in the natural rights arguments of Locke or the biblical grounding of popular perception. But in Weyl's case it must also be said that he sensed the loss of transcendent purpose in his definition of American democracy and that loss haunted almost all of his writing.

The analysis of democracy in Progressive scholarship not only altered the basis of democratic political theory, but it also managed to create an economic model of the American citizen that was only partly connected with reality. For example, America remains perhaps the most religious country in the Western world, and it has been through that religious connection that most citizens identify both their rights and their sense of the Declaration and the Constitution as the authoritative basis of their political rights. While it is true that the Declaration of Independence is not sectarian in its inspiration, it is also true that most Americans have not found it incompatible with religion—nor did the founders. In terms of authority as an issue in any political system, the Declaration fit comfortably with both natural rights and religion in American society.[14] The more secular basis of regime analysis in Weyl is in turn based on an analysis that seems incomplete on the face of it. It is to Weyl's credit that he sensed the loss and instinctively understood that it made authority more problematic than in the founders' political science. But he did not seem to grasp how it could become the Achilles heel of the liberal-progressive science of politics.

The Origins of *The New Democracy*

One reason Weyl was often overlooked during the Progressive Era is because of the company he kept. In retrospect, Walter Weyl looks like the junior partner in the establishment of perhaps the single most influential political journal in the liberal-progressive tradition, *The New Republic*. In 1914 Herbert Croly, with the financial backing of Willard Straight, a banker with J. P. Morgan, and Straight's wife Dorothy, an heir to the Standard Oil fortune, founded the journal that was intended to be a popular organ for the promulgation of the liberal-progressive voice in politics. To assist him with this venture, Croly recruited Walter Lippmann and Walter Weyl as co-founding editors of the journal. Both Croly and Lippmann have attracted more scholarly attention over the years than Weyl. Even Weyl at the time regarded Croly's *The Promise of American Life* as the standard by which the emerging liberal-progressive science of politics, including his own work, was to be measured. Ironically, perhaps, Croly regarded Weyl as the standard by which scholarship in the progressive cause would henceforth be measured.

At the time the partnership was formed, Herbert Croly was the best known of the three. Lippmann was well known both among progressives and to the broader public, but was not yet the journalistic icon that he was later to become. Weyl seemed like a brilliant specialist out of place among the other generalists. But the original editorial organization of the fledgling journal was pretty loose and none of the original editors could truthfully say which one was more influential is shaping the editorial policy: each contributed a distinct personality and line of argument that complemented the others. Although they eventually fell out with each other over the Wilson administration's handling of the Great War and its aftermath, there was initially a broad-based agreement among them over domestic policy concerns and priorities. Indeed, it was Weyl's articulation of these objectives in *The New Democracy* that made him seem to be such a natural fit at *The New Republic*.[15] Among the popular writers who thought of themselves as "liberals" and "progressives," Weyl was deemed "essential" to the fledgling publication because, as Lippmann put it, "He was by far the best trained economist in the progressive movement. He was the only active Bull Moose I ever knew who thought the Progressive program could be justified by statistics of the social facts as well as by moral denunciation."[16]

Weyl was an academic prodigy, much like Lippmann but with a more scholarly background. Born in 1873, he entered high school at age thirteen. Three years later he received a scholarship at the University of Pennsylvania's Wharton School of Commerce and Finance where he entered directly as a junior in 1890. His primary interests were politics and, above all, economics, where he was much influenced by Simon Patten, at the time perhaps second only to Thorstein Veblen as the most influential American academic economist. Neither philosophy nor religion seems to have interested Weyl at all and a student colleague later wrote, "He was almost impervious to the religious idea. He did not admire either the Hebrew religion or its descendant, Christianity."[17] The closest he came to expressing an opinion about philosophy in a formal sense was his approval of William James' secular pragmatism precisely because it rejected moral absolutes, and because, after all, as he put it, "...what have the Cosmic Verities ever done for me."[18] After graduation Weyl spent a brief period studying law, which he despised, before Patten saved him from that unpleasant toil and tried to direct him toward graduate school in economics. Patten wanted Weyl to take a Ph.D. at the Wharton School, but Weyl was more interested in an adventure abroad and Patten encouraged him to study in Germany. Patten had studied at Halle, Germany, some seventeen years earlier and returned home inspired, as he put it, "to help in the transformation of American civilization from an English to a German basis."[19] He hoped Weyl would follow him in this regard but Patten remained far more of a Germanophile than Weyl ever became.

On the strength of Patten's recommendation, Weyl went to Halle for a year and then transferred to the University of Berlin where he spent two additional years of intermittent study, neither of which resulted in a degree. During his sojourn abroad he also studied briefly in Paris and London, but it was the German experience that most impressed him, though he did not return as the prophet of German *Kultur* that Patten had hoped for. Nevertheless he retained a definite sympathy for German culture that Croly and Lippmann, for example, never shared. In particular he seems to have developed an instinct for the German conception of "organic law" as the basis for national political development over the American understanding of natural right. Upon returning to the United States in 1896 he finally entered the doctoral program at the Wharton School under the sponsorship of Patten and graduated a year later with a specialized interest in labor economics. Although Weyl was an early product of the new university system, he did not pursue a career in academics as his mentor Patten encouraged him to do. Instead, he worked for a while with the Bureau of Statistics in Washington, D.C., and later with the Treasury Department. Government work was in many ways a natural fit for Weyl at this time in his life: in a display of intellectual epiphany that probably only an economist could experience, he once said that was his favorite "literary work" was the *United States Census Report*.[20]

The problem of labor and capital was, in many respects, the heart of the policy problem for the Progressive science of politics, and this was certainly true for Weyl. Almost all roads to liberal-progressive reform seemed to end at this one destination. The practical problem, which was also a theoretical problem, was how to construct a science of politics that concentrated power to solve political problems. The separation of powers in the founders' constitution was an insuperable obstacle to purposeful policy government. All of the reformers in the liberal-progressive tradition saw the problem in political terms and understood the economic link, but lacked the intellectual tools to create a non-Marxist economic argument for democracy based on economic analysis. It was Weyl's contribution that he brought together in *The New Democracy* the diverse strands of political thought in the Progressive Era and articulated the paradigmatic character of the movement as a whole in economic terms. In Lippmann's words, Weyl and Croly are to be credited for "gathering up the loose ends of the muckraking era and turning them to constructive use."[21] Economics may have remained the "dismal science," but in the hands of a writer like Weyl it was rendered less dismal than it might otherwise be. He had absolute faith in the faculty of economic reasoning to yield a coherent and complete worldview that would defend democracy. Yet the facts of his economic analysis also undermined his innate optimism. In his doctoral dissertation he hoped to prove that the reduction of railroad passenger rates would stimulate passenger use, in much the same way lowering of postage rates had stimulated mail usage. Unfortunately for his theory, he was forced to conclude that lower rates were not the only, or even the most important, way to encourage railroad travel.[22] Later, in *The New Democracy*, he remained sensitive to the need to mesh economic analysis in a way that hard facts would not contradict broad democratic theory.

Weyl left Patten and the Wharton School with a faith in the faculty of economic reasoning to yield a complete and coherent worldview that would defend democracy on more solid grounds than anything heretofore attempted. Weyl, like most rationalists, was optimistic about progress. After all, economic reasoning was itself a manifestation of rational progress. But Weyl's pragmatism, like that of James, masked a passion for justice that was not derived from the study of economics. One of his student friends at the University of Pennsylvania later wrote of him, "The motive of his vision was an unwavering faith in the dignity of man, the spontaneity and ethical beauty of individual life. He sought to know the material forces chiefly in order to master and control them, to put them into the service of a better humanity."[23] And another close friend pointedly noted, "To him radicalism was not merely the name for a method but the name for a faith, the faith in a new social order, a new democracy, a new republic."[24] Weyl was passionately convinced of the power of ideas to change the world for the better and was equally convinced that economic rationality would ultimately prevail; untenable theories would melt before the hard facts, just as his own theories of railroad rates had melted before the hard facts of economics. The logic of economic analysis would obviate any concern about the motives of such rationalists because they would change their theories to conform to the facts once the facts became known. Weyl was described as having the moral passion of an Old Testament prophet, but with a copy of the *United States Census Report* under his arm instead of the Torah.

Weyl impressed all who knew him as a brilliant and committed economist. But what perhaps distinguished him from more academic economists was his passionate commitment to putting economic knowledge in the service of the liberal-progressive political agenda. Eventually this meant a more radical commitment to a form of socialism than that offered by *The New Republic*. He chafed under the journal's editorial policy that made it virtually the house organ of the Wilson administration, especially during the war.[25] Eventually he thought that first Roosevelt and then Wilson had betrayed the promise of liberal-progressivism by acting too timidly in the face of what he regarded as the crisis of American democracy—its inability to solve the problem of poverty. "That economic determinism is basic he was certain; that economic forces and their responsive human instincts are susceptible to mastery by the concerted will of mankind he was equally certain."[26] It was this sense of the power of economic forces to make and remake the political world that eventually pushed Weyl toward a socialism that he barely repressed in *The New Democracy*.

It was Weyl's commitment to economic rationalism and the methodology of economic analysis that also pushed him toward an increase in state power to solve the paradoxical problem of material want in the midst of plenty. Concentrated political power was inseparable from socialism. The solution could not be found in a democratic system that made political freedom the sole basis of liberal democracy. It was an odd, but perhaps logical, combination of innate optimism and economic fatalism that informed Weyl's democratic theory. While Simon Patten may have been his favorite living economist, his favorite all-time economist was Thomas Malthus. The reason behind his interest in Malthus was the economic power of his "Essay on the Principle of Population." According to Malthus, the "iron law" of economic reasoning was the clash between steady population growth and finite agricultural resources. The clash between people and their basic needs was inevitable, and it was this clash that helped to make economics the "dismal science." Sooner or later the immovable object of scarce resources would meet the irresistible force of population and the result would be disaster at best and perhaps war at worst. And a Darwinian survival of the fittest was little comfort to a man such as Weyl. Woodrow Wilson could make Darwinian evolution the optimistic basis for a more scientific political science if he wanted to, but economists dealt with hard reality, and for Weyl this "iron law" described by Malthus was the hardest reality of all. Facts could not be banished: they had to be confronted. But how? Economics foresaw the problem, but could it provide a solution? *The New Democracy* was the first work in the liberal-progressive cannon of political-economic analysis to try to find a way out of this apparent conundrum.

The New Democracy and the Problem of the Founding

The New Democracy begins with the arresting chapter title, "The Disenchantment of America." It reflects a common theme of the Progressive Era: something has gone wrong with the founders' political architecture. Beginning with Woodrow Wilson's *Congressional Government* in 1885, the critique of the founders' natural rights accepted as an axiom of politics that the American founders are no longer the primary teachers of the science of democracy. Europe has effectively surpassed us and if we want further to develop as a democracy it will be necessary to go to school abroad: "According to some critics," Weyl wrote, "American democracy is in process of decay."[27] The reasons cited by Weyl seem to echo Frederick Jackson Turner's frontier thesis, first promulgated in 1893, that the end of the American frontier had changed the American character. But while Weyl may have borrowed from Turner's thesis, he added to this account what he took to be the economic consequences of this momentous reality. According to Weyl, this meant the end of bountiful natural resources and, ominously, that the great national vacation from the iron laws of Malthusian economic determinism was coming to an end. The problem was that while the economic reality had changed, or had at least finally become evident, the earlier individualist psychology of freedom and abundance that was a hallmark of the founding remained. The conflict was between a political theory that did not know Malthus and was therefore was no longer viable and an economic reality that could not be changed: it defined the present and future challenge of all democracy, but of American democracy in particular.

While the reality is economic in essence, confronting it is a political problem, expressed in the now hollow meaning of "unalienable rights." In the face of unemployment and economic want, these political rights have become virtually meaningless. But in this moment of crisis there is a ray of hope, "when men are beginning to doubt the all-efficiency of our old time democracy, that a new democracy is born. It is a new spirit, critical, concrete, insurgent."[28] Weyl presents it as a dialectical unfolding of a new spirit that is gradually replacing the founding spirit. It is a spirit that Weyl sees as replacing the religious spirit of Protestantism that has driven American sef-understanding since the first colonies: "Protestantism, too, was at first protesting, insurgent, negative, but Protestantism to-day is positive, plenary, and protested against. So our nascent, insurgent, still unfolded democracy, which unites many men in a common hostility to certain broad economic and political developments, is now passing over to a definite constructive program."[29] A political superstructure not grounded in economic reality cannot long endure because reality will eventually overwhelm vacuous theory. "Our newer democracy demands, not that the people forever conform to a rigid, hard-changing Constitution, but that the Constitution change to conform to the people. The Constitution of the United States is the political wisdom of dead America."[30]

The democracy of the founding is what Weyl calls a "shadow democracy." That is to say, it was not really a democracy at all, either in theory or practice: "America in 1776 was not a democracy. It was not even a democracy on paper. It was at best a shadow-democracy."[31] In Weyl's retelling of the American founding, the democracy of the Declaration is, at best, a mythic reconstruction by later generations who understand that something has gone radically wrong with the practice of politics in America: they wrongly imagine a golden past when the theory and practice of democracy were somehow united in the Declaration and the Constitution. It is an illusion that makes it all the more difficult to understand the present forces of the new democracy. "The Declaration of Independence was not an organic law, but an appeal...to the 'natural right' of revolution." Further, Weyl denies that average Americans in fact believed these ideas, because they knew full well that the "better class," those who actually wrote the Constitution and laws of the new nation, did not believe them. The Constitution was, in fact, designed as an anti-democratic document that Weyl characterizes as "reactionary" in principle. "The founders of the Republic, be it remembered, were not quiet old gentlemen in stocks... They were a very human lot of people who, liking to win, were not over nice as to means."[32] Sharp social distinctions remained that made political equality more of a theory than a reality. True democracy is dependent on social equality, and social equality is in turn dependent upon economic equality.

The great merit, and the greatest defect of the Constitution, is that it has survived into the twentieth century.

Following Jefferson, but apparently unaware of Madison's critique of Jefferson on this point, Weyl thinks that it might be well if the American people would recast their Constitution every generation.[33] That the Constitution worked with some degree of democratic spirit "is due less to its intrinsic merits, or the genius of Hamilton and Madison, than to the moderation and political tolerance of succeeding generations of Americans, and to a subsequent rising tide of democracy which has liberalized our organic law, overborne it, or evaded it."[34] Evading the formal strictures of the Constitution was a prerequisite for the growth of democracy.

From an historical perspective Weyl believes that the conquest of the continent took precedence over democracy because the conquest reflected the primordial economic basis of society. Despite the moral fervor of Weyl's critique of the founding, there is also the air of non-judgmental scholarship in that critique. The founders were merely following their natural economic instincts. Even the pioneers in their conquest of the frontier, whom he likened to the "Barbarians which [sic] overturned Rome," were merely acting out their economically predetermined part in the development toward true democracy. The experience with the frontier fostered an individualism that was "self-confident, short-sighted, lawless, doomed in the end to defeat itself, as the boundless opportunities which gave it birth became at last circumscribed." Life in this state of American nature was very much a survival of the fittest in which the robber barons of industry had the upper hand. In turn, these captains of industry corrupted the political process to further their economic ends. Innate American individualism made it difficult to criticize the robber barons because they were, for the most part, merely the American character writ large. And it was this character of intense individualism, born of the frontier experience, that corrupted true democracy. Properly understood, democracy is more communal than individual in its ethos. But, Weyl noted, the individualistic character he deplored was also rooted in the English tradition of the founders as a whole. "Had America been settled by Laplanders, equatorial Negroes, Spaniards, Venetians, or Greeks, our civilization would have developed differently... The roots of these men's characters ran deep into the soil of dead centuries."[35]

Unrestrained capitalism in America, defended in the language of the Declaration, eventually undermined the political rights found in the Declaration. Ultimately, it could not have been otherwise: political rights were built on intellectual quicksand and were revealed as such once economic development revealed its natural character. "The individualist could no longer rely upon his automatic 'unalienable rights' and his fair field and no favor."[36] The protection of property rights, for example, the mainstay of Lockean natural rights, had created a social inequality built on a vastly unequal distribution of economic wealth. We can see the true economic basis of the founders' science of politics more clearly if we restore the original Lockean language. Stripped of Jeffersonian euphemisms, the true principles of the founders' political science of "sacred rights were life, liberty, and property, and the greatest of these was property."[37] The protection of property is the key to understanding the founders' distrust of democracy. It led them to create a system in which the concentration of power was difficult. A true democracy would never make the protection of property the basis of government because the natural consequence would be both economic and social inequality. And to protect the unequal distribution of property it was necessary to construct a weak system of government: "The political philosophy of the 'Fathers' might have been summed up in the phrase 'the less government the better.'"[38] This was the key to understanding the feeble powers of the national government. In a state divided against itself, the individual flourished and the government became a kind of machine that would run itself without central direction.

All of this resulted in the liberal-progressive thesis that the regime had in fact become a plutocracy, whatever it may have been intended in theory. Weyl was not breaking new ground on this point, but he did link the plutocracy to politics in ways that were novel. The plutocracy, Weyl thought, did not rule directly, but rather through the corruption of the representative process: it bought politicians wholesale. When the plutocracy did enter politics, it was as special interest intent on thwarting democracy. It was not, as Madison had argued in Federalist 10, one of a multitude of diverse factions competing in the public square: it was outside the boundary of a legitimate democratic theory. The bond formed between the businessman and the politician "is the nexus of political interest."[39] But the plutocracy spawned its own reaction: this time, a democratic reaction that came from the growth of the city.

The role of the city was an example of how Weyl synthesized the work of others and brought it into his larger picture of economic determinism. Lincoln Steffens had brought the plight of the cities to the attention of reformers with his *The Shame of the Cities* (1904), but he was pessimistic that much would in fact be done. Frederic Howe's well-received work, *The City: The Hope of Democracy* (1905), was perhaps more optimistic, but it lacked the punch of economic analysis and optimistic economic determinism as to the eventual outcome that Weyl could provide. "The American city, destined to become the leader in our new democracy, had suffered most grievously from the spirit of the conquest."[40] The city was the place in American life that experienced the growth of the slum, a social phenomenon unknown in the revolutionary era. And it was in dealing with this new development that European democracies proved superior to the American system of fragmented power. What gave Weyl hope that the problems of the city could be solved was the experience of war.

The Civil War drowned out the nascent reform movement of the early industrialization, but the war had consolidated national power, at least temporarily, and demonstrated the efficacy of nationalism in the consolidation of power to deal with the problems of the city. In turn, this appeal to nationalism as a means to consolidate power provided Weyl and others at *The New Republic* with a rationale to initially support Teddy Roosevelt's "New Nationalism" over Woodrow Wilson's "New Freedom." Nationalism was the foundation for an appeal to consolidate power to make policy. What seemed most significant to Weyl and others at the time was the realization that the source and inspiration for the consolidation of power seemed to come from outside the constitutional system itself. This promised a way to break the constitutional deadlock of the separation of powers and federalism that checked unified policymaking at the national level. It promised a solution to the problem of fragmented power in the Constitution.

The New Democracy and the New Solution to the Problem of the Founding

Reforming the political system by constitutional amendment was, for Weyl, close to impossible. Only a complete starting over, this time on the basis of a true science of democracy, would suffice. "Our hand is stayed by ancient political ideas which still cumber our modern brains; by political heirlooms of revered—but dead—ancestors. Between us and it, the plutocracy thrusts the Constitution of the United States." It is the most undemocratic feature of the American system. The problem is not that the meaning of the Constitution is fixed in the founders' science of politics, however erroneously they may have supposed that its political principles were eternal: the Constitution is amended daily by the process of interpretation. But the actual as opposed to the theoretical interpretation is not through democratic means. "The Chief Justice of the United States is responsible to God and his conscience (as is the Czar of Russia), but he is not responsible to the ninety million people."[41] And while the Supreme Court has come under some of the influences of the new democratic spirit, "it has not so democratized our Constitution as to render possible the carrying out of necessary measures of political and social reform which other nations have adopted."[42] Changing the reactionary nature of the judicial system would require the creation of some stronger popular check, formal or informal, upon the power of the federal courts. The complexity of the institutional checks and balances makes it unlikely that popular control can be effectively exercised through the representative system. Where then will the check be found? Again, the answer will have to be the hard economic reality that has come with the end of the frontier mentality.

The plutocracy that actually runs the country believes in increased economic efficiency and national productivity. And it is true that the plutocracy has increased economic efficiency and created greater national wealth. But who gets the prosperity? National wealth has come to be concentrated in a few hands, which has in turn produced the economic inequalities so evident in the great cities. The natural consequence of these inequalities in the distribution of wealth has led to a widespread desire not for wealth in terms of national income, "but for more economic satisfaction, more widely distributed." The new economic thought emphasizes not toil, "but economic pleasures and satisfaction." As Weyl puts it, "The Achilles-heel of the Plutocratic Economy...is this individualistic and objective conception of wealth."[43] For the individual, the accumulation of wealth without concern for distribution is legitimate. But for the nation it is self-destructive because it merely supports the status quo in a kind of perverse survival of the fittest. This is where the plutocracy proves to be weaker than most reformers think.

Collectively the new democracy uses the plutocracy's economic efficiency in a new sense. "Where the plutocracy means the greatest wealth, the democracy means the widest range of economic satisfactions." Public opinion in the new democracy does not define wealth in the same way as the individualists in the plutocracy. "The democracy interprets utilization as such a production, distribution, and consumption of wealth as will give the highest excess of economic pleasure over economic pain to the largest number of people for the longest possible time. Upon this end all the industrial, political, social, and ethical ideals of the democracy converge"[44] A class conflict naturally has grown out of these economic conditions. The plutocrats are not wicked men, but what is perhaps more significant, they are economically obsolete.[45] The plutocracy, which denies the very possibility of a democratic revolution, makes it inevitable by furnishing a common point of attack to diverse assailants. Thus the pressure of public opinion, despite its essentially fragmented nature, converges on a single point of attack. Economic determinism virtually guarantees it, and although it might be thwarted or misdirected from time to time, it is relentless and the very growth of the economy ensures that it will not disappear but only grow stronger.

While hard economic reality is forcing Americans to look at their country and their political system in new ways, the average American is having difficulty articulating a new philosophy. This is the task of the reformer: to mobilize the masses and give them a voice grounded in reason. "To-day no democracy is possible in America except a socialized democracy.... All the inspiring texts of democracy fall into nonsense or worse when given a strict individualistic interpretation. 'Government should rest on the consent of the governed' is a great political truth, if by 'the governed' is meant the whole people, or an effective majority of the people; but if each individual governed retains the right at all times to withhold his consent, government as a social union becomes impossible.... In the socialized democracy toward which we are moving, all these conceptions will fall to the ground."[46] The reformer is the intellectual who has mastered the tools of specialized economic analysis, exposed the fallacies of the existing system, and can in turn promote the true conception of reality in a way the ordinary citizen can understand.

Ultimately we can know the shape of the new democracy because economic laws cannot be repealed or ignored, as can the natural rights theories of the founders. "In two respects, the democracy toward which we are striving differs from that of today. Firstly, the democracy of to-morrow, being real and not merely formal democracy, does not content itself with the mere right to vote, with political immunities, and generalizations about the rights of men. Secondly, it is plenary, socialized democracy, emphasizing social rather than merely individual aims, and carrying over its ideals from the political into the industrial and social fields."[47] The revolution is comparable, Weyl thinks, to the English Protestant Revolution and the French Revolution that earlier drove James II and Louis XVI from their thrones. If anything, the new democratic revolution is more profound because its stirs more men and stirs men more deeply. "Like other revolutions, it is simply a quicker turn of the wheel *in the direction in which the wheel is already turning*."[48] And most of the new revolutionaries do not even know they are revolutionaries, a factor that gives it an essentially conservative character, unlike the violent class-war revolution of Marxism that he rejected.

His critique of Marxism is revealing because it suggests both the strengths and the weaknesses of Weyl's economic analysis of democracy. However much Weyl's economic determinism pointed him toward some sort of socialism and egalitarianism, he rejected the Marxist version of economic determinism, largely because it rested on the idea of class war. Marxist socialism is what he called "absolute socialism," to distinguish it from the "Utopian socialism" that preceded it and the "conditional socialism" toward which the new democracy is moving. Conditional socialism is scientific because it is "buttressed through...reasoning from science" whereas "absolute socialism remained in its appeal essentially religious."[49] Unlike Marx's predictions, the masses of workers are not becoming poorer: real wages are rising and factory conditions have improved. "In countries where there are income tax figures, a progressive diffusion of wealth can be statistically shown."[50] The hope of society in Weyl's economic determinism lies not in the oppression of men to the verge of revolt, but in the continuous elimination of such oppression. Conditional socialism in Weyl's version is to be pragmatic, whereas Marx's socialism is dogmatic. Marxists made the appropriation of property an absolute right of the proletariat based on the iron laws of history, whereas for Weyl the "whole problem of distribution ceases to be one of absolute right and becomes one of relative utility."[51]

It is at the point of economic utility that Weyl made the transition from political analysis to political prescription. It is what made his work simultaneously so attractive in his own day and seemingly so dated a few years later. Yet, even in the evanescence of his proposals, there are a number of prescient observations on the evolution of the American economy and how it has affected society as a whole. Weyl's work also pointed to a way out of the seeming impasse of the modern state: "Opposed to the theory that democracy is to be attained through class war is the theory that the attainment of democracy will result from national adjustment. Opposed to the theory of democratic progress through impoverishment is the theory of progress through prosperity."[52] That he was able to link economic progress to a Malthusian economics is a testament to the creativity and power of Weyl as a democratic theorist.

Weyl's reading of the *Census Report*, whatever may be said of its literary merits, provided him with the hard facts he needed to support his critique of Marx on the increasing impoverishment of the proletariat under capitalism. The increasing wealth of America is not growing the poverty of any class, as Marx had predicted. Rather it is producing a "social surplus" that is spent wastefully in the manner articulated with considerable wit by Thorstein Veblen in his famous *The Theory of the Leisure Class*.[53] It is as if the iron law of Malthusian economics is broken in American capitalism. The invalidation of Malthus is, of course, a temporary illusion for Weyl, but it presents an opportunity nevertheless. A new leisure class spending surplus wealth on luxury has not meant that people have starved. On the contrary, it has created an opportunity for rational economic planning rather than the free-market system that has been the defining feature of American society since the founding. "The surplus of society, which thus overrides all our traditions and shapes all our philosophies, is a phenomenon of transcendent importance." Without an excess of wealth no democracy on a large scale was possible in the past. But it is precisely this excess wealth that makes the new democracy possible. For the first time in history a majority of people have both a stake in the form of government and the wealth to make that stake not a utopian dream but a reality. "The rising middle class, finding themselves held down by a reactionary class, were compelled to appeal to the lowest class" against the reactionary robber barons.[54] The plutocracy has succeeded in sowing the seeds of its own destruction in the creation of a new, prosperous middle class.

The economic position of the middle class makes the new democracy possible, but not inevitable. Because this middle class has a stake in society it has no interest in the "war ethics" of Marxist class war. This is a novel development in Western political history. "The disequilibrium between social surplus and social misery colors all our thoughts. It is the basis of our social unrest. It causes stirrings of uneasy consciences."[55] But the ideas are born of particular economic conditions, and because those conditions are subject to continuous change, the idea of the new democracy must be seized upon at the moment. The new wealth is a foretaste of the sort of civilized life central planning can create, but it is not necessarily inevitable. The key is controlling the growth of population in the future so that the resources, which are by nature finite, will not lead to a return to the survival of the fittest that is as much Malthusian as it is Darwinian.[56] But the middle class must be persuaded to change many of its most cherished habits: can it be done?

In a key passage, Weyl writes, "The democratic mass represents a residue of the population, after a majority of the very rich and of the abjectly poor have been drawn off."[57] Rather arbitrarily, because, as he admits, statistics are lacking, he estimates that about twenty million people are debarred from the new democracy because they are either too wealthy or too poor. That leaves some seventy million people who are actively interested in democratic reform. It is a clear majority by any statistical computation. But the question is, "Can these potentially democratic masses unite?" The ethnic diversity of America would seem to say "No." But whether they can unite will depend upon the issue they unite behind: solidarity strengthens as the issue narrows. Solidarity, however, is relative, not absolute: "Were the authority of the plutocracy greater than it is, that of the democracy would needs also be greater."[58] But the plutocracy has already begun the process of its own demise by creating the very middle class that is now the basis of a new democracy. "Men who voted as producers are now voting as consumers."[59] This is the basis of conditional socialism. Ironically, perhaps, by making consumer sovereignty the locus of political action in the new democracy, Weyl reintroduced a new, radical form of individualism. And at the heart of consumer sovereignty in Weyl is the concept of the autonomous individual who has the economic right to pursue his or her own self-identity.

The middle class as consumer both narrows the focus of its interest and creates the basis of democratic transformation. "The appeal to the consumer has heretofore been made on the political field. To-day the consumer is represented on party platforms."[60] The consumer has become a force in public opinion that is unique in political development. What later generations would call "consumer sovereignty" represents the wave of the future and the best hope for the new democracy. The social surplus makes for social peace, if it is recognized for what it really is. And it is the task of public intellectuals to make this development clear. It is not socialism as that term has been commonly applied, although others may call it that. The new democracy is pragmatic in the economic rather than the philosophic sense of the term: "The goal of the democracy is a maximum of control with a minimum of regulation. In other words, the democracy, not being slavishly bound to logic, would rather be successful than thorough."[61] And Weyl has no doubt but that the end result of this process will be some sort of socialization of industry with the dividend going to the public as a whole rather than a few wealthy businessmen.

The lynchpin of making the political program work, however, is the social program, which requires, among other things, strict population control. "The demand for large populations is not democratic in origin. It is the despot who wants soldiers; the business prince who wants cheap labor; the jingo who believes in a swaggering, fighting nation... It desires a full life for all who are born, but it does not measure national success by the numbers who are born."[62] All of the economic progress that makes the new democracy possible will come to naught if population pressures on natural resources are not brought under control. New models of education are needed to teach the truth of this Malthusian problem to the many. An increase in population is the ultimate enemy of the new democracy. On this point Weyl makes one of his few gestures in favor of France, which has held its population constant, over Germany, which has seen its population explode over the course of the nineteenth century.[63] Consumption must be socialized if the evils of scarcity and population, the very factors that help make economics the dismal science, are to be avoided.

It will require a strengthened national government to prevent private expenditures on what Weyl calls "expensive toys." These examples of conspicuous consumption are the product of a dying individualism. "To socialize our consumption we must therefore depend upon the direct or indirect action of the state and upon the gradual education of the consumers."[64] And the state can further socialize consumption by furnishing a larger number of common goods, such as public transportation, parks, schools, and the like. The final success of democracy is thus tied to economic progress, and progress implies that the dead hand of the past be overcome. Defenders of the founders, by their very nature, are reactionary and anti-democratic: "The supposed incompatibility of democracy with progress rests on the assumption that democracy means an intolerable 'tyranny of the majority' over the minority, of the ignorant over the wise, of the careless over the prudent, of the mediocre over men of genius and spirituality."[65]

Why Weyl was Influential and Why He has been Forgotten

Any comparison between the American founders and Walter Weyl on the proper science of democracy would do well to keep in mind Aristotle's political dictum that we ought not to expect in politics the same philosophical consistency and precision we expect in mathematical sciences. Weyl's economic analysis is but a disguised political science that seeks to make the inherently unpredictable business of ordinary politics into a predictable science, and for that end he utilizes a methodology that is uniquely mathematical among the social sciences. And perhaps the most predictable consequence of this quest for theoretical precision has been to impoverish the study of politics.[66] This happened because practical politics is so often a matter of concern with equity, treating likes alike and differences differently. But economic calculation tends to separate issues of efficiency from issues of equity and in so doing treats natural rights as incalculable in principle. On the practical side of politics, the twentieth century is a textbook for the study of what happens when natural rights are regarded as mere formalities. That history is the driving force behind Strauss' inquiry into natural right and history. It is where we need to pick up the question of why Weyl was so influential in his own day and yet so quickly forgotten or overlooked.

Twentieth-century totalitarianism has not been madness in the classical sense of the term. Behind the apparent madness has been reason run wild, often rooted in a single strand of logic carried out to its final consequence. Economics may explain some of the workings of totalitarian systems at a mundane level, but is ultimately unable to penetrate to the core attractions and pathologies of such regimes. We are left with the classical categories of good and evil to explain what is involved, and the social sciences, at least to the extent they are prisoners of a rigid empiricism, are left to deal with only the most ephemeral aspects of the most important political phenomena of the century. This realization brings us back to the query posed at the outset by Strauss. How does the rejection of natural rights entail a critique of the founders' experiment in republican government? After considering Weyl and the foundations of the liberal-progressive science of politics as a critique of the founders, we can ask whether any social science that purposefully ignores the natural rights tradition in American democracy is adequate to the task of either analysis or prescription for modern American politics, or any politics for that matter. Would a return to the political science of the founders better provide a basis for the defense of American democracy and the basis for its improvement? We may get a better sense of this in Weyl if we return briefly to his critique of Marxism.

In an economic sense Weyl no doubt had the better of the quarrel with Marxists. If the dispute really turned on economics alone today we would more likely be reading Weyl and ignoring Marx: but that is not the way the twentieth century turned out. Marx was wrong about the distribution of wealth and the impoverishment of the proletariat under free market regimes. Nevertheless, Weyl unwittingly may have put his finger on the appeal of Marx, namely what he referred to, almost in passing, as the "essentially religious" basis of Marxism. The appeal of Marxism has not really been because of its economic analysis of capitalism. Much of Marx's appeal rests on the breakdown of both natural right and religion as a source of authority. Weyl could defeat the economic argument in a few pages, but he could not defeat the "essentially religious" argument by economic analysis. The natural right philosophy of the founders' science of politics is surely a better counter to this issue than economic rationality if only because the former speaks to the soul while the latter addresses only our appetites. Weyl treated Marx as an economist, which is natural enough in one sense, because the mature Marx, the Marx of *The Communist Manifesto* (1848) seemed to be simply an economic analyst of capitalism with a revolutionary call to do something about the injustices it spawned.

But since the discovery of his *Economic and Philosophic Manuscripts of 1844* in the 1930s, students of Marxism have been much more sensitive to Marx as a theorist of alienation. And while Marx may have described alienation in economic terms, the concept of alienation is in essence a philosophic and religious one. In his *Communist Manifesto* it was a portion of the intellectual elite, a class that was ideologically formed and not economically determined, that understood alienation philosophically and historically and went over to the side of the revolution to form a vanguard of the proletariat. The abolition of classes would result in an economic equality that made the formal political equality of natural rights and religious grounded government obsolete. What Marx called "alienation" was, in both the classical and religious natural rights traditions, understood to be a consequence of human separation from the Good or from God; in Marx it was wholly secular in origin and could therefore be overcome by wholly secular political action. If Weyl had had a stronger sense of natural rights or religion he might not have dismissed the Marxist argument on purely economic grounds so readily. And he might have better appreciated how little economic analysis alone can penetrate to the heart of Marxism and hence its appeal, especially to alienated intellectuals. The "death of God" does not mean that intellectuals believe in "nothing": it more often means that they believe in some substitute secularist ideology as a source of authority.

This is not the place to engage in an extended discussion of Marxism, but merely to suggest the problem of applying a purely economic interpretation to anything as multi-layered as democratic theory. Weyl and the liberal-progressive science of politics consciously abandoned both classical natural right and its religious counterpart. And because this abandonment necessarily meant an abandonment of the American founding in a constitutional system rooted in both, the liberal-progressive science of politics has sought and has tended to find authority, such as it is, in methodology. Authority slips through our fingers like quicksilver as academic methodologies have become ever more abstract and divorced from the experience of ordinary citizens. The result has been that what looked like rational progress to Weyl now looks like a truncated reasoning that has had difficulty probing the depths of modern political depravity. It is not a critique of economics to observe that economic reasoning only captures a part of the human condition and it is an abuse of any specific social science reasoning to suppose that it can offer a complete and coherent picture of democracy, or any political subject. The very soul of a project that self-consciously refers to itself as "progressive" is a faith in the future. But reading Weyl some eighty-plus years after his death gives the impression of someone who occupies an intellectual halfway house between the commercial republic of the founders and the socialist state of Marxism-Leninism. Weyl looks dated because within a decade "Communists seem like liberals in a hurry." Weyl was not obviously in a hurry and he got left behind by those who were.[67] Authority turns on "Who owns the future?" and the very methodology of economic determinism suggests the future belongs to the progressives.[68]

Weyl's economic determinism as a halfway house in the development of the modern liberal-progressive tradition of political science is an apt summation of his influence and the reason for its neglect later. Precisely because the liberal-progressive tradition is premised on a faith in a more perfected secular future, it is difficult to really establish a canon of liberal-progressive works. A canon of liberal-progressivism tends to focus on the evolution of methodology or empiricism. The very idea of a canon implies a sense of permanence that is foreign to the very idea of progress. The Declaration of Independence or *The Federalist*, for example, can be considered as part of the canon of a political science of natural rights because the political science of the founders was built on an acceptance of permanent principles. Our understanding of permanent principles may be incomplete or mistaken in any given example, but the very idea of permanence gives a reference point for political reasoning that seems always to be elusive in the idea of progress. *The New Democracy* looked like cutting-edge political science in 1912, but by the time Franklin Roosevelt made "freedom from want" one of his "Four Freedoms" in 1941, it looked more like a single component of the liberal-progressive science of politics.[69]

The halfway house of Weyl's democratic theory became dimly evident to him in the upheaval of World War I. The war distressed him enormously and contributed to the breakup among the original staff at *The New Republic*. Weyl wrote and had published an insightful economic analysis of the war, *The End of the War* (1918)—interestingly, before the war actually ended—that anticipated many of the same themes analyzed two years later by John Maynard Keynes in *The Economic Consequences of the Peace*.[70] When the Bolsheviks came to power in Russia after the revolution of 1917, Weyl could not help but wonder if these were merely liberals in a hurry. He wrote in his diary, "The charge is made that it is undemocratic." But those who made the charge referred only to a "political democracy"—"a democracy with as many holes in it as a Swiss cheese, but in which the holes are the essence of the cheese."[71] Viewing the unemployed in New York, he wrote, "What does equality mean when men are as unequal as these?... There can be no equality, not any approach to equality, except among men economically independent and economically comparable.... What does it avail the poor devil trudging the streets without a chance of bed or breakfast, that he is an equal American citizen, with a vote?... What interest has he in all our fine political schemes, in economy and efficiency, in democracy and progress, when he himself after an election as before is without a job and hungry?"[72] But what would be the political consequences if we no longer faced scarcity in the future? Tocqueville thought we might likely surrender ourselves to schoolmasters who substituted comfort for liberty. The economic formation of citizens as consumers will surely be different from the moral formation of citizens under a concept of natural right: the former can be managed by elites, but the latter presupposes consent.

The New Democracy derived its contemporary appeal because it was one of the first works, and certainly the most influential among progressives, of a science of American democracy cast entirely in the form of economic analysis and not simply as a critique of the founders. Its appeal was based on what appeared to be solid empirical foundations in facts that seemed to speak for themselves. And it seemed to offer a comprehensive analysis of democracy, past, present, and future that prior critiques did not do. But Weyl was tethered to an economic methodology that made a rigid empiricism based on material factors the basis of social analysis. Economic variables are by their very nature products of time, place, and circumstance, and Weyl was painfully aware that economics alone simply would not take him where he wanted to go. When he died in 1919 he was trying to formulate the sort of broad generalization about American democracy that had catapulted Croly to the front ranks of liberal-progressive theorists. One of his friends wrote at the time, "The quality of that unattained objective is the lost key to any valid appraisal of his work."[73] The strength of his work was its economic empiricism, but that was also its weakness. Neither men nor democracies live by bread alone. And Weyl's demand for economic equality, before political equality could be meaningful, broke with the founders' premise that political equality was best protected by limited government with enumerated powers. In order to achieve economic equality, government could not easily be limited and would require unlimited powers in order to achieve a purpose foreign to the founding.

There is a sense in which economic analysis is essential to political calculation. To govern is to choose, and choice always involves tradeoffs: someone loses and someone wins. But that is also why economics is the dismal science, because it serves as a constant reminder that no society can have everything it may want. Yet not all political questions can be reduced to an economic calculus. Some political questions are matters of preference and no particular issue of justice attaches to them. It is appropriate to use economic calculation for these issues. But the great questions of politics are the questions of justice and injustice, right and wrong, and good and evil: these are questions that are philosophic and religious in their essence, even, or especially, when they are debated in the public square. Making them simply values reduced to economic calculation threatens to undermine the very notion of permanent principles or "self-evident truth" altogether and the idea of a permanent constitutional order tends to become unintelligible. Few people are likely to be persuaded to accept what they believe to be injustice simply because it may involve some sort of economic efficiency. Justice and injustice are often experienced, in politics as in daily life, as gratuitous actions that are not easily calculated or explained by means of economic reasoning alone.

Indeed, there was a part of Weyl that did not fully accept the notion that all social and political problems could be reduced to a matter of economic calculation, although his narrowly focused methodology and empiricism left him no serious analytic tools with which to think about the issues. He tried, for example, to write a novel, or rather a sort of allegory, with a modern Christ as the central figure, but he abandoned the project because he became convinced that he did not understand either Jewish life or the technique of the novel. A friend wrote, "He did not admire either the Hebrew religion or its descendant, Christianity. Yet, curiously enough, the Bible was his constant companion."[74] His immersion in economic analysis and methodology left him unprepared to deal satisfactorily with the ethical problems that were at the heart of his work. The basic problem of politics, right and wrong, would not disappear simply because the social sciences reduced the problem to something else—the distribution of wealth, for example, with the implication that there is no ultimate injustice, but only hunger. Weyl had trouble understanding the founders' concern for simple majority rule because he could not understand a problem of majority rule divorced from an equitable economic distribution of wealth. His methodological assumptions precluded any other calculation.

If the natural rights philosophy of the founding is essential to understanding both the founding and the present, then we must conclude that it is unlikely that the compartmentalized social sciences of the modern university will be able to seriously probe the depths of the various disorders of modern politics. The reason, of course, is that they are themselves a part of that disorder. What one writer has accurately called "a fierce discontent" fueled the Progressive revolt against the founders' science of limited, imperfect political order: and in this sense it would appear that the demand for political perfection here and now soon became the enemy of the merely good.[75] It is the tragedy of the liberal-progressive science of politics that as it has helped to obscure the foundations of American democracy it has also obscured the tensions between the liberal-progressive science of politics and the religious-natural rights foundation of both the Declaration of Independence and the Constitution. The founders' science is probably not a panacea for what ails us, and there are some aspects of it, certainly in practice, we probably would not want to go back to even if we could. But we may also ask if any particular political action is possible if we are unencumbered by the past as Weyl thought. Will we have the courage to act in politics if we think the only thing involved is an economic transaction? Why should the middle class as consumers, or any class for that matter, care about democracy as long as the economic pie is distributed in the most efficient way? Do we inhabit a moral universe governed by an order we are called upon to understand and to which we are required to conform to the best of our understanding, or is the universe an arena in which individual selves may construct their own self-defined goals through an elaborate process of economic bargaining? If these questions could be answered definitively, once and for all, we would not need political science. But if we accept a wholly secularized understanding of democracy that is closed to raising these questions and their connection to politics in the first place, we should at least recognize that that will be the end of the peculiarly American experiment with democracy as it was conceived at the founding.

Sidney A. Pearson, Jr.

NOTES

[1] Theodore Roosevelt, *An Autobiography* (New York: Charles Scribner's Sons, 1913), p. 25. The decisive link between Roosevelt's ideas he dubbed the "New Nationalism" and the ideas of Croly and Weyl seems strained, this statement in his autobiography to the contrary notwithstanding. First, Roosevelt's heroes, such as Andrew Jackson, were not the heroes of either Croly or Weyl. Second, the publication chronology of their works and Roosevelt's ideas on the "New Nationalism" does not seem to jibe; he developed his "New Nationalism" ideas before he read either Croly or Weyl. It seems more likely that Roosevelt simply read Croly and Weyl after he had already made up his mind and found their ideas compatible with his own. But even if they were merely compatible without a causal connection, their compatibility is itself revealing.

[2] The only serious exception to this observation is Charles Forcey, *The Crossroads of Liberalism: Croly, Weyl, Lippmann and the Progressive Era, 1900-1925* (New York: Oxford University Press, 1961). Forcey's fine study was completed long before the political and cultural upheavals of the 1960s. His work was prompted by the vague notion that there was a hole somewhere in the soul of the liberal-progressive tradition and he sought to find out where it might be, but he may have been too close to the "crossroads" himself to appreciate the depth of the problem. Forcey assumed that the modern social sciences as they emerged in the modern university would support the liberal-progressive tradition without ever considering whether the reverse would also be true.

[3] Leo Strauss, *Natural Right in History* (Chicago: The University of Chicago Press, 1953), pp. 1-2.

[4] James Madison, *Notes of Debates in the Federal Convention of 1787 Reported by James Madison*, with an Introduction by Adrienne Koch (Athens, Ohio: Ohio University Press, 1966), p. 194.

[5] In some respects the more fully developed form of Beard's thesis can be found in his *The Economic Basis of Politics* (New York: Alfred A. Knopf, 1922).

[6] Irving Louis Horowitz, *The Decomposition of Sociology* (New York: Oxford University Press, 1993). Horowitz makes much the same point and traces its path in academic sociology. His discussion of this domination of sociology by methodology is, as he makes clear, true throughout the social sciences. Only the academic names need be changed to protect the guilty.

[7] An exception to this general point is Walter Lippmann, Weyl's colleague at *The New Republic*, who clearly saw authority as an emerging problem in liberal-progressivism, and indeed politics in general. See Walter Lippmann, *A Preface to Morals* (New York: The Macmillan Co., 1929), especially chapter V, "The Breakdown of Authority," pp. 68-83. See also the more detailed analysis in Thomas L. Haskell, *The Emergence of Professional Social Science: The American Social Science Association and*

the 19th Century Crisis of Authority (Urbana, Illinois: The University of Illinois Press, 1977).

[8] For a brief discussion of this development and Weyl's place in it, see Dorothy Wickenden, "Introduction: Little Insurrections," in Dorothy Wickenden (ed.), *The New Republic Reader: Eighty Years of Opinion and Debate* (New York: Basic Books, 1994), pp. 1-22. A wickedly biting review of Wickenden's account of the politics of *The New Republic* is Hilton Kramer's "Life After Lippmann: *The New Republic* at Eighty," in his *The Twilight of the Intellectuals: Culture and Politics in the Era of the Cold War* (Chicago: Ivan Dee, 1999), pp. 319-333.

[9] Walter Lippmann, *Drift and Mastery* (New York: Mitchell Kennerley, 1914), p. 266.

[10] Herbert Croly, *The Promise of American Life* (Cambridge, Massachusetts: The Belknap Press, 1965), p. 278.

[11] Julie A. Reuben, *The Making of the Modern University: Intellectual Transformation and the Marginalization of Morality* (Chicago: The University of Chicago Press, 1996).

[12] The best analysis of this development remains the work Strauss quoted: Otto Gierke, *Natural Law and the Theory of Society*, translated with an Introduction by Ernest Barker (Cambridge University Press, 1934).

[13] John W. Burgess, "The American Commonwealth: Changes in Its Relation to the Nation," *Political Science Quarterly*, I (March, 1886), 9, 17. See also Jurgen Herbst, *TheGerman Historical School in American Scholarship* (Ithaca: Cornell University Press, 1965).

[14] Mark A. Noll, *America's God: From Jonathan Edwards to Abraham Lincoln* (New York: Oxford University Press, 1962).

[15] Forcey, pp. 52-53.

[16] Walter Lippmann, "As a *New Republic* Editor," in *Walter Weyl: An Appreciation* (Privately Printed, 1922), p. 87. Hereafter cited as *Weyl*.

[17] Howard Brubaker, "In His Workshop," *Weyl*, p. 119.

[18] Ernest Poole, "Exploration," *Weyl*, p. 37.

[19] Quoted in Forcey, p. 59.

[20] Brubaker, *Weyl*, p. 111.

[21] Ibid., p. 87.

[22] Ibid., p. 61.

[23] Martin Schutze, "As I Knew Him in Woodstock," *Weyl*, p. 69.

[24] Francis Hackett, "Publicist and Radical," *Weyl*, pp. 101, 106.

[25] The best account of this can be found in Christopher Lasch, "*The New Republic* and the War: *An Unanalyzable Feeling*," in his *The New Radicalism in America 1889-1963: The Intellectual as a Social Type* (New York: W. W. Norton & Company, 1965), pp. 181-224.

[26] Robert W. Bruere, "An Attempt at Appraisal," *Weyl*, p. 142.

[27] Walter Weyl, *The New Democracy: An Essay on Certain Political and Economic Tendencies in the United States* [1912] (New Brunswick: Transaction Publishers, 2005), p. 3. Hereafter cited as *ND*.

[28] Ibid., pp. 4-5.

[29] Ibid., p. 5.

[30] Ibid., p. 13.

[31] Ibid., p. 12.

[32] Ibid., p. 8.

[33] The Madison-Jefferson exchange can be found in James Morton Smith (ed.), *The Republic of Letters: The Correspondence between Thomas Jefferson and James Madison 1776-1826* (New York: W. W. Norton & Co., 1995), Vol. I, pp. 631-636, 650-653. It is sufficient to point out here that despite Jefferson's better known argument that "The earth belongs to the living," Madison's more cogent reply dissuaded Jefferson from pressing his argument.

[34] Weyl, *ND*, p. 16.

[35] Ibid., p. 36.

[36] Ibid., p. 48.

[37] Ibid., p. 52.

[38] Ibid., p. 51.

[39] Ibid., p. 99.

[40] Ibid., p. 67.

[41] Ibid., p. 109.

[42] Ibid., p. 111.

[43] Ibid., pp. 145, 146.

[44] Ibid., pp. 149-150.

[45] Ibid., p. 151.

[46] Ibid., pp. 162-163.

[47] Ibid., p. 164.

[48] Ibid., p. 166.

[49] Ibid., p. 173.

[50] Ibid., p. 177.

[51] Ibid., p. 185.

[52] Ibid., p. 191.

[53] Thorstein Veblen, *The Theory of the Leisure Class: An Economic Study of Institutions* (New York: B. W. Huebsch, 1899). The chief characteristic of the leisure class is that it is freed from the painful requirement that it must work for a living by virtue, if that is the proper word here, of a wealth that far exceeds ordinary necessities. The result is that this class continues to spend in ways that are both conspicuous and socially useless. Veblen then obligingly goes into great detail describing this "conspicuous consumption." What Veblen calls "conspicuous consumption," and the moral critique of it, is what Weyl refers to, in a more neutral term, as "social surplus." In both cases the object of derision remains pretty much the same.

[54] Ibid., p. 194.

[55] Ibid., pp. 197-198.

[56] Patten undoubtedly introduced the Malthusian problem of population and scarce resources to Weyl. See Simon N. Patten, "A New Statement on the Law of Population," *Political Science Quarterly*, Vol. 10, No. 1, March 1895, pp. 44-61. Patten cast his essay as a refinement of Malthus' basic argument. His ideas were later expanded in his *Essays in Economic Theory* (New York: Alfred A. Knopf, 1924). Forcey, p. 86.

[57] Ibid., p. 237.

[58] Ibid., p. 242.

[59] Ibid., p. 251.

[60] Ibid., p. 252.

[61] Ibid., p. 264.

[62] Ibid., p. 320-321.

[63] Ibid., p. 356.

[64] Ibid., p. 331.

[65] Ibid., p. 351.

[66] Perhaps the best discussion of this turn of mind is Michael Oakeshott's "Rationalism in Politics," in his *Rationalism in Politics* (New York: Basic Books, 1962).

[67] In spite of its age, perhaps the best work on this subject remains Theodore Draper, *The Roots of American Communism* (New York: The Viking Press, 1957).

[68] See Irving Kristol, "Who Owns the Future?" in his *Reflections of a Neoconservative: Looking Back, and Looking Ahead* (New York: Basic Books, Inc., 1983), pp. 253-256.

[69] James MacGregor Burns, *Roosevelt: The Soldier of Freedom, 1940-1945* (New York: Harcourt Brace Jovanovich, Inc., 1970), pp. 33-35. Roosevelt's liberalism, and its ambiguous place as a halfway house in the development of the liberal-progressive tradition, is nicely illustrated in William E. Leuchtenburg, *Franklin Roosevelt and the New Deal, 1932-1940* (New York: Harper & Row, Publishers, 1963).

[70] Walter Weyl, *The End of the War* (New York: The Macmillan Company, 1918).

[71] Quoted in Christopher Lasch, *The American Liberals and the Russian Revolution* (New York: Columbia University Press, 1962), p. 132.

[72] Walter Weyl, *Tired Radicals, and Other Papers* (New York: B. W. Huebsch, Inc., 1921), pp. 34-36.

[73] Robert W. Bruere, "An Attempt at Appraisal," *Weyl*, p. 136.

[74] Howard Brubaker, "In His Workshop," *Weyl*, p. 119.

[75] Michael McGerr, *A Fierce Discontent: The Rise and Fall of the Progressive Movement in America, 1870-1920* (New York: Free Press, 2003).

THE NEW DEMOCRACY

CHAPTER I

THE DISENCHANTMENT OF AMERICA

AMERICA to-day is in a somber, soul-questioning mood. We are in a period of clamor, of bewilderment, of an almost tremulous unrest. We are hastily revising all our social conceptions. We are hastily testing all our political ideals. We are profoundly disenchanted with the fruits of a century of independence.

Our visitors from Europe in the early days of independence were obsessed by the unique significance of our democracy. To liberty or to its excesses they ascribed all American qualities, customs, and accidents. Our native apologists laid equal emphasis upon democracy. In half-ludicrous, half-tragic orations, they acclaimed the rule of the people as the essence and import of the new Republic. America was to be the eternal land of liberty, the refuge of the world's oppressed, the mentor of Europe. The chosen people of the West were to teach the true creed of democracy, in obedience to a divine command, as explicit as that laid upon the ancient folk of Israel.

Four generations have passed since Cornwallis surrendered at Yorktown. We have survived the early days of poverty and interstate bickering. We have grown in wealth, power, and prestige. We have issued triumphantly from a great civil war, which put an end forever to chattel slavery. Our institutions have not become less popular; our patriotism, though less fervid, is perhaps deeper; our hope of equality is not quite dead.

Nevertheless, to millions of men there has come a deep and bitter disillusionment. We are no longer the sole guardians of the Ark of the Covenant. Europe does not learn at our feet the facile lessons of democracy, but in some respects has become our teacher. Foreign observers describe our institutions with a galling lack of enthusiasm, and visitors from monarchical lands applaud their native liberty, while condoling with us over our political "bosses," our railroad "kings," and our Senate "oligarchies." A swelling tide of native criticism overtops each foreign detraction.

The shrill political cries which to-day fill the air are in vivid contrast with the stately, sounding phrases of the Declaration of Independence. Men speak (with an exaggeration which is as symptomatic as are the evils it describes) of sensational inequalities of wealth, insane extravagances, strident ostentations; and, in the same breath, of vast, boss-ridden cities, with wretched slums peopled by all the world, with pauperism, vice, crime, insanity, and degeneration rampant. We disregard, it is claimed, the lives of our workmen. We muster women into dangerous factories. We enroll in our industrial army, by an infinitely cruel conscription, the anæmic children of the poor. We create hosts of unemployed men, whose sullen tramp ominously echoes through the streets of our relentless cities. Daily we read of the premature death of American babies; of the ravages of consumption and other "poor men's diseases"; of the scrapping of aged workingmen; of the jostling of blindly competing races in factory towns; of the breakdown of municipal government; of the collusion of politicians, petty thieves, and "malefactors of great wealth"; of the sharpening of an irreconcilable class conflict; of the spread of a hunger-born degradation, voicing itself in unpunished crimes of violence; of the spread of a social vice, due in numerous instances (according to the Committee of Fourteen) not to passion or to corrupt inclination, but to "the force of actual physical want." According to some critics—among whom are conservative men with a statistical bent—American democracy is in process of decay.

If we are now scourged with whips, we are, it is claimed, soon to be scourged with scorpions. Our evils, if uncorrected, must grow with the country's growth. If in a century we have increased from seven to ninety millions, we may well increase, in the coming century, to two or three hundreds of millions. In the lifetime of babes already born, the United States may be a Titanic commonwealth bestriding the world; a nation as superior in power to England or Germany as those countries are to Holland or Denmark. It may be a nation spreading northward to the Polar Seas, southward to the Isthmus, or beyond, and westward to Australia. It may be the greatest single factor, for good or evil, in the destinies of the world.

It is this very vastness of our future that gives us pause. It is because in America we are about to play the game of life with such unprecedentedly enormous stakes that we are at last taking thought of the fearful chances of ill skill or ill luck. If to-day we have individual fortunes of four or five hundreds of millions, whereas in Washington's day we had not a single millionaire, how overwhelming may not be our fortunes in the year 2000, how overbearing may not be the pressure of poverty upon our hundreds of millions of citizens. Already our free lands are gone, our cheap food is in danger. Soon our high wages may be threatened. It is possible to conceive of a progressive deterioration accompanying an increase in population. We have no guarantee that prosperity, intelligence, discontent, and democracy will be our portion.

To-day, more than ever before in American history, dire prophecies gain credence. Some foretell the dissolution of the Republic and the rise under democratic forms of an absolutist empire, of a malevolent or "benevolent feudalism" of business princes. Others predict a day of "civil war, immense bloodshed, and eventually military discipline of the severest type." Grave men hope or fear a sudden destructive cataclysm, in which the ponderous pillars of our society will fall upon a blind and wretched people. Revolutionary and reactionary agitators are alike disillusioned. They no longer place their faith upon our traditional democracy.

Even the mass of men, — that experimental, inventive, but curiously conservative group of average Americans, — though voting instinctively, is beginning to feel that in essential respects the nation "conceived in liberty" has not borne its expected fruits. No one believes after this century of progress that the children of America are endowed with equal opportunities of life, health, education, and fructifying leisure, nor that success depends solely upon individual deserts. The "unalienable rights" have not availed against unemployment or the competition of the stronger. Our liberty is not yet absolute nor universally beneficent; our right to bear arms, our right to trial by jury, our rights of free speech and free assembly have been sensibly abridged. The slums are here; they cannot be conjured away by any spell of our old democracy. Disenchanted with the glorious large promises of '76, we are even, like our early European visitors, beginning to ascribe all evils to political institutions, and occasionally the unacknowledged thought arises: "Is democracy after all a failure? Is not the bureaucratic efficiency of Prussia as good as the democratic laxness and corruption of Pennsylvania? Are not progress, honesty, security better than the deceptive 'unalienable rights'? Does democracy pay?"

It is in this moment of misgiving, when men are beginning to doubt the all-efficiency of our old-time democracy, that a new democracy is born. It is a new spirit, critical, concrete, insurgent. A clear-eyed discontent is abroad in the land. There is a low-voiced, earnest questioning. There is a not unreverential breaking of the tablets of tradition.

It is not merely the specific insurgent movement in Congress which occupies men's minds. That is but a symptom, but one of a hundred symptoms, of a far broader, subtler, and more general movement of revolt. Men in the Middle West, in the Far West, in the East and South; men in the factory and on the farm; men, and also women, — are looking at America with new eyes, as though it were the morning of the first day. They are using old words in strange, new senses; they are appealing to old moralities in behalf of strange, new doctrines. It is not all "talk" of congressmen, for the man who is represented is more insurgent than the man who represents him. There are millions of insurgents who have never been to Washington.

The new spirit is not yet self-conscious. It does not understand its own implications, its own alignments, or its own oppositions. It does not quite know whether to look backward or forward. It is still inchoate. It is still negative.

Protestantism, too, was at first protesting, insurgent, negative, but Protestantism to-day is positive, plenary, and protested against. So our nascent, insurgent, still unfolded democracy, which unites many men in a common hostility to certain broad economic and political developments, is now passing over to a definite constructive program. It is becoming positive through force and circumscription of its own negations.

As it becomes positive the new spirit seeks to explain itself, and in so doing to understand itself. It seeks to test its motives and ideals in their relation to American history and conditions. Is our new democracy merely the old democracy in a new coat? Is it a return to the past or a turning from the past? Is it an imported creed or a belief of native growth? Is it a high-hung Utopia or an attainable end? Is it a destruction, or a fulfillment, of the fundamental law of American development? Whence does it come? Whither does it lead? What is it and what is it to be? What does it mean, for better or worse, to the common run of us?

CHAPTER II

THE SHADOW-DEMOCRACY OF 1776

WHEN the course of events is not to our liking, and we long for something that we do not have, our most instinctive argument is an appeal to a former golden age. We claim that we once had this property, this right, or this democracy, which in later evil days has been wrongfully taken from us.

Applied to America, this method of thinking presupposes an earlier era of native, full-blown democracy, when men were free and equal, with universal, uncontested political and civil rights. The period of this imagined era is vaguely placed at the dates of the Declaration of Independence and of the adoption of the Federal Constitution. Filled with a zeal for historical orthodoxy, we plead vehemently for the restoration of our one-time equalities and freedoms. Tacitly we assume that the broad and responsible democracy, for which we are now striving, once existed.

What, however, are the facts? To what extent were the democratic ideals of to-day embodied in the laws of a century ago? What solutions does the wisdom of our ancestors offer to the perplexing problems of their descendants? What, in short, was our original heritage of democracy and how have we added to or taken from it?

At the time of the Declaration, as during the preceding one hundred and fifty years, there existed in New England, and elsewhere in America, a certain measure of self-rule. The Puritans were by no means ardent democrats, their government, compounded of English and Hebrew tradition, inclining rather to theocracy. The democratic spirit, however, found expression in the town meeting, in which the good citizens came together to build the road, provide for the school, and pass laws against scolds and Sabbath-breakers.

It was a primitive, unrepresentative democracy in a group small, simple, and homogeneous. It differed widely from the larger colonial, and later from the State and national governments, by which the township was subsequently to be overshadowed. It was a democracy of poverty, — of men of small means, — and herein also it differed from modern democracies of wealth, in which enormous fortunes and their getting and keeping involve the clash of gigantic interests.

The political problems of the formative days of Hamilton and Jefferson cannot be likened to those of to-day. Since Washington's inauguration our population has increased twenty-three fold and our national wealth probably over one hundred fold, while the whole structure of society has been metamorphosed by steam, electricity, railroad, and telegraph. When we realize how the poor, simple, and homogeneous community of the eighteenth century has evolved into our present wealthy, complex, and differentiated society, we need not wonder that we have failed to inherit spontaneously the supposed democratic Utopia of the Declaration. A perfect democracy conceived in 1776 and adapted to those days would not have fitted comfortably upon the men of 1911.

In reality the democracy of 1776 was by no means perfect. The Declaration of Independence was not an organic law, but an appeal — a very special and adroit appeal — to the "natural right" of revolution. It was a beautiful ideal, as wonderfully poised in mid-air as is to-day the golden rule among the thrice-armed nations of Europe. The average American was not a true believer in its doctrines. The "better classes," tainted with an interested loyalty to King George, could not abide rebels, petitioners, and "agitators," and among the signers were many conservative men who feared "too much democracy," though they saw the advantage of issuing a "platform," and of hanging together to avoid "hanging separately."

Although a revolt against despotism swept through the land; although the new State constitutions, conceived in the diluted spirit of the Declaration, breathed a distrust of governors, legislators, and judges, — nevertheless a democracy, in the sense of our present hopes, did not exist in the emancipated colonies. Of the "free and equal" men of 1776, one sixth were chattel slaves. These poor blacks, largely native Americans, were speechless and voteless, were bought and sold, were mortgaged and flogged. Many whites, under the names redemptioners and indentured servants, were also limited in their civil rights, being bound to service and liable to harsh and cruel treatment. A large proportion of adult, white, free males were disfranchised. New Hampshire limited the suffrage to Protestant taxpayers; South Carolina, to free white men, believing in God, Heaven, and Hell, with a freehold of fifty acres, or a town lot, or who had paid a considerable tax. In Massachusetts, Connecticut, Maryland, Virginia, North Carolina, and New York the right to vote was based on the ownership of property (usually real estate) or upon the payment of equivalent taxes. In New Jersey no one could vote unless possessed of real estate to the value of fifty pounds.

The qualifications for office were even more excluding. The right to be elected to the Lower House was usually denied to all except Christians (or Protestants) of means. In Delaware the candidate for office was obliged to "profess faith in God the Father, and in Jesus Christ, and in the Holy Ghost, one God blessed evermore," and to "acknowledge the Holy Scriptures of the Old and New Testaments, to be given by divine inspiration." [1] In South Carolina no man

[1] See John Bach McMaster, "The Acquisition of the Political, Social, and Industrial Rights of Man in America." (Cleveland, 1903.)

could be elected to the Lower House unless he owned five hundred acres and ten negro slaves, or real estate worth 150 pounds sterling and clear of all debt. The qualifications for the Upper House, and especially for governor, were still higher. A governor of South Carolina had to be possessed of ten thousand pounds, a property qualification comparable with that of a million dollars or more for the present-day governors of New York or Illinois. Generally speaking, none but a rich or at least well-to-do Christian was eligible to the office of governor.

The will of the people, aborted by a restricted suffrage, was completely nullified by the "rotten politics" of the time. The founders of the Republic, be it remembered, were not quiet old gentlemen in stocks, living honorable and prophetic lives for the uplifting of us, their putative descendants. They were a very human lot of people who, liking to win, were not overnice as to means. "In filibustering and gerrymandering," writes Professor McMaster, "in stealing governorships and legislatures, in using force at the polls, in colonizing and in distributing patronage to whom patronage is due, in all the frauds and tricks that go to make up the worst form of practical politics, the men who founded our State and national governments were always our equals, and often our masters."

By such devices the balance of power under the Revolutionary constitutions was held in the hands of the "gentlemen," and kept away from those whom John Adams styled the "simple-men." In most States the mass of the people were compelled to accept a subordinate position. Unrepresented by government, press, or public opinion, largely illiterate and comparatively isolated, they were no match for the able, educated, and often unscrupulous gentlemen who seized political power and the fruits and spoils thereof.

Sharp social distinctions remained. What equality existed was due to a level of poverty, a uniform hard striving, and a most unwelcome simple living. On the Appalachian frontier this rude equality of poor men was most clearly exemplified, but in the East, where were the "well-born" and the "opulent," vestiges of aristocratic gradations lingered. The line between the scholarly or sporting Virginia burgess and the poor white of his district, or between the Madeira-drinking Dutch landlord of Albany and his neighboring shiftless farmer, was as sharp as that to-day between railroad president and railroad engineer. You could not mistake a journeyman shoemaker for his Excellency the Governor. The ill-clad, ill-conditioned, foul-mouthed mobs of the little cities delighted to bespatter mud upon the small clothes and silver-buckled shoes of the gentleman, who responded with a deep scorn for the "low-born" rascals.

Nor did the economic conditions reflect the freedom and equality which were the American's inalienable rights. True, there was a plenitude of cheap land, offering itself as an alternative to wage labor; but the industrial organization of the revolted colonies was ineffective, commerce was slow and cautious, and the rude labor of even a hard-working farmer produced nothing but an overabundant supply of simple and unvaried food and clothing. As for the landless laborer, he toiled from sun to sun for a wage lower than that to-day earned by a newly arrived Hungarian immigrant. Such a Revolutionary toiler could not be sure when or in what form his wages would be paid, or indeed, whether they would be paid at all; while, if he fell into debt for a few shillings, he might be cast into a reeking, vermin-infested jail, to fight with half-naked male and female prisoners for the retention of his clothes.

To keep the poor among our free and equal forefathers in their place, a barbarous criminal law, inherited from seventeenth century England, was invoked. Not only was imprisonment for debt universal, but attacks upon property were repelled with savage severity. In Maryland a thief was branded with a T on his left hand, and the rogue or vagabond — the unemployed man — with an R on his shoulder. The sovereign commonwealth of New Hampshire branded burglars on the hand, or, if the crime was committed on Sunday, on the forehead; while in Virginia all "deceitful bakers, dishonest cooks, cheating fishermen, careless fish dressers" (all of them "simple-men") were ordered to lose their ears. In Virginia it was a capital crime to obtain goods or money under false pretenses. Branding, whipping, ducking, the cropping of ears, the pillory, and the stock were ordinary punishments for vulgar rogues. A man could be hanged in Pennsylvania in 1776 on a first conviction for any of twenty crimes; in Virginia twenty-seven crimes were punishable by death. The law fell with especial severity upon the unrepresented, voiceless, and often uneducated "simple-men," who feared the debtor's prison as they feared the omnipresent pillory and lash, or the cloth P which the unfortunate pauper and his wife and children were obliged to wear upon the sleeve. Politically, industrially, socially, the "simple-man" was subordinate, and over this extremely imperfect democracy hung the black cloud of an aristocratic South, with its preponderating population and its wealth based upon the enforced labor of benighted negroes.

America in 1776 was not a democracy. It was not even a democracy on paper.[1] It was at best a shadow-democracy.

Nor was the substance of democracy conferred by the federal Constitution. If our modern ideal of democracy does not lead back to the noble eloquence of the Declaration, still less does it revert to the federal Constitution, as it

[1] Of democracies on paper, Mexico is an admirable example. Our sister republic imitates the forms, rites, and solemn-farcical pretenses of democracy. No one, by merely looking at her unwinking constitution, could surmise that the government is autocratic, or that peon slaves toil on the sisal grass plantations of Yucatan. The American Constitution, on the other hand, openly and unblushingly avowed slavery.

issued, in 1787, fresh from the Philadelphia Convention. Our newer democracy demands, not that the people forever conform to a rigid, hard-changing Constitution, but that the Constitution change to conform to the people. The Constitution of the United States is the political wisdom of dead America.

So intimately has this Constitution been bound up with our dearest national ideals and with our very sense of national unity, so many have been the gentle traditions which have clustered about this venerable document, that one hesitates to apply to it the ordinary canons of political criticism. For over a century we have piously exclaimed that our Constitution is the last and noblest expression of democracy. But, in truth, the Constitution is not democratic. It was, in intention, and is, in essence, undemocratic. It was conceived in a violent distrust of the common people, and was dedicated to the principle that "the minority of the opulent" must be protected from American *sans-culottes.*

There was perhaps some excuse for a reactionary document. Things were in a bad way. Thirteen free and very independent States were issuing paper money and were taxing each other's commerce. The central government, under the Articles of Confederation, maintained a precarious and contemptible existence. The domestic debt was not worth a continental, and the interest on the foreign debt (which was falling due) was regularly defaulted. England and Spain were hemming in the disorganized States on north, west, and south. National preservation was all-important, and the Constitution paid more heed to this problem than to the "unalienable rights" of men.

Some of the men who drew up the instrument frankly preferred a king, and the chief spirit of them all, the brilliant Alexander Hamilton, desired a life-elected president with an absolute veto on all legislation, appointing governors with absolute vetoes over all State laws. That such an abhorrent ideal should have been for a moment entertained indicates the unlimited contempt in which the greatest political leaders of the day held the raw and vociferous American democracy.

No king was set to rule over America. But the Constitution, as presented by the Convention, was more subtly subversive of the popular interest than might have been a dozen Georges. The House of Representatives was conceived to be the sole popular branch of the new government, but even in the choice of this body no provision was made for an extension of the then restricted suffrage. The senators, indirectly elected for long terms and without reference to the population of their districts, were legislators likely to be largely free from popular control. The power and dignity of the Senate were correspondingly augmented. The President by his indirect election (for it was not anticipated that presidential electors would accept instructions) was thought to be even farther removed from the unstable and easily beguiled people, and the Chief Executive was accordingly granted a qualified veto on Congress and enormous powers in peace and war.

All these checks upon a supposedly democratic House were reënforced by what in practice is an absolute veto inhering in the Supreme Court. This veto was intended to enable a small body of jurists, non-elected, but appointed for life by an indirectly elected President and an indirectly elected Senate, to set aside through a nullifying interpretation or upon the ground of unconstitutionality any federal law, approved by any majority, as well as any State law or State constitution. The supposedly undemocratic federal government was thus to be protected from ebullitions of the democratic spirit in the States and the United States.

Finally the altering of the Constitution was surrounded with almost insuperable difficulties, so that to-day less than one fortieth of the voters could conceivably frustrate the wish for amendment of thirty-nine fortieths. This threw the real power of amendment into the hands of the interpreting body, the same Supreme Court, intended by its composition and the manner of choice and the life tenure of its members to be the most remote of all governmental agencies from the operation of popular control. Popular rights were presumably, for all time, bottled up.

The greatest merit — and the greatest defect — of the Constitution is that it has survived. It might be well if the American people would recast their Constitution every generation.[1] We would assuredly do better in 1911 with a twentieth century organic law than with an almost unchangeable constitution, which antedated the railroad, the steamboat, and the French Revolution, and was contemporary with George the Third, Marie Antoinette, and flintlock muskets. In the early days, however, when the States were jealous, exigent, and eternally overvigilant, any bond of union, if only strong enough, was good. Our eighteenth century Constitution was a marvel of judicious compromises and wise evasions, and its ratification was a long step forward towards political autonomy.

This ratification was not a popular one, for the Constitution was never fairly presented for adoption to the people, but was accepted by a small minority during a reactionary year in a fear of foreign aggression and domestic anarchy. Even many who voted for the adoption of the Constitution were opposed to its principles, but by cajolery, logrolling, and questionable tactics the ratification was finally secured. The far-seeing leaders recognized that the Constitution was necessary. With a sop therefore to a jealous people in the form of the first ten amendments, guaranteeing civil and political rights, the dominating, intelligent minority of Americans decided to go ahead.

[1] Jefferson, who believed that each generation has a right to formulate its own organic law, advocated a policy of revising constitutions every nineteen years. In this way "the consent of the governed" could be periodically obtained.

That the Constitution has worked so well and comparatively so democratically is due, less to its intrinsic merits, or to the genius of Hamilton and Madison, than to the moderation and political tolerance of succeeding generations of Americans, and to a subsequent rising tide of democracy which has liberalized our organic law, overborne it, or evaded it. The almost direct election of the President, the enormous influence of political parties and of public opinion, the widening of the suffrage, the increasingly direct election of senators, are democratic features which were unpredicted, and would have been undesired, by the authors of the document.

The new government based upon the Constitution fell into the hands of the conservative class. By 1789 thousands of wealthy loyalists, who had fled in 1775, were reinstated in public esteem, and these men, as well as other "leading citizens," had scant sympathy for democratic vagaries and demagogic vaporings. The Federalists, who had made themselves responsible for the Constitution, realized that the efficiency of a political instrument depends upon the minds which interpret and the hands which administer it. It was in this spirit that they secured control of the new government. The formative American government thus came to be marked with the stamp of Hamilton, Adams, and, later, of John Marshall, men who had faith in the union of the States, but not in the people who formed their citizenry. These leaders recognized that it was necessary to attach to the nascent federal government the interested loyalty of the moneyed classes, which was done through the levying of a mildly protective tariff, the creation of a national bank, and the assumption of the State debts. Through the strengthening and astute manning of the Supreme Court, they created checks upon the people and upon the State governments, while they wisely held aloof from the embraces of revolutionary France and tried to repress internal disaffection by the ill-advised Alien and Sedition Laws.

The democratic spirit, however, was growing. A few months after the inauguration of President Washington, a Parisian crowd stormed the Bastille, and the great French Revolution was launched. When Citizen Genêt arrived in America, he found many thousands sympathetic to the new democratic doctrines. The Declaration of Independence was also bearing fruit. Suffrage was being extended in the several States; property and religious qualifications were being lessened or removed; the limitation of officeholding to men of wealth was made less stringent; and the penal law and the conduct of prisons were somewhat humanized. In 1800, the "Jacobin" and "leveller," Thomas Jefferson, was elected President, and by 1814, after the disastrous Hartford Convention, the influence of the Federal party was forever gone.

During the first quarter of the nineteenth century the progress away from the evil old conditions was even more rapid. The little cities were growing, and the citizens, especially the journeymen workingmen who were forming unions, had no respect for suffrage qualifications based on the ownership of farms. The city poor were asking for public — not pauper — schools, for the right to strike, for the cessation of special privileges, for a mechanic's lien law, and for that most revolutionary of all programs, the abolition of imprisonment for debt.

On the westward-moving border of the States, also, a new and iconoclastic spirit, born of the wilderness, began to arise. In the conflict with nature all strong men were equal; to pass the Appalachians, a social convention had needs be hardy. The pioneer, who blazed a trail through the primitive forest, who fought with Hull at Detroit or Jackson at New Orleans, who drank "hard cider" with Tippecanoe, had no remembrance of pre-Revolutionary gentlemen and no respect for the old-fashioned school of statesmen.

The wave of a new democracy — intensely individualistic, intensely confident, aggressive, dogmatic — passed east over the mountains from Michigan, Ohio, and Tennessee into New York, Pennsylvania, and Virginia. The new crude democratic movement, fed on a number of social and political reforms, culminated in the electoral victory of 1828. Jackson was made President, a democratic ideal was fixed upon America, political traditions were unsettled, and the door was opened to all manner of revolutionary changes, good and bad.

With the inauguration of this popular hero in 1829 began the spoils system, the short tenure of office, the popular boss, and the fresh and wholesale corruption of parties. The suffrage was still further extended and the congressional caucus which had formerly nominated presidential candidates gave way to the theoretically more democratic, but in practice equally unrepresentative, national convention. The prayers to the "gentleman" leaders of public opinion died away, and louder appeals were made to the unquestioned sovereignty of an imperious people. Industrial and social changes also took place. The opportunities of workingmen were widened, and their rights were affirmed and defended. A wave of educational reform along democratic lines swept over the country, and abuses of many kinds, grown old in America or torn from feudal settings in Europe, were attacked and abolished. The people were supreme. A turbulent army of camp followers and spoilsmen accompanied Jackson in his invasion of Washington. Democracy was attained.

It was a crude nation which believed that it had attained democracy, a nation still poor, but little instructed, with raw impulses which might lead it anywhere. It was a dispersed, atomic nation; a nation of "queer,' inquisitive folk; a nation boasting of the armor it was to put on. It was a nation loudly protesting against all artificial distinctions;

a nation in which the servant was the respected and condescending "help," and the policeman, letter carrier, and stagedriver equal and aggressive citizens, proudly refusing to wear uniforms or other badges of servitude. It was a nation in which the doctor or lawyer cultivated his farm, and the factory girl might play the piano and write for a magazine. It was a nation hopefully anticipating the imminent downfall of the monarchs of "effete Europe"; a nation devoutly confident that the ultimate sanction of Divine Providence had been uniquely reserved for the ideally perfect American Commonwealth. It was a nation shamed by filthy prisons, barbarous penal laws, imprisonment for debt, and ill-kept cities. It was a nation cursed with slavery.

The evil, like the good, of the Jacksonian era is still with us, and only slowly are we freeing our larger, newer democracy from the trammels placed upon it by the raw, crude democratic movement of that day. But with all its defects, the democracy of the America of 1829 was far in advance of that of the contemporaneous world. Europe was still lying in the slough of reaction, following the Revolution and Napoleon. In England George the Fourth ruled a slumbering nation, Catholic Emancipation was just being granted, the Reform Bill had not been passed, the "rotten boroughs" sent up their members to an aristocratic Parliament, and the hand of a noble class lay heavy upon the land. In France the Revolution of 1830, which was to turn over the nation from the Bourbon Charles X to the bourgeois monarch Louis Philippe, had not yet occurred. Prussia, Austria, Russia, Spain, were in the grasp of absolutist régimes. The world's hope of democracy seemed to lie to the west of the ocean.

Two years later, Alexis de Tocqueville, the philosophic student of popular government, conceived this land as "the most democratic country on the face of the earth." In

America the people had a sure foot on the ladder of freedom. Again and again De Tocqueville speaks of our equality of political rights, of property, of education, of opportunity. Often he speaks of the unquestioned sovereignty of the people, of the exclusion or voluntary retirement of aristocrats. The inevitable rule of the masses, which De Tocqueville everywhere foresaw, was to be studied in the towns of New England, on the frontier of Illinois, in the halls of Congress. The most youthful nation would teach its elders the lessons of popular government. A child would lead them.

To-day the tables are turned. America no longer teaches democracy to an expectant world, but herself goes to school to Europe and Australia. Our ballot laws come from a nation younger than ourselves; our students of political and industrial democracy repair to the antipodes, to England, Belgium, France, to semi-feudal Germany. Politically, as otherwise, we have made progress, but we are no longer so supremely confident that the men of 1787 could adequately foresee and rightly predestine the lives of the men of 1911. We are beset by bewildering new problems; by portentous, unexpected versions of old problems; by stubborn, staring facts, irreconcilable with our old optimism; by evil, incredible conditions, the impossible offspring of our early hopes. Where we have planted the good, the ill has sprung up; where we have striven for equality, we have achieved inequality.

Why have the promises of the rash young democracy of 1829 remained unfulfilled? Why has the tortoise Europe outdistanced the hare?

There are several reasons. First, we believed that we already had democracy. To the early Americans, democracy was something negative, an *absence* of kings, of nobles, of political oppression, of taxation without representation. It was something which, having, they need not worry about, like their wives, whom they loved but no longer courted. It was an individualistic democracy — not a democracy adapted to the steam engine, the big factory, the great city and the social relations corresponding to a complex, closely knit industrial system.

A second reason was slavery. From 1787 slavery was an acute national problem; from 1820 to 1863 it was *the* problem of America. To have attained a plenary, socialized democracy, we should have been obliged to turn all our national thought upon the problems of the distribution of wealth, the effectuation of the popular will in government, and the creation of a nationa intelligence and a national will to cope with these problems. Such a concentration of our national thought was impossible during the slavery struggle. The South fought desperately in Congress and, later, on the field of battle for the maintenance and extension of its peculiar institution, as a man fights for a drug to which he has become subject. The most democratic nation in the world was distraught over the question of the extension of slavery at a time when the politically less advanced nations of western Europe were agreed that slavery and even serfdom were immoral, uneconomical, and obsolete.

A still more formidable obstacle lay between America and the democracy to which we to-day aspire. In the early thirties, when De Tocqueville was studying our institutions so sympathetically, America stood at the parting of the ways. She had to choose between the attainment and modern adaptation of the rights of men and the conquest of the continent; between immediate democracy and material progress; between the Declaration of Independence and "manifest destiny."

It was not a conscious choice; few determinations of great masses of men are. It was rather a blind inclining to a great task, a blind fulfillment of the supreme need of the epoch. Unless the continent were subjugated by the nation; unless the far distant corners of the Republic were united by road and canal, by railroad and telegraph; unless men and goods could pass freely from Atlantic to Pacific and from Rio Grande to Lakes Superior and Michigan; unless America were united, cemented, and fused, — the Republic and all its idols would perish. Theoretically America might have abjured Louisiana, foregone Florida, refrained from the Mexican foray, and stayed at home and developed her democracy. Actually she was forced outward. The pressing need of America was not liberty, equality, and fraternity, nor yet a perfected and socialized democracy, but the conquest of the continent, the fashioning of a man to conquer it, and the creation of a state which would aid, or at least not hinder, the conquest. The subjugation of this continent from the Appalachians to the American Desert, and beyond, and the search for the wealth which was its embodiment, must set its stamp upon the acquisitive, imaginative, and starkly individualistic American; it must set its stamp upon the feeble, faltering, starkly individualistic state. The nation was compelled to develop along lines hostile to the highest political evolution. It was compelled to sacrifice a large measure of immediate progress in democracy in order that the material substratum might be provided upon which eventually a fuller, deeper, nation-wide democracy could be reared. It was perhaps a way about — an instinctive *détour*.

Thus it came about that America, in 1831 the leader in democracy, gave up its leadership to attempt another task. The immediate task before America, the frontiersman of civilization, was not democracy, but the Conquest of the Continent.

CHAPTER III

THE CONQUEST OF THE CONTINENT

THE conquest of the wide-stretching continent lying to the west of the Appalachians, gave to American development a tendency adverse from the evolution of a socialized democracy. It made America atomic. It led automatically to a loose political coherence and to a structureless economic system. The trust, the hundred-millionaire, and the slum were latent in the land which the American people in their first century of freedom were to subjugate.

That land was one of the most magnificent portions of a fertile world. The immense domain stretched from Appalachians to Pacific, with broad, deep rivers, with a chain of fresh-water lakes unique in the world, and with exhaustless supplies of water power. The varied climate was adapted to all the purposes of civilization; the soil was fertile beyond the experience of European cultivators. A million square miles of forest, with treasures of pine, oak, hickory, and ash, stretched like a shoreless sea before the eyes of the early settlers. In those forests and on the plains beyond were numberless deer, buffalo, mountain sheep, and fur-bearing animals, while overhead passed clouds of pigeons, turkeys, geese, and quail; and in the seas, lakes, and rivers were myriads of edible fishes. Land, sea and sky, forest and prairie, offered seemingly exhaustless supplies to the scattered millions of early Americans.

Beneath the deserts of forest and prairie lay an equal bounty. There were hundreds of thousands of square miles of deposits of coal and iron. In gold, silver, lead, zinc, in building stone, phosphates, and salt, in many other minerals and metals, the country abounded. These buried treasures were not for the unseeing eyes of the first generations. It was the forest which fed and warmed and housed them, which sheltered them from the Indians, and held out its constant lure.

In grandeur the march of the pioneers into the pregnant forest compares with those multitudinous outpourings of northern Barbarians which overturned Rome. The movement was peaceful, continuous, resistless. Wherever the pioneer pressed, boundaries gave way. Napoleon sold a magnificent empire to the young Republic, and vast territories were stolen from feeble and distracted Mexico. Not until it reached the impassable ocean did the westward movement stop. To-day the peaceful conquest moves northwest into the wheat lands of Saskatchewan. It is all the same process, the overflow of a vigorous, fertile race into an empty, fertile land.

It was this emptiness of the wide land which impressed upon the new nation its essentially industrial character. Spain became martial through eight centuries of warfare against the Moors; the ancient Jews became militant because, to win the Promised Land, they were forced to slay root and branch. To the Americans such warlike qualities were not essential. A few hundred thousand Indians could not withstand the prolific invaders. The aborigines were not so much conquered as overawed. They were literally crowded out by men who, themselves wasteful, yet made a better use of the land. The plow, not the rifle, vanquished the Indian.

We must pause to survey this conquest of the continent because it has entrained a series of developments which still vitally affect American life. To-day we cannot tear down a slum, regulate a corporation, or establish a national educational system, we cannot attack either industrial oligarchy or political corruption, without coming into contact with the economic, political, and psychological after effects of the conquest. What our land is, what our state is, what we are, our present problems and our present hopes, are largely traceable to the hasty occupation of the continent, and to the rapid material development of the nation which the conquest visualized.

What was the impelling cause of this vast, harmonious movement? What inspired the men who built the new West?

It is *naïve* to believe that all these men were inspired by a concerted desire to work out a national destiny. Their motive was more personal. Nor may we ascribe the movement to a disinterested love of adventure. Adventure means money. Ordinary men do not break home ties, go forth into a trackless wild or into a new, crude community, do not put their lives, still less their permanent comfort, to the touch without hope of money, gold, farms, a free economic life. The exceptions do not disprove the rule. The great migrations of history have been economic.

In the business, labor, and property conditions of the East of America, as in the unparalleled offerings of the West, we must seek the cause of the Western movement. It might seem that the vast territory east of the Appalachians should have sufficed for the needs of its sparse populations. In 1790 there were far fewer people in all the United States than in New York City to-day; in 1820 the whole population, white, red, and black, on both sides of the mountains was but little greater than the present population of New York State. Had the early Americans been engaged in manufacturing, commerce, and intensive agriculture, there would have been little apparent incentive to a westward migration.

Such were not the conditions. By an adverse policy of the British government, manufacturing had been restricted during the colonial period, and after 1815 it was again injured by the competition of the better equipped English factories. Farming, in America, even according to the then European standards, was superficial and ineffectual. The tools were rude; the plow was essentially that which Herodotus had seen in Egypt. The farmers were neither ambitious nor scientific. The one-crop system prevailed, fertilizers were unused, and the land was subjected to the most exhausting tillage. An ineffectual national production and a rapidly increasing population[1] forced increasing numbers of Americans across the mountains.

So long as commerce offered an alternative, Americans were loath to move westward. A few years after Washington's inauguration, Europe became embroiled in a series of wars which lasted a generation. The slaughter in the East was a golden opportunity to the poor Western Republic. America turned its back upon the forest and expanded toward the sea. She became the audacious blockade-runner, the shrewd trader, who stuck to business while competitors quarreled. American fleets filled the seas, scattered the Mediterranean pirates, carried food to England, ministered to Bonaparte, and engaged in the lucrative, horrific slave trade. Finally warring England and France joined hands to assail our rising commerce. The maritime monopoly of America ceased. Our ships lay idle in the harbors, and grass grew in the Salem streets.[2]

Thereafter the undivided energies of Americans turned westward. The cession of Louisiana in 1803 had brought under the American flag distant lands less known than are to-day the hiddenmost recesses of Central Africa. Into

[1] Prior to the flood of immigration which began in 1820, the white population was doubling every twenty-two or twenty-three years, and the slave population was growing almost as rapidly.

[2] American commerce received so great a setback through the French and English policies, the American Embargo, and the War of 1812, that the tonnage of American vessels was less in 1830 than in 1800.

the Western territory there poured, after 1815, increasing numbers of hardy adventurers. Turnpikes were built between the ocean and the Appalachians. The steamboat, launched on the Hudson, was transported to the Western rivers, and carried passengers from Pittsburg and Cincinnati to St. Louis and New Orleans. The opening of the Erie Canal in 1825 connected the Great Lakes with the Atlantic Ocean, while in the early years of the fourth decade the newly invented railroads began to open up lands inaccessible by water. The forests of the Northwest Territory went down before ax and pyre. Clearings were made, towns grew up, and Territories, and later States, were formed. The population of Ohio, Indiana, Illinois, Michigan, and Wisconsin increased from 50,000 in 1800 to 3,000,000 in 1840. The Appalachian barrier had been turned. The country lay open to the Rockies.

The building of the West was hastened by the wasting of the East. Labor being scarce and land plenty, it seemed extravagant not to waste. Beyond his tumble-down fences the Eastern cultivator saw other boundless farms. The New Englander profitably ruined his land and migrated to Ohio and Illinois. The Georgian moved with the spoils of his ravished acres to the cheaper and more fertile acres of Alabama and Mississippi. In the South both waste and migration were incited by the ignorance, apathy, and mobility of the slave. The Southern planter transported his valuable human property easily and cheaply, and these transitions carried slavery and cotton beyond the Mississippi. The impact of "King Cotton" drove the Mexicans across the Rio Grande, and Texas and Arkansas were settled, while in many parts of the Southeast decayed buildings and overgrown lands were all that remained of once prosperous plantations. The center of population moved westward. The Southwest, shipping its one "pay-crop," cotton, to Liverpool and New York, drew its corn and bacon from the Northwest, which in turn bought plows, railroad tracks, and other manufactured products from the East. The North Atlantic and Middle States went over to manufacturing; the nation's mineral resources began to be tapped; and the country, about the year 1840, emerged from its former poverty and sparseness of population into an era of exuberant prosperity.

To this prosperity and to the almost intentionally wasteful exploitation of resources, two new factors contributed, the railroad and migration. The railroad, bringing the virgin farm of the West nearer to the wasteful farmer of the East, removed the last penalty from the murdering of the soil. The most adventurous and resilient among Americans, men who in still earlier days would have engaged in whaling or the desperate fur trade, turned their energies into the construction of railways. Against the urgent cry for transportation, voiced by the upgrowing nation, nothing could stand. Peculation, speculation, force, fraud, genius, and courage, — all went into the new lines. Tracks were laid upon the smooth prairie into a land uninhabited. The freight and passengers built the road that carried them. Wooden bridges, desperately flimsy, made subsequent iron bridges possible, as iron bridges later paid for steel and stone bridges. Where the iron rail went, pioneer and settler followed, and cities — strident boom towns, born of an insane optimism — sprang up in swamps and forests. The railroads, like their children, the new communities, were a law unto themselves. The savage little lines, fighting for life with tooth and claw, running anywhere and everywhere, cutting, rebating, overcharging, were gradually forced into bigger combinations of continuous railroad, which also cut, and rebated, and overcharged, and fought tooth and claw. Parallel "strike" lines arose, and the struggle for money and land waxed fiercer and fiercer; while pregnant America poured forth ever new torrents of wealth, and men wasted and garnered and laughed and fought, as the continent was conquered.

While the American pioneers were crossing the first range of mountains, a reserve army was moving to their assistance from the fecund lands of western Europe. These men too were adventurers, giving up home and friends for money, food, and a job. The voyage was hard. Success depended upon an ability to survive in the ruthless, fertile struggle of American life. From 1820 on, immigration grew rapidly, and after the bad crops of the late forties, the Irish Famine of 1846, and the unsuccessful German revolution of 1848, millions of men poured into the Western Republic.[1] The cities, which were growing up like weeds, attracted the plastic Irishman, while the Germans swept over the new lands of the West. Here, beyond the Wabash, the immigrants found an unforested prairie, where, though wood and water often lacked, progress was easier. The "prairie breaker," with his team and plow, turned the soil, and farms sprang up instantaneously. Often the immigrants did not settle on virgin territory, but bought from pioneers, who, after disposing of their log cabins and half-burned woods, "cleared out for the New Purchase." The incoming swarms of immigrants pushed the pioneer ever farther west.

Settlement, railroad building, and immigration were in their turn incited by a heedless, precipitate disposal of the public lands. Originally conceived as a common property to be sold for the extinguishment of the national debt, the public domain came to be regarded as an infinite checkerboard of future farms, to be put into the possession of individual settlers as expeditiously as possible. The prices of agricultural and mineral lands were reduced; credit

[1] From 1821 to 1840, 742,564 immigrants arrived; from 1841 to 1860 the number was 4,311,465, of whom over two thirds were Irish and Germans.

was, for a time, extended to every one; a succession of "temporary" statutes permitted preëmption; and finally the Homestead Law of 1862, and certain ill-advised amendments and complements thereto, let down all bars, and gave access to the land without effective guarantee of permanent settlement. These methods stimulated the craziest excesses of land speculation and the crassest inequalities, but they also expedited settlement. An overgenerous land policy, fashioned by corrupt Congresses and administered by corrupt officials, succeeded, at the expense of all future generations, in hastening the already rapid conquest of the American continent.

Uninterruptedly the westward course of the army of settlement took its way. The Mormons, persecuted in the East, turned the deserts of Utah into gardens. The cry of "gold" arose in California, and, dropping their plows and lathes, men rushed madly to the Pacific. Over the desolate, arid wastes, around the Cape, across the narrowing continent at Panama, came the gold hunters. Farmers, truck gardeners, and peddler merchants followed, and a new, rash, gambling civilization arose on the lands of the stately Spaniards. The westward movement, halted by the belief in a great American Desert, stretched out two long, thin trails to New Mexico and Oregon. Then Kansas and Nebraska were opened, and fierce men from North and South came to fight for farms and to decide there the issue of slavery. For, while America grew in its rapid, disorganized way, sprawling over a continent, a nation all arms and legs and no body, the great disruption threatened. Slaveholders and single-handed pioneers struggled for the territories, for the continent of America. Forty years of compromises and evasions had brought the nation to the "Irrepressible Conflict."

The seventh decade decided the question whether the continent wrested from nature should pertain to a single nation, or to a group of clashing nations, representing opposing ideals. The railroad decided the battle and unified the nation and its territory. Backed by the railroad, the Northern armies poured down from East and West and overcame the heroic resistance of the South. At last the North and South, estranged for generations, were united in a nation which knew no dividing line. Four years later, on the 10th of May, 1869, a golden spike was driven into the connecting rails of the Union Pacific Railroad, and the two oceans were united by a rod of steel. The continent was conquered.

The land had been covered. The public domain, opened by the homestead laws, lavished upon railroad corporations, despoiled by timber thieves, by mineral reserve exploiters, and by adventurers, honest and dishonest, showed signs of depletion.[1] When, in 1889, Oklahoma was opened for settlement, the overwhelming rush of land-hungry men showed that the patrimony of the country was lessened.[2] The processes of exploitation and waste were extended to mineral, timber, and swamp lands, and were aided by machinery, which during the century had revolutionized industry and now lent its immense powers to the spoilers of the nation. Trees were no longer brought down by the ax, but vast forests were destroyed by machinery with the rapidity of fire. Iron was shoveled by steam out of the unprotecting hills. The steam drill invaded the coalpit, and wonderful inventions of warfare were turned against the disappearing fauna of the continent.

Our frontier, the actual physical boundary of the coun-

[1] According to the report of the Public Lands Commission of 1905, almost one billion acres (967,667,449) had been disposed of in the United States (excluding Alaska) up to July 1, 1904. Of this, 114,502,528 acres were forests reserves, and over 162,000,000 acres were Indian lands and school and other grants to States and Territories.

[2] On the first day of entry more than fifty thousand people entered to occupy the land.

try, had been attained. For the man who had girdled the trees and built log cabins in Tennessee or Ohio, there was no chance in newly acquired lands in Pacific and Caribbean. The westward wave of migration, checked but still unspent, turned back upon itself. The driving force, the fierce resistless momentum, remained, but there was nothing against which to strike. The alkali lands of the silent desert, the cloudless blue skies of arid America, laughed at the plow and the harrow and the earnest, searching glances of the home builders. The Pacific Ocean, stretching out to the thronged coasts of China, buried the hopes of those who for generations had conquered the continent. The occupation of America seemed gone.

It was not that there were no virgin lands, no unused mines, no primeval forests. All these there were, but they were preëmpted. Appropriation, not use, had cornered the opportunities. The railroads alone had received over a hundred million acres, which they now held at their use and pleasure. From the beginning, the pioneer had taken what he could and had held what he took. The gigantic railroad, with a thousand fold greater power, had done but the same. Farseeing corporations of enormous reserve strength had grabbed legally and illegally, had seized strategic positions, had secured themselves against the time when tens of millions of homeless men would press upon the no longer boundless, but strictly bounded, territory.

While the pioneer had struggled with ax and plow against the resistance of trees and soil, a silent change had taken place behind him. Machinery had become highly specialized and had conquered the world; competition had become tempered by combination. Railroads had become trunk lines, transcontinental systems, and finally amalgamations of systems. The trust had arisen. The trust had tramped into the disordered ring of life as the pioneer had forced his way into the forest. In pioneering itself, once the province of the individual man, in the discovery, appropriation, and exploitation of resources, the trust had excelled as it excelled in the refining of oil and the making of steel.

The old style pioneer, the log cabin man, the placer miner, had been met and held off by his brother of a more modern type. The new pioneer might be a soft-handed gentleman, with a taste for intrigue and percentages, and as ignorant of woodcraft as was Daniel Boone of debenture bonds. Nevertheless the same adventurous, getting spirit which had driven and lured the frontiersman into the forest now attracted the like-minded promoter into the similar business of wholesale preëmption. Like the pioneer, though on a much greater scale, the promoter preëmpted; like the pioneer, though on a much greater scale, he wasted, ravaged, and laid fire; like the pioneer, though on a much greater scale, he built for himself and for the nation. Ruthless, greedy, imaginative, he erected, by fair means or foul, by his own brains and the tributary science of the world, an edifice overpowering in its immensity.

Against that edifice, against the preëmption of financier and trust builder, the naked hands of the pioneer could avail nothing. His self-reliant individualism, formerly the mainspring of his strength, now reduced him to impotence. Preëmption had grown large and prevented preemption. Individualism, fattened on reserve money strength, inspired by an avid appetite for gain, directed by science, system, and the subtlety of invention, had rendered individualism abortive. The new preëmptor circled his appropriations with excluding fences far more effective than those of the early pioneer. About his property, however gained, were legal grants, and legal confirmations, statutes of limitation, corrupt political organizations, pliant judges, and the laws and the constitutions of the States and of the United States. The old pioneer was warned off the farm, warned off the cattle range, warned off the forests, warned off the mines. Discouraged, as though bewildered by the abortion of a primal instinct, the pioneer, the typical American, turned back from the physical frontier to lose himself in the city, in the wilderness of opportunities of the city.

While the pioneer was felling the forest, the city had been growing apace. The city, which all over the world was becoming the new home of civilization, had developed in America even more rapidly than elsewhere. It grew with the progress of the pioneers; it grew even faster after the pioneer period ended. As the supply of free Western farms ceased, as the settlers, with no further place to go, began to exploit what they had, the alternative which the frontier once offered to the city disappeared. The progress of agriculture enabled one farmer to perform what two had performed before, and the surplus rural population moved to the upgrowing cities. The very isolation of the farm, with its sharp limitation of possibilities, sent the most energetic boys to the cities. The immigrants, finding the new lands preëmpted, remained at the ports of entry. The new opportunities, the chances which the pioneer had sought among the trees, on the plains, or in the sands of California's rivers, were now sought in the mysterious, congested, surcharged life of the city.

Here the pioneer met a new frontier. The streets of the cities were underlaid with networks of telephone wires, electric railway conduits and privately owned water mains, so that no new individual or company could compete. The best city sites, those adapted for department stores, office buildings, and fashionable residences, were in the hands of men who held them at enormous prices. The road to political preference in the city lay through bosses who had preëmpted the strategic points of the city control, or through financiers who controlled the bosses.

Everywhere the preëmptor had been. The city, conceived in an individualistic society and composed of men who minded their own business and nothing else, had grown up like one of its own ragged newsboys, untended, reckless, and weak. The preëmptors, divided in grabbing, were united in holding. The politicians exploited the apathy of the public, and the financier exploited the cupidity of the politician. "Deals" and "jobs" had become vested rights in perpetual franchises, and what had been obtained by foul means was held by fair. Our legal traditions and our most sacred political institutions had sanctified the end, though they abhorred the means, and a midnight franchise grab was crowned with the sanction of the Constitution of the United States. And so in the city, as on the wide-stretching continent, men had preëmpted and bribed and stolen and bought in good faith, until preëmption precluded preëmption and grabbing put a stop to grabbing. The chances of the city, like the chances of the forest, became circumscribed. The city, like the country, was preëmpted.

CHAPTER IV

THE INDIVIDUALISTIC SPIRIT OF AMERICA

THE westward march of the pioneer gave to Americans a psychological twist which was to hinder the development of a socialized democracy. The open continent intoxicated the American. It gave him an enlarged view of self. It dwarfed the common spirit. It made the American mind a little sovereignty of its own, acknowledging no allegiances and but few obligations. It created an individualism, self-confident, short-sighted, lawless, doomed in the end to defeat itself, as the boundless opportunities which gave it birth became at last circumscribed.

Based though this individualism was upon the environment of the American, it was also in part an intellectual heritage. National character depends upon the past as upon the present. Had America been settled by Laplanders, equatorial Negroes, Spaniards, Venetians, or Greeks, our civilization would have developed differently. We cannot understand the problems of to-day, nor foresee the solutions of to-morrow, without knowing something of the minds of the middle-class Englishmen who came to Massachusetts in the seventeenth century.

The roots of these men's characters ran deep into the soil of dead centuries. The Pilgrim Fathers imported traditions formed millenniums before by Angles and Saxons in the Baltic dunes. The history of England, from the Heptarchy to James the First, was part of their intellectual equipment. In their beliefs and prejudices might be traced the slow political and legal development of England, the stiffness and harshness of the common law, the tenacious middle-class traditions of the towns, the democratizing, individualizing effects of Reformation and Dissent. The early spirit, strong, narrow, pious, became diluted as the Puritan stream flowed into the ocean of English America. Even in dilution, however, it preserved, and to this day preserves, much of its individualistic, uncompromising, reforming quality.

Another type of man lived in Virginia, and men of still different caliber were to settle Maryland, Pennsylvania, and Georgia. The Dutch in New York, the Swedes in Pennsylvania, the French Huguenots in the South, had still less in common with the men who plowed New England's rocks. But the Puritans prevailed. Though the Carolinian plantation owner scorned the Connecticut divine, though the wealthy and populous South overshadowed New England and New York, though Virginia, not Massachusetts, became the mother of Presidents, it was in the North that the spirit of the nation was evolved.

That spirit was necessarily individualistic. The colonists were more self-reliant than even the original, self-reliant British stock, since, broadly speaking, only selected men essayed the ocean journey. No aid from a hostile, Stuart-ruled England could reach the colonist, who, separated from his neighbors by miles of treacherous forest, was compelled to rely upon himself. With the aid of his family, he plowed his acres, shot his game, caught his fish, made his soap and candles, dressed and cured his leather, spun and wove, did his own carpentering, and sometimes his own smithing. He made what he ate, wore, and lived in, and he made and held his own opinions. His philosophy was that of the lonely, self-contained farmhouse.

When, after the wars with England and her Indian allies, the back country was opened, and the colonists, leaving behind sea and civilization, settled their farms in the virgin forest, a new era opened for American individualism. So long as the settlers had lived on the fringe of America, like shipwrecked sailors clinging to the barren coast of a lavish land, they had preserved some of their old traditions. What revolutionized them was their march into the continent, the erection of a mountain barrier between them and Europe. As the continent was transformed by the settlers, so in turn the settlers were transformed by the continent. It was the continent that created the typical individualistic American spirit.

That influence was not the mere sight of beautiful rivers and primeval forests. Men are affected wonderfully little by scenery and wonderfully much by considerations of bread and butter. West of the mountains, individualism was rooted in the soil. All the elements of the trans-Appalachian life, the free movement, the initial character of the inhabitants, the contemporaneous political theories, the cross currents of immigrant nations — all aided in the development of this national characteristic. On the fertile lands along the Ohio and Mississippi, as on the unforested prairies beyond, success could be attained by the individual, reënforced by the occasional reciprocal assistance of his neighbors. No great irrigation projects were needed, such as made the Mormons a semicommunistic group and are perhaps destined to socialize the future settlers of arid America; and no scarcity of land and no fear of foreign invasion forced the people into villages like those of continental Europe, where all peasants must act in the common interest. The scattering of so small a population over so large an area led to an unprecedented exaggeration of the centrifugal forces of society. The individual stood alone.

The most representative type of this American individualism was the pioneer. It was he who typified the expansive force of American civilization in the rarefied American continent. This backwoodsman, overburdened with land, clamored for more land, for Louisiana and Texas, for New Mexico and California, for Oregon to fifty-four-forty. His almost savage individualism triumphed over forest, swamps, malaria, privation, and solitude. It transformed his rough log cabin into a "castle" and his vague, far-reaching land and his roaming swine into "property." It showed itself in a sense of complete self-containment and in a churlish though free hospitality. Ignorant, dirty, often drunken, frequently brutal, as some of these "solitaries" were, they nevertheless possessed a certain large dignity not unlike that of the Hebrew shepherds. Forever displaced by steadier and more industrious beneficiaries of his adventure, this marginal man, with his eyes ever towards the West, loomed up large in the imagination of Americans, and cast his shadow backwards over the filling land and its cities, over even the national Congress assembled at Washington.

The self-reliant, aggressive individualism of the pioneer was also the spirit of the American factory builder, town boomer, railroad wrecker, promoter, trust manipulator, and a long line of spectacularly successful industrial leaders. During the Conquest of the American Continent there was developing in Europe, as a result of changed economic conditions, a keen, assertive, individualistic captain of industry. The Oldham cotton manufacturers, like the colliery proprietors of Lancashire, Belgium, and France, developed qualities similar to those of Americans. In the Western land, however, individualism was a national, not a class, characteristic. The continent was one enormous workshop, and it was new, not like the scarred European continent, which had been the burying ground for a century of centuries of fighting, starving populations. In America, except the slave (the whipping boy of civilization), all were imbued with something of the spirit that in Europe pertained to a few.

It was not that the American industrial leaders imitated the pioneer, but that they were subject to conditions similar to his. Everywhere in America there was a low external pressure, which resulted in an inflation of individualities. The pioneer acted for himself because there were no others; he knew no law because he knew no society. So, with the others, the vastness of the land compared to the fewness of the people, the richness of the land compared to the labor of the people, induced an instinctive taking, an instinctive wasting, a sense of magnificence, a toleration of others (with whom there was so much to share), and a lawless, traditionless exploitation of boundless resources according to the will and ideas of each.

American individualism showed itself in a certain magnificence, which to this day affects the life of the nation. The American, like a young heir, developed a confused sense of abounding wealth. He did not mind waste, for he throve while wasting with both hands. If the racked lands reverted to desert, if men despoiled and politicians stole, if fires ravaged forest and city, was he not, fortunate mortal, possessor of a continent? He derided small gains and petty savings. Small gains were for small men. The penny-wisdom, which in Europe has built up great coöperative stores, he esteemed but as the beggarly expedient of "pauper labor."

This "magnificence" revealed itself in ways ludicrous and grandiose; in lavish gratuities, disproportionate to services; in the unbelievable — yet believed — prophecies of innumerable Mulberry Sellerses; in a contempt for pennies, nickels, and "shinplaster" currency. More than in anything else it showed itself in American bragging. The nation, its resources, excellences, and virtues were colossal, continental. Even its vices were boundless, and, therefore, admirable. This magnificence invaded the arid intellectual life of America. It inspired our perfervid oratory. It was of the very essence of our humor, with its broad continental exaggerations, and its rollicking, cascading contrasts, like that between the prairies of Nebraska and the turbulent Falls of Niagara. To the Illinois farmer, the Colorado prospector, the California gambler, the New York banker, to the "magnificent" rank and file of America, — all of them individualists, — everything was bigness, wasting, getting, and a theme for a crude, touching magniloquence.

Another side of this individualism was an illimitable, supreme, categorical optimism. As the wasted lands led to new lands, as the ravaged forests led to new forests, as the ruined man rose again richer than before, a feeling spread that all was well with America, that nothing could stay the ultimate success of individual or nation. Evils there were, but the continent was large, movement easy, and what could not be cured need not be endured. The discontented Easterner went West and prospered; the discontented immigrant fared better than he had hoped. Economic crises gave way to newer prosperity. There was never a famine in the land, for the land was a continent, and one crop made up the deficiency of another. Invention, scientific discoveries, improved transportation, opened the continent ever wider, and the optimism of America clung with invincible credulity to a belief in the inevitableness of progress. The continent, moreover, made all the good come true, and the man who believed — with or without reason — was not disappointed in his predictions. Faith in America, faith in one's self, faith in the ultimate good sense of the people, became a creed; the cautious maxims of poverty-bred generations were belied. In America a rolling stone *did* gather moss; in America a penny saved was often a dollar lost. "Waste not, want not" meant nothing to a generation of wealth-getting wasters, while "nothing venture, nothing lose" was not so true as its contrary.

This optimism — then as now — closed the ears of the people to all warnings. The dissenter, the ever-falsified prophet of evil, was derided. Again and again, for one cause or another, for the breaking of economic laws or of the tabled Commandments of God, America, it was predicted, would shatter, and be one with Nineveh and Troy. America never shattered. Despite political corruption and absurd legislation, despite an extravagance of errors that would have doomed another nation, the rallying continent and the invincible buoyancy of the American spirit triumphed. Supply preceded demand and created demand. Confidence, not caution, was the law of business.

A corollary of American optimism was tolerance. This tolerance, which was half-part indifference, extended to slavery, slums, piratical business, and political corruption. The presence on the continent of a great community of unlike, free, and nominally equal men stimulated this toleration, as did also the fluidity of American life, the facile escape from local evil conditions, the easy association in business and society of diverse elements, and the free exchange of goods and ideas between different sections. Prosperity, too, made for tolerance. To a well-fed, well-housed, suitably mated man, few beliefs, opinions, or prejudices are intolerable; and the ready humor of America, tinged with the joy of mere well-being, was both an antidote and an alternative to intolerance.

The potential success inhering in all men, the chance that even the unfortunate might eventually triumph, widened further the application of tolerance. The "crank" must be humored because his crazy device might transform an industry. The ragged and ungrammatical visionary might found a religion or an empire; the log splitter might become Chief Executive. The immigrants — German, Irishman, and Swede — were tolerated, because through this very toleration these people "won out," and lost their alien qualities in the dissolving bath of American prosperity. The continent was big enough for wise and foolish, good and bad. Excepting always the Negro — the helot of North and South —

only the polygamist and the atheist were held outside the pale. Especially the atheist, for it behooved all men to believe in a Creator who had fashioned the continent and reserved it for the eleventh-hour American.

The continent made us a "practical" people. We judged policies by "results"; by immediate, visible, realizable results. We were not thorough. In America, it did not pay to be thorough. We did not think things *out*. We did not generalize. Our political and economic life appeared as a disconnected succession of suddenly arising problems, each of which was to be singly met — or singly avoided. We did not determine on definite long-time policies. To the future — that beneficent but unknowable ally of America — we intrusted the problems of the future. America lived under the dominion of the immediate. The Americans were a "practical" people.

The crass, unbounded individualism of the practical American found its highest expression in private business and the quest of money. Although Americans were idealistic, and even sentimental, although the nation, sympathetic and generous, gave to all alien causes which appealed to the common mind, nevertheless it was with a certain justice that America was called the Land of Dollars. The dollar was omnipotent. Traditions being weak, classes inchoate, and the state inactive, the individual in measuring his success accepted this only available standard. The very fluidity of the nebulous communities, the ease with which one man became successively laborer, teacher, farmer, lawyer, soldier, legislator, and banker, and the prevalence of the creed that any man could do anything, tended to reduce all the inequalities of life to the one equality of the dollar.

It was, moreover, a useful and essential standard, for it was the dollar, not the title of nobility, or the university degree, that could conquer the land. The continent and its conquest fused with the conception of the dollar, and the possession of money was *prima facie* evidence of a man's usefulness to society. There was no cringing to gold, for all had it prospectively. But there was respect for it, since each man worshiped in the millionaire the apotheosis of his individualistic self.

American individualism, applied to business, explained all our then economic arrangements and all our business methods and traditions. Individualism, run riot and rejoicing in its own excesses, led to a veritable pay streak theory of business. The American followed the one lead, raised the one crop, worked the one vein, cut the best trees, took everywhere the cream of the cream. In a search for dollars in a country where a dollar to-day was worth ten to-morrow, there was no wisdom in working poor soils, in preserving fertility, in gathering coal from culm heaps, in securing by-products, or in working for the permanence or salvation of machinery that could be "scrapped," of workmen who could be replaced, or of properties which could be duplicated. The American shipbuilder built ships to sail, not to last. Factories and cities were built for immediate profit, like the cheap shanties of a moving gang of Polish railroad laborers. The six-story house was dismantled to build the twenty-story skyscraper. Naturally, during the brief life of these temporary elements of a permanent civilization, each was worked to its utmost capacity. Intensity became the law of business. The night was made "joint laborer with the day," and in a few years of feverish activity relays of highly paid workmen got out of a new machine its full value. In the North the free workers were lured into intense labor and excessive overtime; in the South, on some of the plantations of Louisiana, it was found profitable to work off a stock of negroes once every seven years, and to buy a new set with the proceeds of the cane. As for the property — the farm, mine, mill, railroad — the goose was worth less than the golden egg.

The sequence of such untrammeled individualism was a brutally unprincipled code of business morals. Every man was presumed capable of playing his own game. The tenderfoot from the East was expected to know a ranch when he saw one. If a simple-minded man bought a broken-winded horse, a salted gold mine, a city lot in Lake Michigan, or the mythical wooden nutmeg, it was *his* lookout. If he bought sand in his sugar, water in his milk, chicory in his coffee, or chalk in his bread, he had no redress. He could not appeal to a spiritless, futile law, cramped like a Chinese foot; he could not protest to a community which would have laughed at the fool and his folly. The buyer did what some men do when they receive a counterfeit dollar. He kept silent, and passed it on.

Upon competitors, the individualist turned the same batteries. Competition, the fetish of America, was largely unregulated by public opinion. The spirit of haggling was everywhere, in the horse trades of country fairs, the bargainings of itinerant peddlers, the real estate transactions of boom cities. The competitive spirit ran high among towns offering rival locations to a prospective railroad, and among the railroads themselves, which during rate wars might carry the passenger free and give him a bonus. The little country newspapers carried a competition for subscribers into their fierce editorial columns, and thousands of lawyers, doctors, and dentists, throwing aside professional restraints, launched into lurid advertising of competitive claims. In the relentless struggle for patronage, bribery, treating, false pretense, the buying off of rivals' agents, the damaging of rivals' wares, ingenious chicanery of all sorts, entered into the game. Competition was war, and in war all was fair.

The apotheosis of American individualism was the rebate. It was the individualistic, higgling spirit carried to its logical conclusion. It was a negation of the public character and public responsibilities of railroads, and an assertion of the principle that each man might be permitted, here as elsewhere, to make the best bargain possible, open or secret, and the devil take the hindmost.

In the early days a man injured by a rebate to a rival did not waste time deploring the demoralization of business. He passed the counterfeit dollar along; he secured a larger rebate for himself. In the eyes of that generation, a shipper who could not, through bribery, cajolery, intimidation, or bluffing, secure a rebate, was as deservedly unsuccessful as the manufacturer who failed to secure customers. The attitude towards the public interest in uniform railroad rates was summed up in the sententious phrase, "The public be damned!"

The individualism of the American led to gambling; competition *was* gambling. In America, as in other countries where the future is large and indefinite (but especially in America), gambling was the core of business. The continent offered a fortune to the lucky speculator; the railroads carried the product, and the advertising newspaper, the words, of the lucky manufacturer to the farthest hamlet. There was no foretelling the fancy of the public, that credulous, million-headed, million-mouthed monster. A man might spend a fortune on factories and advertising — and lose; another might invent a shoe button or glove hook, or coin a happy advertising name for his candy, soap, or cigarette, and millions poured upon him. The incompetent farmer found zinc or oil upon his land, or was overtaken by a great city, so that his pigsty became worth a dozen farms. The easy-going man bought a few yards of "begging" telephone stock and became a financial magnate. Men bought, luckily or unluckily, mines, stocks, great tracts of land; they appealed to the God of Chance as they appealed to the silent continent. They placed the years of their lives and their precarious fortunes upon the cast of a die, upon a future happening — or failure to happen. America was one large gambling "joint," where money, success, and prestige were the counters, and the players were old men and young women, pioneers and workmen, holders of trust funds, and little boys, devoutly reading conventionalized biographies of successful men.

But it is of the essence of gambling that the few win and the many lose. Moreover, as the American game progressed, the rules were changed to suit the big players. More and more, the little gamblers, "the pikers," "the lambs," staked their "piles," not against the resources of the continent, as before, but against what was to them a dead uncertainty and to the big gamblers a "sure thing." The big gambler used the little gambler's money; the little gambler became the stake. The chances of the game seemed gone, but the inveterate little gambler called, not for a halt, but for a "square deal."

It was indeed a strange psychological world in which the American individualist found himself, when, with the reaching of the frontier, American enterprise turned back upon itself. The little gambler was like the belated boy who dreams of a Far West of Indian trails, but finds there only railways and automobile roads. The individualist became bewildered when his familiar rebating became double-cross rebating, and the big shipper received both his own and the little shipper's rebate, and he became still more confused when the big shipper ended rebates by acquiring his own railroads and his own pipe lines. The individualistic American was dumfounded when he saw that favorable terminal facilities, public service franchises, and other special privileges, given to a competitor, had ended competition; when he saw competition become parasitic; when he saw the trusts organizing a fictitious competition against themselves. His psychological development had lagged decades behind the industrial development of the country.

The individualist could no longer rely upon his automatic "unalienable rights" and his fair field and no favor. If he was a farmer, he could not by his own efforts secure just freight rates, fair elevator charges, or equitable grading. The individual manufacturer or merchant might at any time be overwhelmed through the invasion by a gigantic competitor of his circumscribed territory. The man who would not sell out to the trust might be crushed; the workingman who would not join a strong union might be compelled. The city man could not by his sole efforts protect himself against fire, disease, or avoidable accident. He could not determine the quality of his milk or water, the hours that he labored, the sanitary condition of the house or flat in which he lived, or of the factory in which he worked. Individually he was impotent, and he was still an individualist.

The monopolist, the big speculator, was also an individualist, unabashed and unreconstructed. Complacently he sat at the gate taking a tribute which grew as millions were added to the population. Into his hands fell the usufruct of science and invention. Like Pippa he sang, "God's in His heaven; all's right with the world." The big gambler felt that he was an honest man, who, though not a sentimentalist, had merely played "the game." The big gambler could not understand the hostility of the little gamblers.

The little gamblers understood it no better. They too believed that to the victors in the industrial struggle belonged the spoils, and yet *they* had no spoils. Despite themselves they recognized an affinity with the big men, an identity in ambition and in point of view. The little individualists, to find a justification for their enmity, desperately sought a line of cleavage, a something which would separate the vicious who had succeeded from the virtuous who had failed. Lawbreakers accused lawbreakers; rebate takers, rebate takers; the man who stole an invention protested against the man who stole a legislature. The culminating evil was not the illegitimacy of the baby, but its unbabylike proportions.

The very qualities bred into him by the conquest made it impossible for the individualist — so long as he remained an individualist — to solve, or even see, his economic problems. His magnificence estopped him from complaint. His optimism made him still hope for the "luck" which would turn his way. He was still tolerant of abuses and evils, which he hoped individually to avert. The individualist was still a "practical" man, who despised paternalism, socialism, anarchy, and governmental interference, and who still believed, in his downright practical way, that if you could only "jail" a few millionaires, the road to the continent would again be open. The "practical" man saw monopolies, but he did not see Monopoly. He saw corrupt politicians, but he did not see Corruption. He saw evils, but he did not see Evil.

Even to-day, the pure, unadulterated, pre-Adamitic individualist survives. The man who feverishly buys on margin a few shares of "Sugar" or "Smelters," who throws himself into a hopeless competition with a trust, who seeks by his own skill to escape the narrowing circle of the preemptors, is an aborted American gambler. But the man is changing. The little individualist, having asked for the removal of the mote of individualism from his brother's eye, began to discover an identical mote in his own eye. Tweedledum, having accused Tweedledee, learned that they were like-minded brothers. The cure of individualism was not individualism.

Moreover there came to be raised other voices, — not of stark individualists, — and the demand went forth for reconstruction and regulation. The little individualist, recognizing his individual impotence, realizing that he did not possess within himself even the basis of a moral judgment against his big brother, began to change his point of view. He no longer hoped to right all things by his individual efforts. He turned to the law, to the government, to the state.

CHAPTER V

THE SOVEREIGN AMERICAN AND HIS STATE

THE political philosophy of the "Fathers" might have been summed up in the phrase "the less government, the better." The nation was born of a rebellion against King and Parliament, and, in a certain sense, against government in general. At first the colonists proclaimed their rights as British subjects not to be taxed without representation, but since Birmingham, Sheffield, and Leeds were unrepresented, though taxed, this constitutional plea fell upon deaf ears. Then the colonists appealed "to the opinion of mankind," on the ground that *as men* they had natural rights "to life, liberty and the pursuit of happiness." Since "all governments derive their just powers from the consent of the governed," the Americans retained the right to sever their bonds with England.

The doctrine so enunciated, though revolutionary, was not new. It had justified the English Revolution of 1688, as, later, it was to justify the French Revolution of 1789. It presupposed the original and residual omnipotence of the individual, who had been endowed by nature, or by "the King of Kings and Lord of all the Earth," with unalienable rights, which, though temporarily surrendered in a social compact to form a government, were still retained and might be enforced against an unjust or tyrannical government. The author of the Declaration, like many of his contemporaries, was a firm believer in the right of revolution, and he dreaded a strong government, which might infringe the sacred rights of the individual.

These sacred rights were life, liberty, and property,[1] and the greatest of these was property. Property gave men the right to vote, to hold office, to serve on juries. It permitted, through the payment of a bounty in war time, an escape from military service. It enabled the rich man to incarcerate his poor white neighbor for debt, or to buy his Negro neighbor at the auction block. The majority of offenses were infractions of the right of property. This right, held to be invaded by the stamp tax and tea tax, made up the core of the unalienable rights with which man was "endowed by his Creator." It is this emphasis upon the natural, unalienable, uncontrollable right of property which molded our state and our law, and became the vital fact in our political development.

It was the philosophy of the new economic world then coming into being. In 1776, when Jefferson, a leading exponent of this political anarchism, was writing the Declaration of Independence, a quiet Scotch professor issued a famous treatise on the "Wealth of Nations." This book proclaimed that in economic life the greatest good of all resulted upon the whole from the unimpeded and enlightened egotism of each, and it proposed the restriction of state[2] activity to the narrowest limits.

The tenets of Adam Smith, exaggerated and distorted by more passionate disciples, became the gospel of the rising manufacturing class in England. The men who were to revolutionize Great Britain with their iron foundries and their cotton and woolen factories wanted a free hand. They begged relief from oppressive state taxes, from state-

[1] In the Declaration of Independence the third in this trinity of rights was designated "the pursuit of happiness."

[2] Where I use the word "state" in the sense of a community of persons, living in a circumscribed territory, under a permanent political organization, I spell the word with a small "s." Where States of the United States are intended, I use a capital "S." In quotations from other authors, I do not apply this rule.

granted monopolies, from laws which kept up wages. They wanted the unregulated power to draft into industry the men, women, and pauper children of agricultural England, to carry them to the alleys of new manufacturing towns, to keep them employed as many hours as "competition" required. For the sake of business the state must be dwarfed.

In the Western world the new philosophy of a weak government and a strong individual, of unalienable rights and non-interference, was echoed approvingly. The philosophy fitted in perfectly with the conditions. In those days a strong state could not have scientifically directed the exploitation of the continent, as Japan to-day is doing so successfully in Korea. The unknown continent could not have been curbed, for no legislators could have foreseen the development which millions of uncontrolled experimenters were to force. That he might go into the forest without his hands tied, the pioneer desired a state too weak to interfere, but strong enough to protect property. If, by the hope of a permanent gain, men were to be incited to conquer the wilderness, the most absolute safeguards to property were essential.

So the Americans starved their state, and made of it the weak, sprawling, free-handed thing it became. The old Confederation pleased the early individualists because it was weak. But it was too weak to live. The Constitution also provided for a sufficiently feeble government. The House, Senate, and President held each a checkrein upon the others; the Supreme Court held one upon all; the State limited the Federal government; the Federal government, the State; while between the two grew up vague areas of unknown jurisdiction, "twilight zones," to which powerful evildoers repaired, as to-day gamblers repair to an interstate river to avoid the jurisdiction of neighboring States. The state — the entire national, State, and municipal government — was hedged in by restrictions, set against itself, and weakened. In a state divided against itself, the individual flourished.

Once created, the government was left to itself. It was an alarm-clock government, which, properly wound up, would run automatically and awaken the individualistic American at the right moment. It was a duty to vote once so often, and the citizens, when they possessed the right, voted. But it was not necessary to keep one's eyes on the government. The American eggs were not in that basket.

The government grew up complaisant. It had little to do. The Americans did not want to fight. They desired no entangling alliances or foreign policies. They had, or thought they had, no internal problems. The government was there, not to govern the people, but to hold them together. Its spirit was eternal compromise. Slavery was undemocratic, but the government was half free and half slave because the people were. The equal representation of the States in the Senate was undemocratic, but it was necessary to get the little States into the Union. The Mexican War, the Gadsden Purchase, the Alaskan Purchase, were to enlarge the continent; the Monroe Doctrine was to preserve it. The goal of the government was union of any sort, and it attained this by giving all citizens a right of exploiting the continent, as an indulgent nurse succeeds for a time in quieting the children by acceding to all the demands of each.

The Federal government being the "business agent" of the pioneer, all of its policies converged upon the one idea of permitting the uncontrolled exploitation of natural resources. Infant industries were given protective tariffs; settlers and great railroad corporations were given public lands; inventors were accorded patents. The freedom of the national domain was conferred upon sturdy immigrants, who were to aid in the Conquest of the Continent.

The government, while thus encouraging the conquest of the continent, scrupulously refrained, for its own part, from participating in the resulting gains. The nation largely paid for the trans-continental lines, but private capitalists reaped the profit, including exorbitant rates for the transportation of the mails. The government dwarfed its own unprofitable postal service rather than lessen the income of express companies. Tariff schedules were for the "revenue only" of protected manufacturers. The whisky taxes, levied during the Civil War, were intentionally arranged to divert most of the proceeds to distillers and whisky speculators. During the same war, "the boys in blue" wore expensive shoddy uniforms and slept under rotting shoddy blankets — all for the manufacturers' profits. Rather than compete with private contractors, the government gave out its work, buying its supplies at the highest market price. The State, like the nation, carried out a policy of subsidy to, but non-regulation of, private business; while the city equally abjured profits, and became, what it was intended to be, a weak, wasteful, exploited public corporation, the appanage of more vigorous and powerful private corporations. So insanely solicitous was the government of the rights of all profit makers, that it offered itself for exploitation to two rival firms — the dominating political parties in America.

The political party had not been contemplated by "the Fathers," who objected to party or, as they called it, "faction." The federal Constitution did not mention the word, and so foreign was the idea to Washington that he united in his Cabinet the leaders of the Federalist and Republican parties, Hamilton and Jefferson, men more divergent in views than were, later, Lincoln and Jefferson Davis. But, because of the very weakness of the government, because of that *intended* weakness which was to strengthen the individual, a strong, centralized, extra-legal power was inevitable. The party to some degree cemented a government which, otherwise, would have been too dispersed for even the moderate degree of efficiency demanded. Moreover, the party grew naturally out of our current political philosophy. The American individualist wanted power vested in the people and not in legislators, who soon came to be regarded as intrinsically dishonest servants. But the American, with his own business to attend to, had neither leisure nor inclination for the drudgery of running the government. Consequently, the making of nominations, the control of elections, the divisions of spoils, and other profitable labor came to be the work of a despised ruler, the professional politician. The government of the nation passed from legislative halls and executive chambers to the unknown meeting places of party bosses. The election became subordinate to the party primary; the voter, to the ward heeler. The party became supreme.

The politician was a business man, for politics was — and is — business. No great body of men ever continuously devoted itself to a non-honorable service without the hope of monetary reward. Our officials were poorly paid, as though the nation showed what it thought of its lawgivers and administrators when it fixed their salaries. We did not, like the Germans, have "honor offices," places which though unpaid and even inconspicuous, are nevertheless so honorific that high-grade men are proud to serve. In America a man of leisure would rather have become Director of a local Charitable Society — which brought social prestige — than be Supervisor of Highways or School Commissioner. When after 1828 the old-time aristocrats went out, the position of politician — of caretaker of American liberties — was offered to whomsoever would accept.

Politics was business, but in America it was low-grade business, like saloon keeping. Not offering the boundless possibilities of other enterprises, it attracted a poorer quality of men. In De Tocqueville's day an American was not ordinarily intrusted with public business until he had signally failed in his private business. Nevertheless, out of this unpromising material something could be made. Politics took the stones rejected by business and cemented them into the edifice of party.

The party attracted its active men by the most sordid rewards. There were tens of thousands of places and a dozen prospectively grateful seekers for each office. The spoils system was incredibly inefficient and demoralizing, but by providing positions, salaries, and munitions of war, it strengthened the politician and fortified, while debauching, the party. Moreover, the system was speciously democratic and generally popular. The average man believed in "rotation in office." He believed that the government service, like the continent, should be appropriated for private gain.

As population and wealth increased, the government had more favors to bestow, and the right to determine the recipient became extremely valuable. The bank, wanting government deposits; the newspaper, clamoring for city advertising; the saloon, the brothel, the gambler, begging protection, — were willing to pay, as was the railroad wanting terminal facilities, the public service corporation wanting franchises, or the individuals wanting tax remissions.

Nor was the venality of politicians harshly condemned. Americans were too tolerant, too humorous, too optimistic, above all, too busy, to protest overmuch. We had no traditions of public service. Moreover, the individualist really believed that the politician was worthy of his hire. As there seemed no other way of remunerating the despised but visibly useful ward heeler (who was admittedly "not in business for his health"), he was allowed to "graft."

The "honest" politician grafted moderately. He "stayed bought."

The public — the great mass of individualists — came to regard official venality as a plague, which could be abated but not ended, like the depredations of rats, birds, and burglars. The most practical plan was for each citizen to attend to his own business, and restrict the amount of public money stolen by limiting the number and length of legislative sessions, on the assumption that less could be taken in one month than in two. The citizen was satisfied if left alone — as he was; if his cherished personal rights were uninvaded. He was "magnificent" towards the politicians. He was quite willing to spend a million and a half for a million dollars of improvements, and he was willing to pay for his police protection as he was for his railroad rebate. "We pay," said the citizens, honest and dishonest, "but we get."

Occasionally the politicians became so flagrantly extortionate, and legislated so patently against the public interest, that the mass of individualists forgot for a moment their farms and their businesses, their franchises and their bonds, and went in to "punish" the politician. Sometimes the outraged public succeeded; sometimes it failed. In the long run it always failed. For after these electoral lynchings, the righteous indignation passed, and the voters went back to their businesses, while the politician *remained* at his.

Political corruption was ineradicable because the party was extra-legal, and, therefore, irresponsible. In the eyes of the law the men who nominated the candidates for office were a group of citizens assembling for private purposes. The whole machinery of party, from the local primary to the national convention, was beyond the control of the voter. Theoretically, he might give his ballot for any candidate for mayor or governor; practically, the only persons with any chance of election were the candidates of two opposing parties. In the choice of those candidates, the voter had no rights which the party need respect. In the district primary, his vote might be refused or left uncounted; he might see with his own eyes bribery, intimidation, and false counting. He had no redress. The honest voter, who had not even a legal right to go to a primary, found the public servants of the nation selected by the most individualistic person of all, the professional politician, ruling within an irresponsible party.

No wonder the professional politician exploited his advantage. He too had hold of a great resource. Able, aggressive, determined, he had fought for political control as the pioneer had fought in the forest, or the speculator in the Stock Exchange. The city boss might begin as a "bruiser" in a district. He might serve an apprenticeship at ballot stuffing, repeating, or the drudgery of ignoble, but important, political work. For the sake of his party he might even have killed his man. Such a leader was as straight and simple an individualist as the man who bought franchises or the voter who made money by evading the building laws. The political boss recognized that he was not a "good" man, according to his own ethical ideal, but he held himself equal with "them fellows" of the Stock Exchange. He was simply in a business unregulated by law — as were many of the businesses of the voters. Of course, his particular business — that of running a political party — was of paramount public importance, but so were the unregulated businesses of many of the individualists who assailed him. Politics was business, and the politician was diligent in his business.

He was also worldly-wise in his business. The politician had the strength of the man who is not respected, of the man excluded from the top and finding his support at the bottom. The politician was not above his trade nor superior to his client. The party — the gaping tent of the politician — was catholic in scope. It welcomed millionaire and pauper, saint and sinner; in fact, it welcomed the pliable sinner rather more effusively than the uncomfortable saint. A man who would be kicked out of a low saloon was welcome to a party on the ground of his vote. The party embraced all governments, national, State, territorial, city, county, township, school district. It appealed to all ambitions. It attracted the man who aspired to St. James or the Supreme Court and the fellow who begged the poor privilege of picking an occasional pocket. The parties, non-principled and compromising, as was the state, kept down problems but raised issues. They clothed themselves with all the passing prejudices of all the people. They were all things, and more, to all men. They became the ideal.

It was inevitable. A man had to cling to something, and in America, where traditions were weak and where men, following their social instincts, became "joiners," the temptation to cling to party became resistless. Nor was this in itself bad. The party gives cohesion and unity to like-minded men, and professional politicians have their place, as have railway conductors, letter carriers, and paid agents of charitable societies. But party loyalty in America did not always remain subordinate to patriotism and honor, and in so far as it was an unthinking loyalty, it became a weapon in the hands of the more mercenary of party leaders. After 1820, this loyalty grew stronger through the admission of millions of immigrants, grateful for the franchise and for their party membership, and again, after 1867, an added impulse was given to an unthinking party loyalty through the sudden enfranchisement of the Negroes, and their admission to the Republican party.

This party loyalty found expression in a traditional

voting, which obscured contemporaneous issues and enrolled men under banners which they could not read. The Civil War blazoned certain ideas upon the minds of men. The North "waved the bloody shirt"; the South rallied to the cry of "negro domination." The party fanned these dying fires into flame, and appealed with skill to an enthusiasm which in other countries would have attached itself to state, king, or army.

The men who were in politics for money built upon this loyalty, which was their asset, as a farm, mine, or franchise is an asset. They developed their property and secured it, as the pioneer and the preëmptor developed and secured their properties. The professional politicians soon saw that they must be protected against the competition of amateurs, and they formulated the rules of the game to exclude interlopers. By force and fraud at primary and convention, by party rules strengthening strategic and pivotal points, already preëmpted, by securing for themselves immunity from criminal prosecution, by developing a special code of honor and *esprit de corps*, they obtained, subject to the right of the people to rebel, a strong, firm grasp on party and government.

When the frontier was reached, and the pioneer found his way to the continent barred, he ceased to ignore the state and turned to it for protection against the preëmptor. He now wished to do collectively what he could no longer do by his feeble, individual might. But the state, though it had grown, had been so checked, cramped, confined, that it was hardly a match for the great corporation, which had not been cramped but encouraged. Between the state and the pioneer, moreover, lay the overgrown, unregulated, individualistic political party and its representative, brother to the pioneer and brother to the preemptor, the individualistic politician, the party boss.

The attitude of the American had changed towards the

politician as it had changed towards the preëmptor. The average man no longer had quite the old "magnificent" view of the politician as a weed hardly worth while to tear up, so small was its influence on the growing corn. He was no longer so tolerant of evils which had grown with the country's growth. The politician was a dishonest servant, who should be forthwith dismissed. Hereafter the American would run his own public business.

To take away, however, was not so easy as to give. It had been part of the political game always to preach to the people that the party existed merely as their servant and by their leave. But the people had been losing their political prerogative through non-user, and the more they hugged the delusion of effective self-rule, the more strongly did the corrupt party entrench itself.

Moreover the business of political leadership had become centralized. Municipal corruption was now a part of State corruption; State corruption, a part of national corruption. There was always a man "higher up," often very much "higher up." Corruption had become subtle, pervasive. An abler type of man had gone into politics, restricting the potentialities of the earlier, bruiser type, as the preëmptor had restricted those of the pioneer. The new politician was perhaps a college-bred man, who could talk tactfully of the eternal verities. He enjoyed unexceptionable social connections and good business affiliations. Like the preëmptor, his ally, he laid under tribute the best legal and administrative talent. Politics became *big business*, and it assiduously studied the methods of the still bigger business outside. The big business politician was far more formidable than had been the little politician who had preceded him.

A still higher obstacle was to be thrust between the individualistic, sovereign American and his "servant," the political party. As business became synthetic and integrated, as the railroads, coal mines, banks, trust companies, and insurance companies drew closer together, politics, which had grown from a small to a large, independent business, became in some parts of America, *a mere branch* in a still larger, integrated business. The state, which through the party formally sold favors to the large corporations, became one of their departments. The biggest client bought out the concern, as the railroad buys up the factory which once sold it supplies. The weak state, free to bestow its treasures on its favorites, was controlled by the party; the party was controlled by the ring; the ring, by the boss; the boss, by the trust. The petty forms of graft, the tribute levied on vice, crime, saloons, and holders of petty rights and small immunities, persisted. But they had become mere by-products. In many States the fount of legislation, the wells of justice were controlled. Legislation was no longer bought, but *owned.* The big individualist, the giant gambler, had gained his last strategic hold.

CHAPTER VI

THE PLUTOCRATIC REORGANIZATION

IT is not possible to set an exact date for the end of the conquest of the continent. Successive eras in a nation's history do not fit nicely like the flagstones of a pavement, but overlap, and the future is born before the past is dead. Even to-day, the single-handed grabbing of the period of the conquest occasionally appears, naked and unashamed.

However, we may somewhat indefinitely mark off the last three decades of the nineteenth century as a transition period in America. By 1869 the Union Pacific Railroad had narrowed the continent to a week's railroad journey; by 1901 the main outlines of our new trust system had become apparent. Between these two dates the period of mere expansion was merging into a new period, of which the trust was typical and representative.

In 1876, when the Philadelphia Centennial Exhibition opened its doors, America reviewed the achievements of a hundred years. The world was invited to compare the pack horse with the locomotive, the sailboat with the steamboat, the straggling, struggling colonies with the compact, secure States. With a pardonable pride America exhibited as its century's accomplishment the Conquest of the Continent and the Evolution of a Nation.

The nation had been born in the West. The Virginian, Pennsylvanian, Rhode Islander, commingling in the Western territory, had lost some of their fealty to their native States, and had accustomed themselves to a common loyalty to a larger political unit. The Western States, created out of a national territory by the fiat of Congress, could not, like the thirteen original States, claim parenthood of the nation. Their artificial boundaries were a confession that these States had been made, not born. Their problems were national. Their domain was national. Evolved in the West by migrants, American and European, the national consciousness was a fruit of the conquest of the land.[1]

Immigration had contributed to the same end. An ethnic amalgamation of many stocks proceeded at an unprecedentedly rapid rate. Under the free, buoyant spirit of America, the Irish peasant, the English farm laborer, the German refugee, became more American than the Americans. Peoples estranged for centuries in Europe knew but slight antagonism in the Western land. The native tongue, the native customs, the traditional methods of thinking and acting, were forgotten by the sons when not abandoned by the fathers. Intermarriage, the Anglicization and abrasion of foreign names, above all an assimilation in language, dress, and methods of making and spending money, reduced all the peoples to one almost uniform mass. The gratitude of these immigrants attached to Nation, not to State. A nationalism arose, and was tried out during the Civil War.

The building of a nation was not the only fruit of our first hundred years of independence. Wealth, also, we had achieved. The continent, wrested from nature, had been converted by a century of intense labor into a vast, complex, delicate, wealth-creating tool. Our industrial organization had attained a high degree of efficiency. The

[1] In America nationalism and patriotism attach themselves to soil, which is one and indivisible, and not to people, which is diverse. We claim no miraculous descent and no Levitical pureness of blood, but rather robustly pride ourselves on being more mongrel than other nations. Our blood is stirred less by Lexington and Antietam than by the joined shares of a wide-stretching continent. So our dithyrambic Fourth of July eulogies of the American nation describe its habitat as "bounded on the north by the Aurora Borealis," etc.

product of our labor, thanks to the fertility of the continent, was greater than anywhere in Europe. Our railroads were more effective (as they were also more necessary) than those of any other country, and our cities, with all their evils, were among the most wonderful workshops in the world. Our farms, though wastefully and unscientifically conducted, produced more *in toto* than did those of any other land. The country was filling with new millions of hard-working, easy-spending men, gaining steadily in knowledge and the ability to produce and intelligently consume. Our labor was being crystallized into factories, cities, machines, railroads, bridges, wharves, and other productive capital, and we were making our production ever more efficient by making it more indirect; by creating tools to produce tools to produce goods; by delaying the consumption of wealth to make that consumption greater. American prosperity was assured.

In the conquest of the continent America had become a wealthy and powerful nation, with a strong national consciousness. America had prospered. Nevertheless, when the traveler from Europe turned from the records of material progress, displayed at the exhibition, and cast his eyes over the back yard of America, he discovered that the progress of growth had not been unaccompanied by an accumulation of waste products. Out of the American's contest with the wilderness had developed certain barriers to future progress: a scarred and wasted continent; a brick-and-mortar substitute for a city; an unregulated and anarchic industry; a city slum; and an appalling and shameless political corruption.

The continent, incalculably fertile and wealth-giving though it was, showed signs of a century of rape. Regions formerly blessed with a plentiful rainfall had become arid, and rivers which once kept their measured beds now alternated between trickling, unfructifying streams and torrential floods. Everywhere were the evil results of the destruction of forests, the denudation of soils, the impoverishment of rivers, the annihilation of animal life, and the insensate wasting of natural resources by men who knew no responsibility, and who in the midst of a self-created desolation were astounded at their own moderation. The continent, which had evoked the spirit which meant its ravishing, was now like a nursery, with its broken toys strewn upon the floor.

Like the continent, the city had been scarred by the same waste and preëmption, the same insensate optimism, the same utter lack of prevision. Cities destined to be the home of multitudes had grown up with the abandon of petty villages. Streets had been made narrow; parks had been forgotten; houses had been built upon the theory of packing boxes; drainage, water supply, fire protection — everything had been left to chance and the play of the instinct for gain. The theory of the American city was that of the pioneer's camp. People were there for business. Their living conditions must work out themselves.

The citizen of 1876 contentedly voted for crude political bosses, as his son to-day votes for bosses of a more refined type. The citizen of 1876 contentedly rode in rainy weather on the roof of a crowded horse car, as his son to-day rides on the outside platform of an overfilled electric car. The citizen of 1876 contentedly died of typhoid, because his city drank water befouled by other cities. Then, as now, municipal heedlessness consigned thousands of citizens to unnecessary deaths from tuberculosis. The filthiness of American towns was a stench in the nostrils, and the houses, tenements, and factories, constructed under a *régime* of unregulated individualism, were a menace to health and an affront to decency. The American city, destined to become the leader in our new democracy, had suffered most grievously from the spirit of the conquest. So onerous was the burden of brick and mortar that a conflagration, which wiped out a whole city, was often an unmixed blessing.

American business — reckless and implacable — showed even more the traces of a barbaric immoderation than did forest and city. To only the slightest extent did the organized national consciousness determine what should be produced and sold, or how the human resources of the nation should be industrially utilized. Our psychological and moral perceptions and our ponderous legal machinery had not kept pace with our money-winged, profit-dreaming business development. The industrially strong had been given what they wanted; the industrially weak might keep what they could hold against the subsidized strong. The small investor had a legal remedy, but little real protection. The consumer had less. The competitor had none. As for the worker, male or female, adult or child, skilled or unskilled, he had the right of a freedom of contract, but was not always himself economically free. He had the protection of the law of supply and demand, but the supply of his labor was artificially stimulated. In 1876 — as now — the American Commonwealths were far behind the leading countries of Europe in laws regulating hours of labor, conditions of work, the prevention of accidents; in laws regulating truck stores, sweat shops, the employment of women, the employment of children.

While some American manufacturers had been protected against the competition of foreign manufacturers, our resident laborers had not been protected against the competition of European laborers. Immigration had brought in nation after nation, each with a lower standard of living. Whether the ultimate effect was good or bad, whether the immediate burden upon the city toiler was tolerable or intolerable, the nation had not cared. The labor market might be glutted or anæmic, the city tenements and shanties might be crowded, the political machine might already be creaking under the weight of illiterate and inarticulate voters. Nevertheless if immigrants came — or could be made to come — they must be admitted; if admitted, they must be rudely digested, or at least devoured. They must pay their way to an army of little "grafters" and to the great respectable tribute-takers of city and country. Unrestricted immigration aided an ultra-rapid development. It pyramided production. We viewed the dense forests of foreigners, as we viewed the pregnant continent, as a boundless, exploitable resource. Into our anarchic industry we poured these millions, adults and children alike, just as in working the Maine woods we felled the saplings, the growing children of the forest, the more readily to get at the full-grown trees. There was no gain in it except the saving of a little time, but a minute to-day was more than a forest or a generation to-morrow.

It had been feared by European observers, even as late as the fifties, that the wide dispersion of the early Americans would result in a reversion to barbarism. No such regression took place. We always carried with us a certain fringe of backwoods savagery (which still persists in remote mountain districts), but the main current of American life moved far too swiftly to permit of intellectual or moral stagnation. Nevertheless a barbarism, different in type from that of the backwoods, did parallel the civilizing, pioneering movement. With the growth of America grew the slum.

Our worst slums are not so hopeless as the slough of Whitechapel, or the horrid slums of English towns, where literally rot the descendants of Crécy and Poitiers. The poverty of even our most destitute negroes is opulence compared with the bottomless misery of south Italy or Russia. The enormous wealth of the continent, and our long immunity from serious foreign war or the fear of war, lessened our pauperism and held up even our lowest standards of living to a point where they annually attracted, and still attract, hundreds of thousands of immigrants. Many of our poorer city wards are not slums at all in the European sense. They are not cesspools of society, into which the hopeless human refuse inextricably sinks, but are rather trying-out stations, out of which are promoted rising immigrants, who have survived the corroding experiences of the first years of American life.

Nevertheless, we have slums, pauper slums and criminal slums, the heirlooms of our sweaty haste, our headless, soulless egotism, our fragile, apologetic, emasculated state. The slum, like the grim, malevolent ogre of the fairy tale, was feasted with children, ground out, destroyed, and corrupted in their weakness, and thrown aside in adolescence, like a dry orange. To the slum came eventually the men who were maimed in factories, in mines, on railroads, and could not recover the cost of crutch or bandage. To the slum came the wives and babes of men killed outright in industry, or poisoned systematically, and for profit, by advertised foods and medicines. The state, the natural representative of the people, fed the slums. It did not interfere when women staggered under excessive tasks; when old men were thrown out upon the pavement; when young girls, unable to support themselves decently, sold themselves outright to indecency; when strikes broke out and men were starved or shot or bayoneted, or in their turn broke the arms of strike-breakers, or set fire to their employers' buildings. The state had no eyes, senses, dimensions. It was nothing but a paralytic old man with a club.

The serenely stupid indifference of the state, the granting of a free hand to all the money-makers — gamblers, speculators, jerry-builders, franchise grabbers, employers of child labor, — to the whole confraternity of "grafters" — helped to muster the ignorant and despoiled denizens of the slum. The turbulence of business gave the slum its quota of cripples, tramps, and paupers; the savage intensification of factory labor created thousands of brutalized workers, and tens of thousands of bloodless persons, incapable of further labor. Our slums became filled with sick who need never have been sick; with derelicts who need never have been abandoned. The slum became the abiding place of "free and equal," but superfluous, Americans.

In these crowded, squalid quarters, with high tenements towering above dirty, narrow streets, lived the poor, the wretched, the ill, the dissolute, the criminal. Flimsy partitions separated families from all corners of the globe. The congestion aided in the spread of vice and infectious disease. In reeking tenements, in horrible streets and mews and alleys, alcoholism, dissipation, consumption, and poverty bred a weakly race, while thousands of wretches, food for the jail, almshouse, and brothel, were thrown out as unconsidered waste products. Upon this festering, weltering mass of sodden humanity, the offspring of a careless society, the frontier no longer exercised an attraction. There was no gateway from the criminal slum. The valves turned inward, to allow the seeping in of the worsted in the battle.

A philosophic traveler might well have turned his back upon the "exhibits" at Philadelphia to wonder how the slum had found its home in the nation "conceived in liberty," in a nation of free and equal men with free access to a continent. And yet the underworld of America was but part of the price of our continental adventure. The recklessness of the slum dweller, bred of the recklessness of the state; the sullen discontent of men whose vision was bounded by mean streets and mean sights — this slum-stamped, seamy side of American life was but the reverse of the daring, optimistic spirit which had conquered the continent. The brilliant, imaginative impulse of the conquest, that impulse which had felled the trees, ravaged the forests, built, as by magic, the instantaneous cities, ground up, or evolved, the incoming millions, turned the energies of a nation and the resources of a continent into an apotheosis of the individual — that all-conquering impulse had ended ingloriously in the slum, the nadir of modern life. The individualist, conquering the primeval wilderness, had erected upon the cleared land a *city wilderness*, an overgrown, tangled, rank, and morass-filled forest of distorted and dying human plants of all countries, of all natures, ill-assorted, struggling for a dwarfed life and — poisonous.

It had not been entirely unforeseen. From the first the conquest of the continent, and the triumphant, ruthless materialism which it evoked, had aroused an opposition from within the nation. A thousand dissidents had risen in rebellion against the crudities, brutalities, and immoralities of the conquest. Amid the shrill clamor of money-making individualists had been heard the low minor note of protest.

Some of this opposition came from quiet stay-at-homes, who, loving an orderly existence, could not abide pioneers, gamblers, or pushing business adventurers. "These men," says a great New England divine, speaking of the early nineteenth century pioneers, "cannot live in regular society. They are too idle, too talkative, too passionate, too prodigal, and too shiftless, to acquire either property or character. They are impatient of the restraints of law, religion, and morality; grumble about the taxes, by which rulers, ministers, and schoolmasters are supported, and at last, under the pressure of poverty, the fear of a jail, and the consciousness of public contempt, leave their native places, and betake themselves to the wilderness." [1]

It was not, however, reserved to New England divines to protest against the pioneer, nor against the stark materialistic and individualistic spirit of America. Great moral and religious movements were in conflict with that dominant spirit. Transcendentalism, idealism, perfectionism, the cult of a Utopian socialism, swept over the land. Communistic

[1] Dwight, Timothy, "Travels in New England and New York." London, 1823.

experiments were tried at Brook Farm, Icaria, and elsewhere. The Mormons, united by a newly revealed religion, developed Utah, without relying upon the individualism of other pioneers. Men arose in protest against the ugliness and callousness of American exploitation.

For the most part these protestants were ineffective. The man of refined taste, who demanded that material progress should be beautiful, had no message for his highly inartistic generation. The average American of 1840 did not object to the smoke of factory towns, nor to the defacing of sylvan glens by advertisements of malaria cures and plug tobacco. He had little understanding for purely artistic or philanthropic plans, and even the vast moral weight opposed to our theft of Mexico's land could not divert America from her task of individualistically exploiting a continent. Waves of religious and ethical emotion rose and fell, but they no more decided the course of America than the Sunday sermon against greed determines the price at which the monopolist sells on a Monday. All these early moral movements — all but one — failed because they lacked confirmation by economic necessity. The voices of the reformers were drowned in the cannon of 1861.[1]

It was not these reformers, but a quite different group

[1] The one exception to the rule that the purely moral movements were without much influence was abolition, a moral movement directed against the crassest and most archaic form of human exploitation. This exception, however, was only apparent. It was because slavery *was* archaic and uneconomical; it was because abolition was not only a moral, but also an *economic*, movement, in harmony with (and not opposed to) the conquest of the continent, that it was so transcendentally successful. Free settlers clamored for free land. The antislavery movement, which in 1831 found few followers (because there was still an empty continent before us), became a potent force in 1860, when the final disposition of our available territory was within sight. Upon the Northern side were not only the uncompromising Garrisonians and other idealists, but also the settlers, the railroads, the corporations, needing more land. The fierce, conquering, individualistic spirit, which was overrunning the continent, armed the Federal soldiers in their assault upon the Confederacy.

of men; it was not the generous aspirations of transcendentalists, but motives of a far tougher fiber, which took us out of the old world of planlessness, unregulated grabbing, and unrestrained wasting. Not men with a new moral ideal, but financiers anxious for profits, put an end to the old single-handed individualism. Brook Farm, a community built upon ideals, failed; Gary, a city made to order, a city planned for profits, succeeded.

It could not have been otherwise. When we struck the frontier, we were still in the full momentum of a profit-seeking individualism. We were still listening to the cry, "Go West, young men," when, suddenly, to our surprise—*there was no West.* The headlessness, the low social pressure, the waste and brutality of the old period could not at once give way to socialization. What followed was the monopoly age, the age of utilization. Its specific feature was the trust; its typical class the plutocracy. It represented the old individualism of America, upon which was grafted the new ideal of continental reorganization.

What was necessary was to supplement the mere appropriation of resources by their wiser utilization. It was necessary to cultivate intensively, now that mere extensive culture had struck against geographical obstacles. Instead of waste, economy became the order of the day. There was money in by-products—in cottonseed oil, in coal-tar derivatives, in the utilization of the whole hog. There was money in a standardization of plants, of product, of labor. There was money, above all, in monopoly. The era of lowering prices gave way to an era of rising prices; the era of industrial anarchy, to an era of industrial subordination. Fighting for one's own hand became coöperation for the sake of profits. From top to bottom American industry was in process of reorganization.

In this reorganization a new spirit entered business. It was an analytical and an objective spirit. Every industrial operation, from the laying of a brick to the building of a subway, was divided into its constituent parts, subjected to a minute and searching financial analysis, and reconstructed on a more paying basis. The rule of hand gave way to business methods of scientific precision. The statistician took his place in the office, and the accountant, the business engineer, and the business statesman introduced a totally new efficiency into industry. The chemist in business gave a new meaning to the search for by-products, discovering a continent greater than that of the pioneer. The inventor opened up new sources of wealth, and the forester and the agricultural expert showed how conservation meant increased production, how you could get more from your land while keeping more in it, how a sanely intensive conduct of industry could give a greater product with less effort than did the former wasteful and sprawling extensive conduct of business.

While chemists, engineers, inventors, statisticians, agriculturalists, foresters, factory organizers all contributed to the reorganization of American business, the greatest contribution was that of the financiers, of the trust builders. These men, the true representatives of the new era, were quantitative gentlemen, who held inventors, scientists, and factory engineers in the leash of their figures. It was these financiers who created the trust, the typical expression of the plutocratic reorganization.

The trust, at its best, represented a more economical and more profitable form of business organization than did the former competing business. It was made up by the union of many thousands of little fortunes, by the coöperation of many individualistic manufacturers, who had not wished to sell to the trust, and had capitalized their reluctance at a high figure. The trust, though in certain respects antisocial, did at least prevent some of our earlier reckless wastes. To a certain extent it saved needless duplications of plants, the useless sending of cross freights, the absurd vagaries of a boundless, competitive advertising, the unnecessary complications of an industry with a hundred heads and a hundred pairs of flapping and entangling arms.

At its best, moreover, the trust tended to bring order out of chaos; to substitute prevision and a broad outlook for the taking of a chance and a narrow view of the situation. It was more likely, because better able, to save to-day, to have to-morrow. It could better preserve monopolized natural resources against the time when depletion would be imminent. It could keep down prices to a reasonably extortionate level. The trust, safely entrenched, was not driven by the fearful, individualistic competition in which mercy, decency, and even foresight, might place a competitor *hors de combat.*

Finally, the trust could refrain, if it wished, from many foolish, short-sighted and antisocial actions. It could afford the long view; it could even afford an ultimately profitable decency. The trust, especially at its worst, with its unfair competition, its tyranny, its over-charges, and its political corruption, was by no means the last word in industrial development, but it was superior to what had preceded it, and *it was necessary.* Because we could not escape from our former utter planlessness and anarchy except by reorganizing our whole business (and allowing acquisitive and imaginative men to make billions out of the process), we were obliged to go over to a highly centralized trust system of production. We were obliged to call in a receiver to take charge of our assets. We were compelled to raise up despots to put an end to the civil strife in our industry.

It fares ill with a population when it is obliged in its own defense to call in mercenaries, military or financial. We have paid a high price for the reorganization of our business, and everywhere in our industry, in our government, in our organs of public opinion, we find the traces of a swaggering plutocracy which has claimed its reward as it performed its work — and faster. To-day our problems are enormously complicated by the presence in our midst of a powerful and cohering plutocracy, with vast power and antidemocratic temptations.

CHAPTER VII

OUR RESPLENDENT PLUTOCRACY

FOR a long time, disliking the idea of a plutocracy, we simply denied its existence. We informed our foreign critics that our great fortunes were evanescent, accidental, due to temporary disturbances in a permanently equalizing economic process. We tried to believe that there were but three generations from shirt-sleeves to shirt-sleeves. To-day, however, the evidence is overwhelming that American fortunes do not vanish, but grow ever larger. Our plutocracy can no longer be concealed.

What is this American plutocracy? It is not, as the Century Dictionary defines plutocracy, "a class ruling by virtue of its wealth," for it is at most a class in process, and its rule is only partial, undefined, and unadmitted. Our American plutocracy is rather a more or less fluctuating group of very wealthy men, loosely united (primarily by pecuniary bonds) who, through their wealth and prestige, and through the allegiance of like-minded but poorer men, exert an enormous, if not preponderating, influence over industry, politics, and public opinion.

This plutocracy does not aspire, and dare not aspire, to personal rule. There is a tenacious political myth that our millionaires aim at the subversion of all constitutional guarantees, and at the creation of an American Empire upon the ruins of our present republic. But our over-moneyed men do not indulge such romantic and belated notions. True, an occasional millionaire succumbs to the pitiful ambition of "founding a family," and accordingly ties up his estate for a generation or two. True, there are sons and daughters and sons-in-law — young and decorative fashionables — who dislike the robustness of American life, and feebly long for those signal recognitions of leisured wealth which only royalty can confer. These facts, however, are of infinitesimal significance. Our titled marriages and our sudden appetite for heraldic quarterings are an unconscious confession, not a boast. The strident inanities, the "conspicuous waste," and the advertised idleness of a few transcendent spenders are not to be dignified by an imperialistic interpretation.

After all, our money kings are groundlings. They are, for the most part, workmen, or business men evolved, without the class traditions which protect British peer or Prussian *Junker* from the resentment of the masses. The American multi-millionaire reads his evening paper, and (though he owns it) forms his opinion, in part at least, by what he reads therein. So thin is the wall of wealth, that great business magnates, who did but what their predecessors had done, have actually died of shame, when an aroused public contempt had been concentrated upon their financial dealings. Individually the great men of America are much like the little men. They are a small group with intense ambitions and enormous power, but they still remain intellectually subject to the current philosophy of the nation.

Our loosely cohering plutocracy is of very recent birth. "Until the twenties or thirties of the nineteenth century," says Mr. Bryce, "there were no great fortunes in America and few large ones." "Now," he continues, "there is some poverty, many large fortunes, and a greater number of gigantic fortunes than in any country of the world." In the twenty years since Mr. Bryce wrote, accumulation has been proceeding at an immensely accelerated rate. To-day, more than ever before, a plutocratic group has power, prestige, and pretensions, with a favored economic position and a wide notoriety.

Whence came these sudden millionaires? What seed carelessly dropped upon the fertile American continent brought forth this strange, exotic fruit?

A curiously significant change has come about in our attitude towards the origin of millionaires. In the early days when our society was less differentiated, and wealth-gaining represented exceptional ability *of approximately the same kind* as that of the average man, mere possession was *prima facie* evidence of shrewdness, force, and *savoir faire.* The rich man was the respected "leading citizen" (with a strong local flavor). He was the ordinary obscure citizen raised to the *n*th degree. The penniless individual, on the other hand, was too often a known wastrel, a man of evil life or neglected opportunities. With customary American immoderation we are now swinging from an excessive laudation of wealth to an exaggerated blame, and our great fortunes are regarded almost as an admission of personal dishonesty. The driver of an ice wagon is now coming to recognize his own abilities as distinct from and therefore as ethically superior to the abilities of the secret financier who reorganizes a railroad or floats a trust. "No man," so runs a solacing maxim, "can make a million honestly."

There is only too much evidence to associate the getting of many of our great fortunes with a swaggering financial brigandage. The story of our railroad wreckers, of our distributors of worthless stocks, of our gentlemanly, manicured thieves of public lands, is repeated year by year with nauseous iteration. The incredible rascalities of the old Erie Railroad; the historic shifts, lies, violences, and illegalities of the Standard Oil Company; the dubious financial manipulations of the United States Steel Corporation; the fraudulent operations of the Ship-building Trust; the dishonest promotion of notorious asphalt companies; the labors of the forty thieves of public service franchises—link the present with the past in one malodorous chain of financial infamy.

It would be invidious to specify more nearly the most tainted of our money-makers, to confer a distinction of blame where so many are deserving, just as it would be invidious to compile an incomplete directory of our contemporary pickpockets or "strong-arm men." Even an outline of the corrupt accumulation of fortunes would require more volumes than one would care to read or write. For lovers of the picaresque, there are hundreds of edifying books, reports, and court decisions, and thousands of magazine articles, constituting a veritable financial Newsgate Calendar. Let us take our feet out of the mire, after noting where the mire lies.

For the true genesis of our plutocracy, we must go deeper. The charge of a universal personal dishonesty is too sweeping. Fortunes have been made by men of sterling integrity. Others have been acquired by men neither better nor worse than their contemporaries. Moreover, the explanation does not explain. Even in the thousands of cases where rogues obtained millions of unguarded public treasure, we must look behind the criminal intent of the fortune-getter to the carelessness, ignorance, and political ineptitude of society. Our laws, institutions, and philosophies aided, instead of preventing, these vast accumulations. We have in this country thousands of hopeful and predestined safe-crackers. We have also burglar-proof safes, but for which we should be despoiled, however loudly we threatened the cracksmen with prison and social ostracism. Our gross private accumulations arose because we had a great social surplus, and knew not what to do with it, how to appropriate it, or how to guard it. Our unseeing society took the vow of poverty, and gave away all it had — to the rich.

Many avenues have led to American fortunes. Men who, by accident or through foresight, held tracts of city land, became innocently rich. Others drew fabulous dividends from unconsidered coal lands, oil fields, iron mines, forests. Some rode to wealth on the wings of a patented device — a telephone, typewriter, harvester, glove-hook. Men fell heir to the inventions of others — as when the owners of rusty horse-car lines profited by the discovery of electric traction. Other fortunes were found on the dump, on the waste heap. Large scale production led not only to direct economies, but to the discovery and utilization of by-products. Quite apart from its rebates, the Beef Trust, through sheer effectiveness in utilizing such waste products, would have been able to overcome the little butchers who used to fill our cities and towns with their redolent abattoirs.

Standardization also made fortunes. As the grading of wheat enabled a man to deal in millions of bushels without seeing them, so the grading of industrial plants, the standardization of labor, and the adoption of uniform systems of cost-keeping allowed a single concern to maintain factories all over the country. Consumption, too, was standardized. By advertising, by sheer repetition of a request to buy, manufacturers could directly appeal, over the heads of shopkeepers and middlemen, to the consumers of the nation. The growing needs of the people were reduced to one common denominator. Individual preferences were accommodated and compromised. The cigarette factories and biscuit factories compelled the people of Los Angeles and Boston, of Jacksonville and Duluth to ask for the identical cigarette or biscuit. The babies of a continent were induced to cry for a single cathartic.[1]

Although most businesses, from the selling of roach foods to the manufacture of battleships and newspapers, have pro-

[1] Standardization also appears in the organization of department stores, nation-wide mail-order houses, etc., which are examples, not of specialized, but of integrated, businesses. A great department store of to-day is merely a federation of independent concerns, for each so-called department is an autonomous business, being charged for rent, light, heat, and being compelled — in order to keep its place in the store — to contribute its share of joint profit.

duced considerable fortunes, the chief source of our stupendous accumulations has usually been some great monopoly advantage, not shared by competitors; some advantage secured legally or illegally, with the consent of the people or in their despite.

This monopoly, which in its simplest form inheres in land and is at the basis of the Astor and the Field fortunes, finds its typical modern expression in a great group of railway, public franchise, and industrial combinations, all of which we may conveniently group together under the vague and inexact term, "the trust." In this large, loose, and somewhat unusual sense of the word, the trust is the business address of our plutocracy, and our plutocrats are the trust-builders, "insiders," the men "on the ground floor." The trust has preyed on the community's surplus, and the insider has preyed on the trust. From those who work for the trust, seek to compete with the trust, buy from the trust or sell to the trust, a steady stream of wealth flows *to* the trust. From the trust and from investors in the trust a steady stream of wealth flows to the insider.

Not all industries are susceptible to the trust process. Our farms are relatively small. Our retail trade is only slightly in the hands of big organizations. Our many businesses of making small special articles, of furnishing personal services, are largely under the competitive control of small business units. Where, however, a business has a natural monopoly element, or where it may be readily standardized, or where economy and efficiency are greater in large establishments than in small ones, there, large scale production (which, though not inherently monopolistic, lends itself to monopoly) is a necessity of business and a permanent symptom of our industrial life. In certain great industries we have definitely and irrevocably committed ourselves to production on the largest scale. Our railroad systems will never again be disintegrated. Our street railways will never be broken up into mutually competing parts. The Standard Oil Company, under perhaps a new organization and another name, will continue to unify the oil business of the country. A steel trust, either the present or some future one, will continue to exist. In many important industries we cannot possibly return to an unlimited competition or to production on a smaller scale. Until we understand this fundamental fact we shall have nothing but hard knocks and chaos.

It is thus possible to speak of the plutocracy not only as a group of excessively wealthy men, with their business and social retainers, but also as a system of industrial organization. We may describe the plutocracy, or the plutocratic economy, as that system of industry in which a large and increasing portion of the income of society flows into great reservoirs (usually natural or legal monopolies) which are preëmpted and controlled by private corporations. The plutocratic economy is based upon a narrowing control of enlarging funds; upon a unity of command in the industrial world; upon the leadership of the large purse. Its ideal is the conquest of the world's market. Its creed is freedom of large industry from political interference. Its weapon is monopoly and large scale production.

Not only are monopoly and large scale production permanent, but they are rapidly trenching upon small scale and formerly competitive industries. The businesses in which there is a visible monopoly element are already overpowering in magnitude. A totally incomprehensible amount of capital, estimated, a few years ago, at thirty-one billions of dollars (par, not actual, value), represents the stocks and bonds of our railroad, public franchise, and large industrial corporations. The United States Steel Corporation alone has emitted securities which actually bring on the market over one billion of dollars. Despite prohibitory legislation, our railroads have continued to unite legally and actually.

There are believed to be six compact railroad groups, each with a capital of over one billion dollars. A single group of financiers is supposed to dominate railroads with a combined capitalization of three thousand millions of dollars.[1]

These great amalgamations are still growing.[2] The big business concern, with a natural or artificial monopoly, or merely a short cut to the savings of the people, prospers exceedingly. It grows fat by indulging the right to levy an increasing toll upon an increasing number of millions. Secure from competition (sometimes even from potential competition), the trust grows in value with the birth of each child and the advent of each immigrant. It raises prices, and each increase is immediately reflected in increased earnings, and in the issue of new capital.[3] Not only does the public pay the increase (though not without humorous grumbling), but it allows the trusts to sell their surplus products more cheaply abroad than at home, to sell cheap abroad *for the very purpose* of selling dear at home. Though the trusts have not been uniquely responsible for the rise of prices during the last fifteen years, this rise has taken place simultaneously with a cornering of a protected market and with the absorption of an increasing proportion of the social surplus by industrial combinations.

The trust succeeds because it is a unit. Consumers, laborers, and competitors, on the other hand, are many and largely unorganized. The trust can profitably employ a

[1] Not even an approximate exactness is claimed for these figures, which are at best but vague estimates.

[2] This does not apply to what may be called pseudo-trusts — mere loose, industrial aggregations, with no monopoly advantage, and with an aqueous capitalization which reveals the motive of their formation. These clumsy business Leviathans merely cumber the ground, and tend to disappear under the competition of more active, because more economically constructed, industrial creatures.

[3] Some ten years ago the railroads, by a mere innocent change in freight classification, were able to add tens of millions to their earnings and hundreds of millions to their capitalizable value.

one-hundred-thousand-dollar man to determine when the scattered millions of consumers will stand an increase of a tenth of a cent per pound or gallon. Over its employees the trust enjoys similar advantages. A hundred mill managers are pitted against each other in a competition to secure — not necessarily the lowest paid employees — but the lowest possible, the lowest conceivable labor cost. Long hours, excessive speed, Sunday labor, night labor, the employment of women and children, the casting aside of middle-aged men, the cutting down of wages, even the running of truck stores enter into this reduction of labor cost. To preserve the advantage of unity over multiplicity, to remain one, and to keep its opponents many, the great trust usually manifests an antagonistic attitude towards labor unions. The hundred-million-dollar corporation, to rescue its honest workmen from the clutches of the walking delegate, prefers to bargain individually with each of its employees. Such bargaining between the lion and the hare — though recognized by our legal traditions as normal — usually redounds to the advantage of the lion.

In its relation to surviving competitors, the trust often, though not always, enjoys the same advantage. There are in industry many small nooks and crannies in which the trust's competitors, because of their very inconspicuousness, may survive, while profiting by the high prices maintained by the trust. Other corporations thrive by preying upon the trusts and especially upon the essentially unstable pseudo-trusts. Usually, however, the big industrial undertaking can defeat the little one by superior banking, railroad, or legislative facilities, or by turning practically unlimited resources to a contest in a limited market. The United Cigar Stores Company (the Tobacco Trust) destroyed, in detail, innumerable tobacconists. The Beef Trust ruined, one by one, many individual butchers. The trust fights on inside lines. It concentrates all its forces on a single point. The trust has the overwhelming advantage of unity.

The trust magnate has an exactly analogous advantage. As the trust is a powerful unit opposed to an unorganized and comparatively defenseless industrial society, so, inside the trust, the "magnate," the "insider," is a powerful unit opposed to unorganized and comparatively defenseless stockholders. The trust rules despotically over business. The magnate rules despotically over the trust.

This despotic rule of the trust magnate is due to a fundamental revolution in the nature of investment. The average small investor of to-day — with a capital of twenty, or of twenty thousand, dollars — does not take a mortgage on his neighbor's farm nor become a silent partner in his neighbor's business. Those investments exist and attract billions, but the greater billions go into large unknown, unforeseeable ventures. The little capitalist may not even own the house in which he lives, and he may run his business on credit, while maintaining a balance at the bank or investments in the great industries of the country. Enormous numbers of small capitals are gathered by banks, trust companies, and insurance companies, and are invested ultimately in securities, which are bought on the stock exchange. Hundreds of thousands of men give to brokers large or small funds to invest, and thousands of millions of dollars, invested in savings banks and in trust and life insurance companies, find their way, unknown to their owners, into enormous agglomerations of capital. The stocks and bonds of "the trusts" are in many cases widely distributed.

This revolution in investment is a necessity of our modern production. It renders capital perfectly mobile. It directs the savings of many men with many minds to one great, concrete enterprise. It enables a man to "realize" immediately; to know, day by day, how much he is "worth." Under present conditions, however, as a result of no laws, bad laws, and of good laws badly enforced, the little investors are not always the controllers or chief beneficiaries of the great corporations which they "own." The very disproportion between the unit of investment (which is one share, worth one hundred dollars or less) and the industrial concern (which in the steel business is the billion dollar corporation) tends towards a divorce between ownership and control, and by encouraging irresponsibility, and discouraging wisdom and caution in investment, enables the insider to profit hugely at the expense of his stockholders. Our enormous private fortunes are largely due to this control by a few men of the blind investments of the many.

It is an old adage that a fool and his money are soon parted, and a modern commentary, that a fool is born every minute. There is no known way to prevent the men without brains from contributing to the support of the men without conscience. We have always had financial manias, when men parted with their savings for stock in companies "to make deal boards out of sawdust," or "for a wheel of perpetual motion," while during the South Sea bubble, men eagerly bought stock in "a company for carrying on an undertaking of great advantage, but nobody to know what it is." In finance high and low, most men are fools some of the time, and some men are fools all of the time.

The defect of our corporation arrangements, however, is not that they fail to provide a guardian for each speculative fledgling, but that they compel even the cautious, honest, and reasonably intelligent investor to work more or less with his eyes shut. Owing to business secrecy and uncontrolled financial methods, the safe opportunities are so few compared to the enormous masses of capital seeking investment, that not only is production made more expensive, but the return to capital is so discouragingly low that men are tempted through the hope of a greater gain to invest in enterprises of which they know nothing.[1]

While the legal constitutions (the charters of incorporation) of our giant trusts are sometimes speciously democratic in form, they are often autocratic in practice. Theoretically the owner of a single share of stock has a voice in the election of directors and the determination of policy. Actually the mass of the capital may be invested in bonds or in preferred stock not carrying voting power, or the individual shareholder may be deceived, overawed, or disregarded. The sovereign stockholder is deluded by misleading circulars, by diversions of profits, by a confusion of securities, piled one upon another; by bond conversions in the interest of dominating bankers; by the arbitrary transfer of profits from one constituent company to another. A company, with a capital of three thousand dollars, solemnly purchases plants worth tens of millions. Dummy directors act as purchasers in the real interests of the vendors. Stock is issued, and huge debts are contracted, without adequate consideration. Stocks rise and fall as dividends are declared or passed, and the insiders not only know, but determine, dividends. The corporation laws of several States, enlisted in an ignoble competition to legitimize robbery, give the insider every possible advantage, as does also a business secrecy which, because it is permissible in a village grocery store, is retained by corporations with hundreds of millions

[1] Moreover, the certificate of ownership — the share of stock — has, by becoming standardized, been made immediately vendible. When a thing is immediately vendible, its selling price becomes of paramount importance. The stock becomes worth what some other person wisely or foolishly is willing to pay for it, and we cease to care about intrinsic values, but buy in expectation of sale. Losses on the stock exchange often represent the delusions of purchasers as to the extent to which other purchasers can be deluded. The man who is seeking investment runs a gauntlet of clashing financial giants and of a mob of speculators seeking to out-guess one another.

of the people's savings. More or less, though less than formerly, the financial magnate works in the dark. By a stroke of the pen he changes the fortunes of thousands. To his stockholders and directors he may thunder, "Vote first, discuss afterwards."

In the lawless days of feudal England the lordless man was so unsafe and so despised that he sought out a lord to whom he might become a serf. In our financial world to-day we have a somewhat analogous institution of lordship and vassalage. We have moneyed oligarchs controlling the capitals of financial retainers, and we have lordless little capitalists seeking a financial lord. There is in all the domain of finance no one absolute monarch, since the greatest of all must secure the support of neighboring rulers, as well as the loyalty of his own money-bound subjects. Nevertheless, the great lords of finance do most confidently depend upon the unquestioning allegiance of their financial vassals, who contribute millions to blind pools without knowing the purposes for which the money is to be used, and without subsequently receiving any adequate accounting. The custom of profits — obtained at the expense of the industry — seals the mouths and the consciences of reorganizers and silent underwriters. They do not ask to know. As for the little investor — the theoretic sovereign of all this financial realm — he is utterly ignorant and absolutely impotent. Oligarchy in business is more strongly entrenched than in politics, not only because it is more secret and profit-bound, but because the little investor gives his proxy or buys his single share with a lighter heart than a voter gives his ballot.

Our plutocracy, based on the trust's position in industry and the trust magnate's position within the trust, is composed, to a great extent, of strong, unscrupulous, far-seeing, and ultra-individualistic persons, who secured hold of our national monopolized business while we as a nation were dreaming of competitive beatitudes. These men, who built up our competition-destroying trusts, are themselves graduates of a ruthless competition. Our plutocracy made its profits under the new *régime*, but it formed its habits and gained its appetites under the old.

Under the guidance of these leaders of the plutocracy, our industrial concentration continues to grow. Our protective tariff aids the trust as against the American consumer. Our internal free trade aids the trust as against less favored competitors in various parts of the country. Our almost unrestricted immigration, by creating a surplus of labor, aids the trust as against its workmen. Finally, our rapidly increasing national wealth aids the trust builder, as against the trust investor, by enormously widening the sources of capital and by making capital cheaper.

It is impossible to set limits to the future development of our trusts. Just as the control by industrial groups of capitals amounting to one billion dollars would have been almost inconceivable a generation ago, so in the future this control may reach even greater proportions. The giant trust, which long since eclipsed city and State, now aspires to overshadow the nation. Difficulties of mere organization have been overcome. It is as easy to control a billion-dollar, as a one-hundred-million-dollar corporation, and it will be no more impossible to organize a five-billion-dollar corporation than it is impossible for the President of the United States to administer a government of ninety-two million citizens. It is quite conceivable that in the future, railroad systems or industrial corporations, or enormous federations of both, or Titanic holding companies with interests in all industries, everywhere, may come to be, in which the capital may aggregate three or five or more billions of dollars, the working spirits being half a dozen, and the leading and responsible executive, one man.

The diffusion of stock, and the resulting divorce between

the ownership and the control of these large corporations, will make for such a progressive amalgamation. The channels through which the billions of savings move toward investment tend to approach each other and to coalesce. The very nature of big business tends towards a narrow control of enlarging funds. The small railroad, swallowed by the large one, often prospers by the swallowing, and as its stock rises, other railroads shyly clamor to be devoured. Gradually it is perceived by great financial powers that their interests are not mutually exclusive, but are capable of adjustment, and, in spite of friction, an inner momentum tends to bring them together. It is largely a problem of psychological adjustment, of the gradual removal of giant financial leaders with separatist tendencies. When the conditions are right, when the minds of the rulers of money and of the people are attuned to the new conditions, there may come, in some period of overwhelming prosperity and optimism, a series of combinations compared to which the formation of the billion-and-a-half-dollar Steel Corporation was a small and timorous venture.

Stupendous and incomprehensible as such future amalgamations may be, their consummation, immediate or ultimate, will bring no absolutely new factor into the field, but merely an exaggeration of a situation already here. What we already have is an industrial oligarchy existing in, and almost overshadowing, a more or less democratic political community. It is an oligarchy which is the reverse and complement of the political society with which it coexists. It is based upon the billions of dollars of millions of people. It marshals these billions as our political parties marshal the voters.

The industrial oligarchy is based not only on the dollars but on the allegiance (if not the affections) of the stockholder. This putative owner of a huge, incomprehensible property is still held by the old idea of the perfect liberty of economic action, of secrecy, of competition. He is still the "magnificent," optimistic American, who believes that he possesses enough liberty of action so long as he has the right to buy, hold, or sell stocks (of the value of which he knows little). He identifies his interest with that of the corporation in which he holds stock, although his true interest lies in a public control, which will make for knowledge, certainty, and equal rights. While he is gradually changing, while a progressive disillusionment is bringing him slowly to the position of critic, his present attitude is still one of belief in the ultimate rights of the trust builders. He is still a humble and devout upholder of the plutocracy.

Thus the plutocracy, based as it is upon a strategic position in our enormous industry, consists not only in the votes and the money power of the trust builders, but in the adherence of millions of men owning billions of dollars. Our resplendent plutocracy, which at the top flowers out in enormous fortunes, magnificent benefactions, and absurd ostentations, is rooted not only in our political non-regulation of economic conditions, but also in the traditions, ideas, and ideals of millions of relatively poor men. Without the support of the small investors and of many men who have not even the wherewithal to purchase a single share of stock, the pillars of our resplendent plutocracy would crumble and fall. The plutocracy can only maintain itself so long as the mass of investors, large and small, are its adherents.

Still more fundamentally the plutocracy maintains itself because as a nation we still do not know what to do; because we support the plutocracy by attacking not causes but symptoms. We object to the false scales of the Sugar Trust, as we object to all the devices, honest, dishonest, and semi-honest, by which a few men maintain a business despotism. We object rhetorically to an oligarchic control of industry, especially when such control leads to spoliation and to an immoralization of business. But as a nation we still believe in the universal efficacy of competition, and we still expect that as soon as we have killed the trusts, our one time independent, but now merged, manufacturers will awaken from sleep and begin competing again where they left off twenty years ago.

In the past we have tried to end our plutocracy by merely "smashing" the trusts, not realizing that with all their imperfections and immoralities they represent a stage in our development from the anarchic industry of half a century ago to the completely socialized industry of half a century hence. We have turned towards the trust a countenance less in sorrow than in anger, and we have tested the vitality of industrial combinations by whacking them over the head, as the military engineer gauged the strength of bridges by prolonged cannonading. Our Sherman law — a law with more fist than head in it — and our crude antitrust legislation generally, are attacks not upon the economic foundations of the plutocracy, but upon the integrity — the wholeness — of business. We cannot kill the trusts without taking away our own bread and butter.

We are at last beginning to realize that while the "criminal record" of many of our trusts is a fact important historically and ethically, nevertheless the recognition of this fact does not teach us how in the future we must run our national businesses. We are beginning to see that we can moralize, we can socialize the trusts, and can build more wisely upon the economic tendencies of the age. This we are slowly, painfully learning. The trusts are teaching us — as we are teaching them — that the end of it all must be production on the largest scale compatible with efficiency, but a production so regulated as to ownership, stock issues, dividends, prices, wages, and profits as to safeguard the whole community. Unless we are to take the *saltum mortale* of a complete and immediate governmental ownership and operation of all large industries, we must work out a more perfect system of corporation control in the interests of society.

Against such measures of regulation, against even the creation of a state and of democratic machinery capable of such regulation, the plutocracy opposes the dead weight of its resistance. Our business magnates, to get what they could and hold what they got, have long since occupied the political positions which the democracy must gain before such regulation is entirely effective. The leaders of the plutocracy are giving direction to their pecuniary aspirations by carrying over their activities from the economic into the political field The key to the citadel which the plutocracy has established in industry lies in the law; the law depends upon legislatures and courts; the legislatures and courts upon parties; the parties upon the powers, open and occult, which control them. To prevent the democracy, through its control of politics, from conquering the industrial field, the plutocracy enters politics.

CHAPTER VIII

THE PLUTOCRACY IN POLITICS

CORRUPTION is the natural weapon of a wealthy minority, as deception is of the weak, and force of the strong. Our plutocracy in its invasion of the political field corrupts legislators, administrators, judges, and parties.

In any rapid view of our present-day political corruption, it is difficult to avoid exaggeration both as to its volume and significance. We find the trail of evil influence in so many places that we are prone to generalize political depravity, and to ignore the large fields of public life in which venality is absent or quite subordinate. "Graft" is more spectacular than the gray honesty of ordinary life, and it is far easier to point out evil than to determine its exact boundaries.

Before stating the influence of the plutocracy upon politics, therefore, it may be wise to emphasize certain considerations which limit the universality of our conclusions. In the first place it is not to be supposed that all, or a majority, of our financial magnates have exerted an improper influence on legislation, or have sought to do so; nor is it contended that the level of political probity of this group (in proportion to its opportunities and temptations) is sensibly inferior to the general level of our whole population. Secondly, it is not assumed that the development to be described has taken place in all cities and States, or that it has been unimpeded; for, as will later be shown, countervailing forces have developed so rapidly that the corporate influence upon politics seems far weaker to-day than it was five or ten years ago. Finally, however amiable the intentions of our more unscrupulous industrial leaders, they cannot lay claim to the distinction of having invented corruption.

Corruption, in fact, is no new thing in America. Charges of venality were preferred against the founders of the Republic, and from 1828 to 1860, during the ascendancy of the Democratic party, public officials openly boasted of their "stealings." The history of the Civil War was streaked with graft. The administrations of Grant, both in the reconquered States and at Washington, were an orgy of venality. The State governments, among which New Jersey maintained a bad eminence, were often degraded, while many cities were corrupt beyond conception. Municipal venality was downright, abject, open, chronic. Vicious elements in the population were mobilized under the banner of graft. Almshouse inmates marched *en masse* to the polls, and were voted wholesale. Elections were carried by colonization, intimidation, ballot-stuffing, and false counting of votes. A succession of bandits, of whom Tweed was not the first, protected and blackmailed vice, crime, and franchise-seeking corporations. Indirect filchings coexisted with the custom-honored method of openly stealing money from the public treasury.

The peculiar significance of our present-day American political corruption lies not in its novelty, but in its change of character and source. It has become subtle, scientific, organized. It has become a pendant to large business, which is also subtle, scientific, organized. To-day political corruption is menacing, not only because all corruption is immoral and antidemocratic, but because it represents the intrusion into politics of a disciplined and aggressive plutocracy.

Wealth invades politics to gain new wealth and to safeguard that already won. It seeks to prevent "interference" and repel "socialistic and demagogic" attacks on property. It is willing to fight for peace; to bribe for "justice." It seeks the things to which it feels it has a right. Our political corrupters are animated by a specious, self-justifying philosophy of business, and their actions are condoned by thousands of beneficiaries, who, though good and patriotic (as goodness and patriotism go), desire above all to conserve material and moral interests, believed to be endangered by the "uncontrolled" representatives of the people.

Corruption is not unilateral. It does not descend from business into politics without reascending. Corporations bribe legislators. But legislators also bludgeon and blackmail corporations. Our legislators were not all uncorrupted creatures of God before the Fall, nor was every industrial magnate an insinuating serpent, crawling into the political garden. The share of obloquy may fairly be contested.

Our lawgivers had a "feeling of their business" long before trusts were conceived. They knew their value to citizens who profited by a "lax" enforcement of laws, and they delighted to levy tribute on prostitute, gambler, and pickpocket. Laws were passed for the purpose of selling exemptions and granting indulgences. Crooks in and out of office joined dirty hands. Outside partners of ruling officials secured the adoption of faulty building plans. Lawyer friends of judges won doubtful cases. Bondsmen, runners, lodging-house sharks, and the whole underworld of business and corrupt politics learned to "divide" and conquer. There was no limit to the evil sphere of influence of the lesser politicians; no end to the "rake-offs" and "shake-downs"; no graft too petty or disgusting to escape the humble ambitions of small political fry. These men were venal before the advent of the latter-day large-scale briber. They escaped corruption because already infinitely corrupted. When, however, in the fullness of time and fate, the wholesale briber, the business lobbyist, appeared upon the scene, the venal politicians gravitated towards him with the spontaneity of beings fulfilling natural and predestined instincts. They were like parasites which benefit the "host" they prey on.

Petty graft has now declined into a mere adjunct to organized big business graft, which gives tone to a multifarious corruption, and welds it into one noxious, formidable system. The blackmail of vice and crime — petty in detail, though enormous in its threatening aggregate — is like the humble forest floor, the matting of lichens, mosses, and ferns, protected by and protecting the upright trees and their flowering branches. The president of a councils-buying traction company is in real, though unsuspected, league with the woman on the street who passes a stealthy dollar to the patrolman. The august board of directors of the legislature-owning railroad are own brothers to the second-story man, who to pursue his lesser calling must also seek legislative connivance. The bond between these groups is the nexus of political interest. The great men who escape taxation through representation in the tax office, who defeat needed legislation because it interferes with their profits, have no sympathy with the tolerated street thugs or the little men who finance vice. And yet, like citizens of a feather, they vote and bribe and steal together. The big corrupters could not hold their own but for the votes and the fists of the little scamps. The little scamps could not survive but for the money, intelligence, and protecting respectability of the princely corrupters.

The organizing skill of the business magnate in systematizing political corruption has changed it from a local though chronic phenomenon to one which is organic and nation-wide. "Every time I attempted to trace to its sources the political corruption of a city ring," says Lincoln Steffens, the acute political pathologist,[1] "the stream of

[1] Steffens, Lincoln, "The Struggle for Self-Government." New York, 1906, page 3.

pollution branched off in the most unexpected directions and spread out in a network of veins and arteries so complex that hardly any part of the body politic seemed clear of it. It flowed out of the majority party into the minority; out of politics into vice and crime; out of business into politics, and back into business; from the boss, down through the police to the prostitute, and up through the practice of law into the courts; and big throbbing arteries ran out through the country over the State to the nation — and back. . . . Not the political ring, but big business — that is the crux of the situation."

The industrial oligarch, on entering politics, raised corruption to a higher power. He was above party (as were the corrupt party leaders), and he abetted both contestants for office, or the one more likely to win in the particular city or State. He cared little for platforms or other oratorical effects, but limited himself to the constitution of the party machine, the elevation of the boss, the choice of utilizable, though inconspicuous, officials, and the judicious manning of important legislative committees with men pliable, purchasable, or purchased, or whose antecedents were known and approved. In conjunction with party bosses, the business corrupter created an intricate scheme of progressive promotion, an elimination of the stiff-necked, and the proper rewarding of all men according to their utility.

In many cities, this corrupting leadership fell into the hands of speculators in street railway, gas, electric light, water, and other franchises. The city was openly and contemptuously despoiled. In New York, Chicago, Philadelphia; in Cleveland, Toledo, Pittsburg; in a tediously long list of American cities, grants in perpetuity of stupendous value were obtained for the bribing. Unscrupulous finance went hand in hand with a light-hearted betrayal of popular rights. The man who stole a franchise and sold it again to the people while still keeping it — a commonplace of financial legerdemain — took, while he was about it, the city government. He dominated conventions, made and unmade mayors, and, where necessary, selected and elected his own governor.

It is held by some that the city is originally sinful while the State is endowed with a larger portion of political grace, and that, therefore, the erring municipality should be subjected to minute State-made laws. We now see, however, that this maternal ligament between State and city is a channel as much for the spread of corruption as for the contagion of political innocence. City corruption is but part of a ramified State corruption, and when city grafters are in danger, State grafters rush to their assistance. When, as Mr. Steffens points out, Minneapolis sought reform, Minnesota interfered; the reformers of Pittsburg were checkmated by corruptionists at Harrisburg, and the people of Cleveland, after defeating the city traction interests, were obliged to take up the battle anew with adverse forces at Columbus and — Washington.

While the franchise corporation, and sometimes the railroad, secured control of the city, the State government in many cases came under the dominion of the railroad and the industrial corporation. The corporation appointed its own men to office, escaped its fair share of taxation, defeated legislation, and secured franchises and privileges. The autocratic control of politics spread from State to nation, so that the United States Senate, as well as the House of Representatives, became in part bulwarks and defenders of unfair privilege.

One of the simplest methods of obtaining power over legislation was by direct bribery of the lawmaker. This was especially easy and efficacious where the object was simply to defeat legislation, for in our multiform government, with its split responsibility favoring the *status quo*, a bill, in running the gauntlet, may be dispatched without its real assassin being discovered. The bill may be killed in a committee of the Lower House, or not reported out. It may be emasculated by amendment, or so "strengthened" as to insure either its legislative defeat, or its ultimate rejection by the courts. It may be voted down on the floor of the House. It may be talked to death. It may meet any of these fates in the Upper House. It may be vetoed by the Executive. It may fall without a positive veto by the adjournment of the legislative body. It may be annulled by the courts for any of a hundred reasons, intrinsic or technical. Finally it may be placed on the statute book and be affirmed by the courts, and yet remain unenforced or malenforced. Who killed Cock Robin is often an unsolvable problem. Upon the vote of one man, given in the obscurity of a committee room, may depend the fate of a measure desired by a majority of the people, but unwelcome to a corrupting corporation.

The bought legislator may betray his trust without arousing suspicion. It is easy to destroy by delay; to kill by seeming kindness; to smother a bill in very excess of love. The need of information is urged by men who want not knowledge but postponement. Incidental and hypothetical hardships of a measure are paraded before willingly credulous legislators, and multimillionaires hide behind the skirts of widows, and mingle their tears with those of destitute orphans. A poor woman, threatened with a law reducing her labor to ten hours a day, pawns her furniture to make a long trip to the State capitol, there to add her protest to that of some benevolent manufacturers' association. Corrupt legislators are reasonable beings and can find a reason for what they are paid to do.

In legislative crises the pressure upon wavering men is increased until resistance breaks down as under a thumbscrew. Money, cajolery, flattery, and intimidation furnish the arsenal of the bribers, — those adept miners and sappers of human steadfastness. The bribers believe that every man has his price, and whether it be "legal fees," stock-exchange tips, social recognition, political preferment, flattering newspaper paragraphs, or the subtler flattery of a private interview with the Olympian employer of the briber, the price is paid. Even more devious means of "persuasion" are employed. From nowhere, from the depths of an ominous anonymity, arise vague rumors concerning the political or personal morality of the recalcitrantly honest. Traps are laid, and the tempted legislator, because of his very straightforwardness, finds his actions clouded over by a veil of false appearances. Gradually he loses a certain fine Puritan fervor of reform. He feels that he fights alone, unaided by public knowledge or sympathy, or the assurance of an ultimate popular justification. At last, by contagion of example, he comes to believe that in this political labyrinth the direct road, hewn out by sheer strength, leads to nowhere, while the sinuous, seductive deviations, the well-grooved convolutions, are the only possible course. Beset by ugly penalizing rumors on the one hand, and the seduction of money and political preferment on the other, he succumbs. He sins in his own defense; he "loses his virtue to save his reputation." Thereafter he becomes more circumspect — for his purchaser cares little how he talks, so long as he votes straight.

No such system of specialized, standardized, subtilized corruption could exist without capital to finance it. This capital is thriftily furnished by unscrupulous magnates, who, though they bribe, consider bribing beneath them, and have sovereign contempt for their own wretched brood of political procurers, who furnish what is demanded — and no questions asked or embarrassing explanations given. The investigation of the life insurance companies showed that the money of the insured — of those very widows and orphans, the patron saints of corrupting millionaires — was turned into a "yellow-dog fund" for the purchase of legislators. Predatory corporations assign to "advertising and publicity accounts" expenditures which need not be advertised and could not be published. Franchises are stolen by free lance bribers, who sell their "interests" to "innocent third parties," who in turn invite the public through stock subscriptions to repurchase their own. It is a Thieves' Market, in which the beneficiaries stand in no ascertainable legal relation to the thieves, and in which the public has no redress except the melancholy satisfaction of locking the stable door.

While the predatory corporation often stoops to purchase a single legislator, to pick up a human trifle at a sacrifice, the main channel through which this corruption flows is the party. Through obedience to party many wavering legislators are secured. The corrupter buys wholesale, and the party machine becomes his agent and sponsor. In our present American political system, we have corruption of, by, and through the party.

The rank and file of political parties is not corrupt, for this rank and file is practically the adult male population of the country. Nor is a majority, or even a large minority, of party agents venal. The virus of corruption runs through the party simply because in America it is the channel of representative government. Like the advocates of social regeneration, so the debauchers of men repair to the party to set the seal of their ambitions upon this instrument of popular sovereignty.

The party is corruptible because largely irresponsible. In our complicated government, where responsibility has always been as diffused as the light of Arctic spring, it was difficult to bring all powers of government under the dominion of one party, and it was often impossible to know whom to punish for known and felt abuses. The party which strove for reform in our national government might stand for bottomless corruption in city or State. Not believing that it possessed the power of carrying out its promises, the party made promises all the more rashly. Statesmen unable to control corrupt associates abandoned the effort, surrendering their places to self-seeking men, who aided in the conversion of the party into a piratical business enterprise.

The root of this party deterioration was money. The party became a beggar, a sturdy rogue without visible means of support, yet living riotously, and insisting that the world owed him a good living. Instead of taking the vow of poverty, as a popular party should, instead of being supported openly and democratically (as is to-day the Socialist party) by the pennies and nickels of its members, the party demanded, and received, an endowment from men willing to invest in political organization as they invested in railroads and timber lands.

For however independent the party became of the people at all times except election day, it never became independent of money. Money it must have — and much money. Mere cohesion was expensive. At election time there were parades, torchlight processions, open air meetings, crowded halls, the securing of speakers, the obtaining of straw votes, advertisements in hostile newspapers, the sending out of thousands of tons of campaign literature, chowder picnics, the payment of loyal but hungry workers, to say nothing of the "illegitimate" expense of "blocks of five" in doubtful districts. Politics was business; business required capital; and to the capitalist belonged the revenue of the enterprise. Corporations did not contribute to campaign funds without hope of influencing legislation, administration, and justice. The secret campaign contribution, the logical outcome of our political philosophy, was Esau's mess of pottage.

This corruption of legislators and parties, this attainment

of strategic positions in the political field, was not due, in the beginning at least, to a thought-out, class-conscious campaign of a cohesive plutocratic group. It was not one correlated system of interdependent parts. Each man merely acquired the political facilities which he needed in his business, without much thought of the simultaneous actions of like-minded men in other places.

These individual spheres of political influence are now beginning to coalesce, just as big businesses themselves are coalescing. There is in process a political integration, similar to our industrial integration, and due to precisely the same causes. Corporations, financially interlinked, are brought together automatically on the political field. Men who for years have grumbled about telephone charges find themselves opposing the State regulation of such rates, because an "attack" upon one "interest" is a peril to all. There is a political, as well as an industrial, "community of interest."[1]

The progress of this political integration, though gradual, is rapid. Political "holdings," like financial "holdings," are "merged," first for a single political "operation," and later for a whole political policy. The like-mindedness of financial magnates, like the like-mindedness of political mercenaries, gives rise to a secret, interstate, *bi-partisan* political machine. Democratic Congressmen, vassals of financiers above party, support a Republican oligarchy; Republician repeaters in one State are loaned to a Demo-

[1] Not only does the plutocracy possess this political solidarity, which money bestows, but also the power of scenting danger a long way off. Our whole industrial system is based upon an intelligent estimate of future happenings, and the present value of a railroad corporation declines if there is real reason to fear that five or twenty or perhaps even fifty years hence the property will in whole or in part be confiscated, or its profits reduced. When the sensitive Wall Street barometer registers a danger, immediate or ultimate, to one listed security, other securities plunge downward in sympathy.

cratic boss in a neighboring State. Political gladiators forget to fight. A sweet vision of gilded peace, of a veritable *Pax Romana*, stirs hearts long inured to bitter partisan strife. The two parties, united at last in a competitive devotion to a generous plutocracy, sleep on their arms in an affectionate embrace. A political trust comes into being.

This political trust is more ramified, systematized, and powerful than any in the history of American political institutions. It represents trust methods applied to politics. It is a secret, effective, card-index scheme of government, based on the elimination of surplus political machinery, the standardization of corruption, and the organization of all legislative bodies on the approved model of the dummy board of directors. The system, crossing party lines and State lines, is built like a pyramid from the ubiquitous ward heeler up through the ward boss, the city boss, the State boss, to a shadowy — as yet non-existent — national boss, seated perhaps in the Speaker's chair or in the Senate of the United States.

The mortar of this edifice is money. It is money which negotiates the direct purchase, for immediate or "future delivery," of individual legislators and of whole party machines. But the power of the political trust has even a wider base. Though money has been used and is still used in national State, and local politics, though men occasionally buy their way, almost openly, into the Senate of the United States, though the dollar mark is placed above many portals to political life, still it is safe to say that political corruption is only the immediate, and not the ultimate and determining factor in the invasion of politics by the plutocracy. If the contest were simply one between men and money, between millions of clear-eyed voters on the one hand and silent bribers on the other, the issue would soon be determined. Despite race and sex limitations, we have a practically democratic suffrage, and if we were once fairly united in opposition to any institution, however protected by money, we could vote it off the face of the continent.

What retards such united action is an ideal, a tradition, an affection for political institutions and modes of thought which have become endeared to us through a century of national life. It is not because we love it that we press the plutocracy to our bosom — on the contrary, we hate it devotedly — but because we love the things which give to it life and extension. Our hand is stayed by ancient political ideas which still cumber our modern brains; by political heirlooms of revered — but dead — ancestors. Between us and it, the plutocracy thrusts the Constitution of the United States. Defeated in the legislature it seeks sanctuary in the courts.

There are many things in the business and political world of 1911 which were undreamed of by the men who drafted the federal Constitution. Nothing in the minds of Hamilton and Madison could remotely have paralleled the interpretations which high-priced trust attorneys have placed upon this instrument. Yet the Constitution was especially designed for a class which bore a similar relation to the America of 1787 that the plutocracy bears to the America of 1911. In any event, it was possible for the plutocracy to capture the Constitution, just as it was possible, several generations ago, for a like capture to be effected by the slave power.

The Constitution aids the plutocracy in many ways. It is like an old, rambling mansion, which cannot be lighted, and in the dark places of which our enemies secrete themselves. The plutocracy benefits by the sharp limitations which the Constitution places upon national and State efforts for reform. Most undemocratic feature of all, the Constitution furnishes no adequate opportunity for popular amendment.

Thus the Constitution — to which we have owed and still owe much — is a stiff, unyielding, and formidable — because venerable — obstacle to a true democracy, and a strong bulwark of the plutocracy. It stands firm largely because of an unlimited admiration, which forbids adverse criticism, and almost precludes discussion. According to current theory, the Constitution of 1787 is good enough for the people of 1911 or 2011 or 3011, its principles and solutions being eternal. It consequently happens that the ancient squabbles of jealous, petty commonwealths still afflict a great nation, infinitely more civilized than the community which gave birth to this organic law.

Actually our Constitution is amended to-day (as it has been amended for the last one hundred and twenty years) chiefly by process of interpretation. New senses are given to old words; the growing political foot, by sheer pressure, changes the old stiff shoe. This amendment by interpretation, however, is carried out not by direct representatives of the people, but by the Supreme Court, a body of nine honorable, estimable, and politically irresponsible jurists.

This irresponsibility was intended by the Constitution, and has been approved by a century of acquiescence on the part of the people. Yet the latitude of this irresponsibility might well give us pause. Not only does the Supreme Court decide questions of far greater moment than that of war or peace, not only does it hold a constitutional veto upon the most fundamental exercise of national sovereignty, but this right is exercised by men who have never received the suffrages of their fellow-citizens, and who, once seated upon the bench, are practically forevermore irremovable. The Chief Justice of the United States is responsible to his God and his conscience (as is the Czar of Russia), but he is not responsible to the ninety million people. Politically, he is more irresponsible than a city alderman, for the alderman needs our votes, and the Chief Justice does not. If eighty million people want a law and five of the nine judges decide that the measure is not constitutional, then, legally, the eighty million will not prevail against the five. There is no appeal from the five jurists to the eighty millions — for the people are not presumed to know, until told, what is constitutional and what is not. They cannot, except through the impracticable process of impeachment, remove the judges or appoint other ones. They must wait until the judges die and new judges take their place. In the meantime, the people who need the law also die.

It must be admitted that, in the ordinary course, our highest federal judges have shown wisdom and patriotism, have sought to interfere little with national executive and legislature, and have been free from even the vaguest suspicion of venality. But whether it be exercised wisely or unwisely, virtuously or viciously, this right of the Supreme Court, finally and unreviewably to declare a law void, in opposition to the opinion of a majority, constitutes, in the absence of ample facilities for a popular amendment of the Constitution, a flat and uncompromising negation of democracy. Though the veto of the court is presumed to be based upon the sole ground of constitutionality, nevertheless the probable tendency and economic effects of the law actually enter into the determination of constitutionality, of which the nine jurists are final arbiters.

Even though the decisions of the Supreme Court were invariably democratic, and made for an extension of popular power, still so long as these decisions were not reviewable by the people through the power of easily amending the Constitution, it would be an undemocratic way to achieve democracy, and we might well look this gift-horse in the mouth. But the general trend of the court decisions, at least until recently, has not been unduly favorable to a rapid extension of democracy, to the effectuation of popular control over industrial and social relations. While the Supreme Court of the United States, like other bodies, has come more or less under the ripening influence of a new democratic spirit; while it has shown greater hesitancy than have many State courts in nullifying needed State laws, it has not so democratized our Constitution as to render possible the carrying out of necessary measures of political and social reform which other nations have adopted. According to Prof. Frank J. Goodnow,[1] there are some measures "which many believe to be absolutely necessary either now or in the future . . . which we in the United States are probably precluded from adopting because of the attitude now taken by the courts towards our practically unamendable federal constitution." Among these measures "may possibly be mentioned some which are apparently regarded as essential parts of a program of effective social reform; such as pensions or public insurance in case of old age, accident or sickness where the recipient of the pension or insurance is not actually a pauper and where the fund from which such pension or insurance is obtained is derived from taxation; the regulation of the hours of adult male labor in any but the evidently most harmful trades; effective regulation of the use of urban land; and the use of the powers of taxation and eminent domain for the purpose of furthering schemes to provide aid for the needy classes. Furthermore, it is somewhat doubtful whether without amendment of the federal constitution our political organization can develop in such a way as to be in accord with even existing economic conditions, not to speak at all of the future." Whatever may be the attitude of certain groups in the community towards such measures, continues Professor Goodnow, "it is believed that there are few persons having the welfare of this country really at heart, or not blinded by prejudice or class interest, who will assert that the conditions of the American people are so peculiar that we should close for them the avenues open to other peoples through which orderly and progressive political development

[1] "Social Reform and the Constitution," New York (Macmillan), 1911, p. 332.

in accordance with changing economic and social conditions may proceed."

It is not to be assumed that the attitude of our highest court, where it has favored the pretensions of the plutocracy or obstructed the expansion of the democracy, has been the result of a conscious, let alone an interested attempt to influence the balance of power in America. It is possible that occasionally there has been a subtle bond of sympathy between the politically irresponsible judges, raised to the very pinnacle of our social structure, and the more statesman-like and cultured of our irresponsible business princes. The road to the federal court runs through the practice of corporation law with the business magnates as clients, and points of view and social interpretations imbibed in one's youth are likely to survive middle age. But the real cause of the excessive conservatism of our constitution, as it is interpreted by the courts, seems to be the comparative inflexibility of the judicial mind, a certain blindness to the changing social and economic order, an exaggerated veneration for ancient principles of law, established under conditions which no longer apply. The very excellence of the federal judge's qualities carries with it certain limitations, a stubborn respect for the prestige of precedent, and an impatience of the cruder strivings of a raw democratic spirit. When we reflect that our higher federal judges have for the most part been old men, with the inelasticity of old men; when we examine into the sources of their nomination; when we trace their activities during the twenty years immediately preceding their elevation, we need not wonder that instinctively, and with perfect mental honesty, they have gently inclined as a rule towards the side of privilege, towards a strict interpretation of the Constitution of the United States favorable to the plutocracy.

All of this is remediable through the education of the judges and of ourselves, and through the creation of some stronger popular check, formal or informal, upon the general determinations of our federal courts.[1] There exists, however, under the name of respect for the courts, a cult of judicial infallibility which, in its usual interpretation, is profoundly undemocratic, subtly demoralizing, and a menace to popular rule a hundred fold more damaging than a hundred adverse court decisions. The decision of the judges (in the absence of any present possibility of an appeal to the people) must be accepted until reversed, but whoever is opposed to such decision should be entitled to express his views in the same manner and in the same terms as against a decision of President, congressman, governor, or alderman. The judge is entitled to respect, as is the senator, railway director, farmer, car conductor, or head waiter; but to shield him, or them, from candid adverse criticism, to create about him a special atmosphere, is extremely bad for clear thinking and democratic enlightenment. The political institution which requires "prestige," pomp, or laws against contempt; which cannot rely frankly upon popular support, is in a bad way. The courts will maintain the respect of the people by being the servants of the people.[2]

[1] It was a sign of progress when a great political philosopher made the discovery that already the "Supreme Court follows the election returns."

[2] Some fifteen years ago, President William Howard Taft, then United States Judge, expressed himself as follows: —

"The opportunity freely and publicly to criticise judicial action is of vastly more importance to the body politic than the immunity of courts and Judges from unjust aspersions and attack. Nothing tends more to render Judges careful in their decisions and anxiously solicitous to do exact justice than the consciousness that every act of theirs is to be submitted to the intelligent scrutiny and candid criticism of their fellow-men. In the case of Judges having a life tenure, indeed, their very independence makes the right freely to comment on their decisions of greater importance, because it is the only practicable and available instrument in the hands of a free people to keep such Judges alive to the reasonable demands of those they serve." For a full statement of Mr. Taft's position, see Taft, William H., "Present Day Problems." New York (Dodd, Mead & Co.), 1908, p. 29 *et seq.*

Through the action of the courts in interpreting the Constitution, the widest possible powers have been given to a growing and entrenched plutocracy. According to President Arthur Twining Hadley, "the power of control by the Government was weakened and the rights and immunities of the property holders correspondingly strengthened by two events whose effect upon the modern industrial situation may be fairly characterized as fortuitous." One of these was the decision in the celebrated Dartmouth College case in 1819, which made a charter granted by a State a contract, the obligation of which could not be impaired, and which thus protected midnight franchises against all future attacks by the legislature.[1] The other was the Fourteenth Amendment to the Constitution, which, designed to protect the freedmen, has been interpreted primarily in behalf of the modern corporation. Since no State shall "deprive any person of life, liberty, or property, without due process of law, nor deny to any person within its jurisdiction the equal protection of the laws"; and since a corporation is a person in the sense of the amendment, therefore any corporation desiring to resist a State or local law may appeal for "equal protection" to the federal courts. The jurisdiction of the federal court having been sustained in 1882 in a case brought by the Southern Pacific Railroad Company, the door was opened in all cases of attempted regulation or taxation to an intervention by federal tribunals, with resulting delays, and a weakening of the State and local authorities. The mere expense of prosecuting these cases in the federal courts, while of little moment to wealthy corporations, was often sufficiently onerous to the city or State government

[1] The evil force of this decision has been greatly lessened by subsequent decisions of the courts, limiting the extension of the Dartmouth decision, and by provisions in later State constitutions, requiring that all grants in future be made subject to revision by future legislatures, and that companies, desiring their charters amended, should subject themselves to similar conditions.

to prevent needed regulation. President Hadley maintains that "the two ("fortuitous") [1] decisions together have had the effect of placing the modern industrial corporation in an almost impregnable constitutional position." "The fundamental division of powers in the Constitution of the United States," says Professor Hadley, "is (not into executive, legislative, and judicial, but) between voters on the one hand and property owners on the other." The property rights so defended are essentially those of the "modern industrial corporation" in its "almost impregnable constitutional position."

If the judicial appeal could be short, sharp, and decisive, if our justice were the simple and summary decision of an Eastern cadi, we might have a more even chance of an inclining of the courts to the will of the democracy. Under present conditions in many States, however, the democracy would fare better by pitching up a penny or consulting a fortune teller than by appealing to the courts. Our whole judicial system is so complicated and involuted that it often has the effect of breaking the force of the popular will. A bill, late after passage, may be declared unconstitutional, and arrangements made in conformity with it may be retroactively voided. By a graduated system of appeals from courts of lower to courts of higher instance, by a subtly intricate and technical body of rules of evidence, by interminable delays working in the interest of the long purse, by a multiplicity of reversals and self-reversals, no law, if contested, is sure of being carried into effect for many years. Even if, after a lapse of years, a State law is approved by all the courts, the political party originally advocating it may long since have passed out of power, because it has lost the support of people

[1] "I call their effect fortuitous because neither the judges who decided the Dartmouth College case nor the legislators who passed the Fourteenth Amendment had any idea how these things would affect the modern industrial situation." President Hadley, *The Independent*, April 16, 1908.

who want " to see something done." Later elections may have thrown the power back into the hands of the very interests who, by their injunctions and judicial appeals, have thwarted the will of the majority. New, often fictitious, issues have arisen; the case of the people is defended by its secret enemies; and gradually the reforming zeal dissipates itself and the proposed reform is forgotten.

One might believe that the force of reaction could no farther go. As a result, however, of our rigid Constitution; of our checks and balances and hindrances and delays and vetoes, executive, legislative, and judicial; of our split authority and our attenuated responsibility, we have allowed to grow up still other obstacles to the effectuation of the popular will. For decades we tolerated in the almost avowed interest of the plutocracy an oligarchic control of the House of Representatives. Our system of congressional committees, says Professor J. Allen Smith,[1] "virtually gives a small body of men constituting a committee a veto on every legislative proposal," while according to Mr. Bryce,[2] it "gives facilities for the exercise of underhand and even corrupt influence. In a small committee the voice of each member is well worth securing, and may be secured with little danger of a public scandal." The limitation of debate on the floor, the haste of the House, the hitherto arbitrary power of the Speaker to recognize members add to the irresponsibility of the individual legislator, who, moreover, though he votes contrary to the expressed will of his constituents, cannot be recalled. We still needlessly hold to the traditional and indefensible custom of convening the new Congress not four months but thirteen months after election, and in the second session beginning in the December of every even year, our legislation is enacted by a "lame-duck" Con-

[1] "The Spirit of American Government," New York (Macmillan), 1907, pages 193–194.

[2] "The American Commonwealth," Vol. I, Ch. 15.

gress, by a House of Representatives which has already been superseded, and of which many members have been retired and are no longer held by the hope of reëlection or the fear of defeat. "It is then," said Congressman John F. Shafroth, "that some (Representatives) are open to propositions which they would never think of entertaining if they were to go before the people for reëlection. It is then that the attorneyship of some corporation is often tendered and a vote is afterward found in the record in favor of legislation of a general or special character favoring the corporation." [1]

Our plutocracy secures its favored position in politics through the existence of a governmental system too complicated to be easily run or easily understood by a busy and engrossed people. It is through these complications and traditional absurdities of our political life, from our long, incomprehensible, and intentionally complicated ballot to our excessively complicated nominating systems, and from our gerrymandered electoral districts up to our needlessly complex judicial system, that the plutocracy is enabled to confound legislators and voters; to set off one public body against another; to confuse issues and to throw a cloud of dust over the whole business of legislation. The plutocracy gains, and the democracy loses, through the complexity and artificiality of our governmental relations.

Thus the plutocracy going into politics in order to defend its position in industry not only bribes and corrupts legislators and parties (as its lesser predecessors had done before it), but intrenches itself in the intricacies and convolutions of our federal system, and hides itself behind the most undemocratic features of our Constitution. Not only does it secure the legislation which it wants, and kill the legislation which it fears (or is merely vaguely suspicious of), but

[1] "When Congress should Convene," *North American Review*, Vol. 164. Mr. Shafroth recommends that the first session begin shortly after election day and the second session end before the succeeding election.

it seeks to prevent even the beginnings of a real democracy, which may grow up to regulate the plutocracy. As politics become integrated, and political enterprises, like business enterprises, are carried out on a larger scale, the plutocracy relies less even on its own standardized corruption and begins to depend more upon its almost impregnable constitutional position and upon favoring judicial interpretations. Finally, the plutocratic influence on politics, once a series of unrelated forays by independent financial interests, tends to became merged; and the political trust — in process — appears.

This political trust, like the industrial trust of which it is the reflection, fights on inside lines. It is able to concentrate all its forces at one point, to turn its organized energies upon any single, isolated manifestation of rebellion. Like the industrial trust it seeks to hold a monopoly of power.

Inevitably, however, this political trust, like the industrial trust, becomes visible, and with its visibility, the countervailing and curative forces of democracy multiply astoundingly. Antagonists spring up. At first the political trust seeks to "buy up" all these strike competitors; especially the demagogues and "tribunes of the people," who spectacularly hate the trust, but who, without surrendering their invectives, endure, then pity, then embrace. Yet the more they are bought up, the more there are to buy up, since opponents, like rabbits and rattlesnakes, thrive best when there is a bounty upon their heads. The party machines which the political trust buys tend to lose their effectiveness as the fact becomes known, just as newspapers, known to be owned by antidemocratic interests, tend to lose their influence with the democracy. The alignment of the people beyond party lines, or in new parties, or in old parties reconstituted, proceeds as the workings of the political trust become visible, so that he who votes may read.

This development, with the resulting conflict, is as yet only in process, but with each year the opposition to the plutocratic control of politics become more obdurate and determined. New methods are devised to prevent bribery of legislators, executives, and judges; to place political parties under popular control; to simplify legislation and administration; to facilitate appeals from legislators to public opinion. Step by step the invasion of the plutocracy into politics is accompanied by an invasion of the democracy into politics; by the creation of a more tenacious and intelligent interest in political affairs; by the rise of a new democratic spirit.

As a result of this growing conflict, certain new truths are being learned by both sides. It is being recognized, both by democratic and anti-democratic leaders, that our political forms are not a last will and testament of a dead sovereign, but are themselves as mutable as the things which they regulate. Our laws and ordinances, our constitutions and precedents, even the inflexible Constitution of the United States, are all subject in final analysis to revision, review, and abrogation by the deliberate judgment and the determined will of the even now potentially sovereign people. Our checks and balances and vetoes, our political qualifications, prerogatives, conditions, and statuses; our statutes of limitation and perpetual guarantees; in fact, all our political institutions, however ancient and honorable, are but creatures of a people who, having made, may unmake, who, having given, may take away. In a nation which contains within itself the qualities which make for true democracy, the final arbiter of all relations, industrial, political, and social, is the people; the ultimate standard of values, the ultimate sanction, is not legal but moral.

To this definitive moral judgment of the people, in process of becoming sovereign, the plutocracy must finally appeal. Just as it went into the legislature and the secret chamber of the political boss to defend its franchises and privileges, present and prospective, so now it far-sightedly comes into the larger arena of public opinion. It is its right. What it has to say in self-justification should be said out loud in newspapers, magazines, and books; in the pulpit, on the stage, in the schools and universities, wherever two or three gather together to discuss public things. Whether the nation will be democratic or plutocratic in its philosophy, whether it will learn from both parties and borrow from both, must be decided by open discussion in an open forum. The ultimate struggle is a struggle for public opinion.

CHAPTER IX

THE PLUTOCRACY AND PUBLIC OPINION

THE plutocracy, to control the market and the ballot box, must control also the mind of the nation. It therefore invests the last citadel, public opinion.

There can be no fair objection to an open advocacy of the plutocracy's ideals and purposes. To every shade of thought, religious, scientific, political, economic, and social; to every craze, fad, dogma, heresy, and inspiration; there should be accorded a forum, a soap box, a ton of type, and, subject to a subsequent responsibility for utterances, full liberty of speech and print. The more frankly the plutocracy speaks out in its accredited journals or elsewhere under its signature, the better for it and its opponents. It has a perfect moral right to flood the country with its "literature," provided such writings show their source as clearly as does a legal brief.

When, however, we speak of the conquest of the press by the plutocracy, we have in mind not an open and candid advocacy, but a subtle, devious, and anonymous campaign of suppression, misrepresentation, and falsehood. In securing publicity, as in securing political power, the weapon of the plutocracy is the weapon of all wealthy minorities, the corrupt and secret use of money. The plutocracy quietly plants itself at strategic places on the avenues to the public mind, where it can exact its toll of the news and temper the truth to a shorn people. When it buys a journal or a politician, it does not advertise the fact. The pirate ship flies a peaceful flag; the wolf in sheep's clothing is sedulously taught to browse.

The broad avenues leading to public opinion are the daily

newspaper, the weekly or monthly magazine, the trade journal, the book, the acted play, the sermon from the pulpit, the lesson in the class, the lecture in the university. Of these, the most influential is the periodical press, and more especially, the penny newspaper.

Americans are voracious newspaper readers. Our problems are so manifold that no one can understand everything; our ninety million neighbors are so unutterably beyond direct personal contact that we must trust to the printed word. In a small Swiss canton or a New England township, public opinion may be independent of a periodical press. The public opinion of a great and dispersed nation is halt and blind and dumb without its morning paper.

Now the newspaper is conceived to be a mirror and a mentor. It is expected to give the news with the gusto of a town-crier and the impartiality of a phonograph. Its function is to narrate to every section of the community, from the baseball "fans" and the chess players to the financiers and the men about town, all the happenings which they require to know for their business or pleasure. As news-gatherer, it is not presumed to be above its patrons, and it dutifully gives information about prize fights which in its editorial columns it becomingly condemns. At the same time, by reason of a virtue inhering in the editorial "we," the newspaper is supposed, like the chorus of an antique play, to provide with the news a running moral commentary, to expound, interpret, prophesy, and enthuse.

But the newspaper, for better or worse, is not a heaven-endowed instrument, independent of terrestrial conditions and considerations. Journalism is a business, like politics, brewing, and agriculture. Like all businesses, it is subject to the prevailing money economy. A journal may be ever so independent in politics, but it is never, except in a few negligible cases, independent of money or the need of profits. It is through profits, that coursing life-blood of all commercial enterprises, that the virus of corruption enters into the body of journalism.

A generation or two ago the influence of money upon journalism was smaller than it is to-day. The thin little newspapers of those days depended for survival and success upon their subscribers, other sources of income being practically negligible. Frequently these papers were poor, usually intemperate, often ignorant, but they were always stripped for action, and were not readily muzzled or bought. The untempted editor, perhaps a college graduate, perhaps a semi-informed typesetter, towered above the inconspicuous and adventitious advertiser, and high above Wall Street, Lombard Street, and all the serried hosts of Mammon. After all, it did not pay to corrupt newspapers which sprang up like mushrooms in many dark places. So long as men had as free access to journalism as to the continent, so long as any youth who could borrow a hand press might start a new journal in garret or hall bedroom, there was no great encouragement to the financiers to pit their influence against the omnipresent influence of the newspaper reader.

Within the last generation the fundamental conditions of the newspaper business have so changed as to make journals far more susceptible to financial blandishments. Advertisers, finding printer's ink more efficacious than painted signs, sandwich-men, and barkers, invaded the newspapers. As a result of the standardization of business, the producer was enabled to appeal with his one standard soap or fountain pen over the heads of the middlemen directly to the people, and this big producer advertised through newspaper and magazine, whereas the middleman had used the modest handbill. Advertising became increasingly profitable, and the advertisement-swollen journals, especially after the advent of the lineotype, grew in bulk, if not in specific gravity. Since advertising value depends upon circulation, the newspaper, in order to secure circulation, was forced to offer itself to the reader for much less than cost. Two thirds of the newspaper revenues came from advertising business interests; news and editorial became a pendant to commercial offerings. The newspaper reader, though he had never asked for alms, had become pauperized.

Year by year, the subservience of the editorial to the business policy of the newspaper becomes more apparent. It is a matter of common knowledge, reënforced by much direct evidence, that many journals will not print news adverse to local department stores. Rather the loss of a thousand subscribers than the slightest animadversion upon these Atlases of city journalism. Public franchise corporations, banks, railroads, and other great undertakings enjoy a lesser, though still considerable, immunity. Some journals maintain a black list of proscribed people, to be ignored or persistently ridiculed, and a corresponding white list of happy immunes, who may indulge in treason, parricide, or sacrilege without fear of the interviewer. Scandalous actions by protégés are covered with the cloak of kindly silence, for our press, though communicative, knows how to keep a secret. A sensational suicide is omitted from the newspaper to make room for an advertisement from the suicide's father. Of course, if any journal turns State's evidence, and, from good motives or bad, blurts out the truth, the conspiracy of silence gives way to a conspicuous competition to furnish the greatest number of columns upon the hitherto forbidden topic.

Such suppression of specific news (some of which might well be generally suppressed, or at least telescoped), while, under the circumstances, immoral and invidious, does not constitute a transcendent factor in the society-wide struggle between plutocracy and democracy. It is rather a transgression *pro domo;* a taking care of one's friends.

Of greater importance is an influence which the plutocracy learns to exert upon the *general tone* of newspapers. There are many ways of exerting this influence without an actual purchase of the journal. In a choice between approximately equal mediums of publicity, a great advertiser often favors journals which more closely approximate his views. A trust pays directly or indirectly for the printing of news or comment, valuable to it individually, or to big business generally. It furnishes free copy, together with paid advertising. It subsidizes the furnishing of "boiler-plate" material to country papers. As the great journalistic enterprises grow, as the margin of loss on each copy is spread over a larger circulation, as the necessity for credit facilities increases, the plutocracy, through its control of a hierarchy of banks, sets its seal upon the policy of an increasing number of journals. The owner of the paper, usually a man of wealth and debts, is subjected to financial pressure upon his newspaper and outside ventures, as well as to social and political pressure.

The trend of plutocratic domination of the press has been from influence to control and from control to ownership. The newspaper in the course of time became for men of large wealth a personal asset greater than was represented by its actual money profits. It was like the old court which went with the manor, in which justice might be dispensed, immunity sold, or private vengeance wreaked. The purchased newspaper might offer sanctuary to the wealthy transgressor, who knew not where to lay his reputation. It might, with every semblance of virtue, surreptitiously connive at its owner's raid upon the public treasury. The progressive development of the newspaper business tended to increase this plutocratic ownership of papers, in whole or in part. Divorced from the dwindling personality of its editor, become a thing of stocks and bonds, the newspaper soon became vendible in parts, and subject to that law of business integration by which small enterprises tend to become subsidiary to larger ones. As the trust often bought out the political party, instead of continuing to buy its product, legislation, so it now bought out its needed newspapers, instead of continuing to buy their products, predigested news, and sterilized editorials.

This influence of the plutocracy over the press, like its influence over the political party, was not obtained in the first instance as the result of a class-conscious policy, but by each man securing the publicity facilities which he needed for his business or preferment. As time went on, however, the plutocracy's control of publicity, like its control of politics, became standardized, systematized, and subtilized. It became possible for large corporations to lend each other their respective publicity, like their political, facilities. The daily of an Eastern street railway magnate defended all manner of spoliation in West and North and South. A "ring" newspaper in a Middle Western city fought direct primaries on the Pacific Coast. A newspaper taking the popular side in a local contest found that it was offending a larger advertiser, who was a financial dependent of a beneficiary of an ally of the interests attacked. Large corporations conducted publicity departments through astute newspaper men, who knew the journalistic ropes as the paid lobbyist knew the legislative ropes. The campaign of the corporation was specific and subtle. So long as it secured what it wanted, silence or a defense, the corporation did not care how rabid was the newspaper in general discussions. In publicity as in politics, bought demagogues had their place and office, and were not without their reward.

The control over publicity becomes more systematic as the newspaper business becomes concentrated. During the last fifteen years the number of newspapers has been rapidly declining in proportion to population, and an enlarging share of the circulation is going to a relatively decreasing number of journals. Chains of newspapers are established in various cities, and unacknowledged alliances are formed between papers controlled by allied business interests. The old resort of the public — to start a new journal — is no longer so available. The success of such new and independent journals becomes problematical, because of the competition of venal periodicals, subsidized by advertisers, or maintained by big business interests at a profitable loss. The strategic value of the venal paper may be heightened by its being a member in a powerful and rigorously exclusive press association, membership in which gives a monopoly value, superior to that of membership in a stock exchange. A new journal of protest might not even secure a news service.

In the matter of journalistic independence we are losing the safety which inheres in a multitude of counselors. We are putting our eggs into one basket.

But the advantage of putting your eggs into one basket is that you are more likely to watch that basket. Despite the greater control of newspaper publicity by the plutocracy, that control remains qualified, partial, and subject to certain counteracting and curative forces.

In the first place many of the faults of our garrulous and somewhat slipshod and unveracious press are due not to the plutocracy, as we love to believe, but to our own careless, exaggerating, and scandal-loving selves. On our sober days we protest against the journalistic purveying of lies. We long for a pure food law which would apply to intellectual aliments, which would compel an editor to give with each newspaper "story" the exact proportions of suppression, indirection, false emphasis, subtle detraction, and other ingredients. And yet, we millions of readers do not skip the highly improbable and dubious details of a murder, accident, or divorce to improve our minds with an editorial on the "Reform of Procedure in Magistrates Courts." In our discursive newspaper reading we seem to prefer recreation to culture, vivacity to exactness, and two half-truths to one whole one.

Still more important is the fact, almost invariably overlooked, that much of the vilification in which some of our newspapers indulge is in the supposed interest, not of the plutocracy, but of ourselves, the great crowd.[1] Many unpopular causes, good and bad, are subjected to an habitual misrepresentation; many men, good and bad, who do not square with popular beliefs and prejudices, are overwhelmed with an unbelievable mass of printed falsehood. There are some plutocratic journals which are above these man-hunts, just as there are some democratic journals which delight in them. The cure for these journalistic lynchings, unlike the cure of other newspaper evils, lies not in the democratization of the press, but in the intellectual and moral progress of the democracy.

Not all the evils connected with our rapid newspaper growth are due to the plutocracy. Not all attempts to "influence" the press are successful. Our editors have their full share of our common instinctive honesty, and journalistic probity does not succumb to a single temptation.[2]

[1] Newspapers, like statesmen, generals, authors, saloon-bullies, and the rest of us, like to have the backing of the crowd. Even the debauched journal, hugging the illusion of its innocence, delights to gain even the temporary approval of a public to which it is bound by the dual hope of subscription and advertisement. Like Falstaff, it will not "turn upon the true prince," but is "a coward on instinct." But when, backed by a million careless readers, it attacks one friendless man or one lonely woman; when, in defense of things which have been believed for all time, it makes a desperate charge against the first, halting, half-formulated conception of a new truth, not the Numidian lion may compare with it for courage.

[2] While some struggling journals buy their independence at an enormous financial sacrifice, others, with greater money resources, lightly sell themselves on a cold calculation of profits. There are great newspapers — prominent and decorous — who surrender themselves to a sleek political prostitution without the excuse either of passion or poverty.

A certain safety lies in the multiplicity of forces influencing the newspaper. It seldom if ever happens that all advertisers, or a large majority, desire the suppression of the identical news, or the printing of the identical falsehood, even though many of them may be agreed upon a more or less definite deflection of newspaper policy. Many advertisers have the same interests as have the readers. Advertisers are, after all, primarily interested in selling goods, not in distorting facts or in expounding political philosophies. Again, the value of the newspaper to the advertiser depends upon its readers, and, since readers fall off if they do not get what they think is the news, the paper is often obliged to sacrifice an advertiser or two for the sake of a pregnant circulation. Such a policy pleases advertisers unaffected by the particular "story," since it gives the "independent" journal a prestige which casts a reflected glory on the men who advertise in its columns.

Although much news is suppressed and other news is colored, although, by reason of the veto of moneyed men, the editorials often tend to become vapid and timid, yet it is perhaps no great exaggeration to say that the man who pays his penny for the newspaper exerts in the mass, even to-day, a more open, if not actually a stronger, influence upon its expressed opinion than the ten-thousand-dollar advertiser or the million-dollar creditor. The pressure of the plutocracy is less insistent upon the journal than upon the political party, because the newspaper reader votes every day and enjoys the privilege of initiative, referendum, and recall. If he does not like the paper, he changes without so much as a letter to the editor.

The venal newspaper is thus like the rope in a tug of war. The subscribers pull it their way by the implied threat to withdraw their pennies; financial groups exercise their "pull" through the threat of withdrawing advertisements or credit. The editor, once a power and a voice, has ceased to be anything but an umpire, the paid servant of the owner, who in turn is the servant of his customers. The journal, acknowledging a double or even a multiple allegiance, becomes intellectually and morally cross-eyed.

The result is that each element in the community receives from the venal newspaper what it is able to extort or willing to purchase. In many of our great city journals, workingmen, who (because of their smaller general purchasing capacity) are among the less valuable of subscribers, do not receive fair treatment in news or editorial, but are promise-crammed, and fed with large phrases. Ignorant groups receive a counterfeit sympathy but no real assistance. The intelligent reader, on the other hand, is a formidable and imperious person, who gets in journalism what he wants, or something like it, not only because his penny is needed, but because if he does not read the paper, the advertiser will not advertise in it. As for the bias of the paper, the intelligent reader learns it and discounts it. He does not follow the editorial — at least, not very far. The editorial follows him. As for the news, he does not believe what he reads, but reads what he believes.

Potentially, the subscribers are more powerful than any corrupting financial interests, because in the final analysis, a journal is not a journal unless read. Actually, the subscribers are effective in proportion as they are intelligent and unitedly determined that the news shall be unsophisticated, and the editorials their own. Adulteration of news, like adulteration of other products for sale, is incited by profits, but is limited by the public's recognition that the article *is* adulterated.

The influence of the plutocracy on the newspaper, even on the newspaper which it secretly owns, is thus so circumscribed that its teachings are necessarily subtle, and its suggestions indirect. The plutocracy does not proclaim that political corruption, misery, slums, unequal distribution of wealth, and other present-day evils are good. We could not be made to believe it. Nor are we taught that democracy is bad. We could not be made to believe that. We are rather taught that while evil exists, proposed remedies are always worse. We are cautioned against flying to evils that we know not of; against following our natural leaders; against adopting any of the means necessary to attain the democratic ends so grudgingly approved.

The plutocratic influence on public opinion, in so far as it is not merely an effort to justify certain men or particular financial manipulations, is directed in this covert manner against innovation. The doctrine of "let well enough alone" is advocated by those who prosper inordinately. Our conservative traditions are fulsomely praised, while democratic experiments are derided and their inevitable failure prophesied. The appeal is always to the old. New laws and constitutions are too likely to be democratic. For the mass of new ideas fermenting in popular movements (in the democracies of 1800 and 1828, in the Abolitionist, Free Soil, Early Republican, Labor, Populist, Socialist parties), for all manifestations of democratic humanitarianism, the plutocracy has, and has always had, nothing but contempt — and fear. The plutocracy exalts good, old, judicial precedents, and its patriotism takes on a mellow, meerschaum, retrospective tinge, which is mere reactionism, as opposed to a patriotism which looks forward to a better America.

The plutocracy preaches individual liberty, the glorious fruits of free contract, the doctrine of the influence of good men, the survival of the fittest in business, an untrammeled individualism, a tame state with a ring through its nose. It believes that while government is wise enough to put us in jail, it is not honest enough to be intrusted with our money or our business. The plutocracy throws the mantle of property rights over things improperly obtained. It decries confiscation, specifying measures of taxation and regulation, not confiscatory in intention. It tolerates discussion but opposes "agitation." It admits popular rights but decries the "mob." It combats the representation of the weaker elements in the community by "agitators," "demagogues" and "walking delegates." Finally, in its appeal to the God of things as they are, the plutocracy places its faith in checks, balances, safeguards, and the letter of an obsolescent law.

But the plutocracy, much against its will, must defend too much. Sharing the same political bed with little crooks, it is obliged from time to time to plead their cause before the tribunal of public opinion. The respectable journals of respectable, free-booting financiers must occasionally defend the immigrant bank against the defrauded immigrant, the sweatshop against the sweated, the loan shark against his dupe, even the ward bruiser against the complaining citizen. Democracy in small things must often be checked, because by a rigorous logic it may be extended to big things. The plutocrat does not like the stunting of the poor, but laws intended to prevent poverty may shatter the very foundations of privilege. The plutocracy — no wiser than the rest of us — is a little confused. It has bad dreams. It is alternately too rash and too timorous. It does not always know what to do with its newspapers after it has bought them.

Moreover, in its control of the newspaper, the plutocracy has not to deal with an inert public opinion, which cannot strike back. Just as the plutocracy's control of industry and of politics evokes a spirit of revolt, so its more partial control of the newspaper, as it becomes visible, evokes a more or less distinct reaction within public opinion against the plutocracy. Newspapers which too openly espouse the plutocracy's cause often lose in circulation to journals assuming a more popular attitude. Simultaneously new journals of protest arise, winning their way against great financial obstacles, and a fresh outlet for public opinion is evolved in the popular, "muck-raking," reformatory magazine.

The magazine suffers, like the newspaper, from the very conditions which make for its extension and popularity; in other words, from a preponderance of advertising revenues, and a circulation at a price below cost. Being national in scope, however, it is at least freer from local pressure, and it is never so dependent upon a single class of advertisers as is the city newspaper upon the department stores. Moreover, because of its freedom from narrow geographical limits, it is able to seek from the enormous population of the country a larger number of like-minded people. Consequently, the popular magazine is perhaps more simple, direct, progressive, and dignified than is the daily newspaper, and despite the narrow gauntlet which it runs, between its increasing cost of production and its lowered price, it has hitherto managed better than the newspaper to maintain its independence. To a considerable extent the reformatory magazine is a powerful antidote to those of our newspapers which, while much-protesting against distant evils, are singularly charitable towards offenders nearer home.

While the magazine, like other business organs of publicity, does not therefore enjoy an absolute freedom in choosing sides, still the tendency during the last decade seems to have been towards an increasing circulation and profitableness of periodicals representing democratic ideals, or, what is even more important, of periodicals impartially presenting in a popular manner the facts of our contemporary life, upon which democratic action may ultimately be based. It is not impossible, of course, nor even improbable, that an increasingly determined attempt will be made by financial interests, hostile to democracy, to secure control of the magazines. In repelling such attacks, however, the magazine reader should be more successful than is the newspaper reader, for the reader is less dependent upon the magazine than upon the newspaper, while the magazine is even more dependent than is the newspaper upon the reader. The reader's preferences in magazines are balanced to the finest point, and the slightest change in policy, by pleasing or displeasing the million, may mean stupendous success or irretrievable failure. Our magazines, like ourselves, are very far from our ideal, but their merits are our merits, and their faults, our faults. The magazine, though often trivial, sometimes banal, and occasionally vicious and timidly obscene, is on the whole more representative of the majority of the people than is the newspaper.

Even were *all* magazines and newspapers to be controlled and muzzled (which is hardly conceivable) it would not be possible to hold down the popular intelligence. The medieval method of cutting off thought by cutting off the head is no longer applicable. Truth to-day is a volatile gas, a great deal of which will escape through a very small hole. Close up the newspapers, close up the magazines, and truth will flow out through other outlets.

Of such outlets there are many. A wide and free forum is provided by books, which, whatever their tendency or bias, can be printed if a thousand people will buy them. An enormous amount of uncontrolled literature in the form of pamphlets, circulars, reports of societies, etc., is constantly circulated. Nor is there an effective censorship of the play. The Theatrical Trust, although on pleasure bent, preserves a frugal mind, and this obedient, undiscerning servant of the two-dollar-an-evening public would as soon scuttle a ship as sacrifice box receipts to the preachment of reactionary principles. As for pulpit utterances — if sermons are directed too exclusively to the solace of the wealth-burdened, the poor stay from church.

Even our privately endowed universities, dependent for the bulk of their revenues upon the free gifts of the plutocracy, follow the general direction of the popular mind, and give to it tone, character, and an ethical interpretation. Although men have been released from University faculties because of their expressed opinions, and others have not been appointed because of their anticipated views, still academic freedom seems to be rather on the increase than on the decrease. Curiously enough, while there has been a certain pernicious influence of great fortunes upon University teaching, it is quite credible that every million contributed to universities out of our existing inequality of wealth renders a similar inequality less probable in the future. Political economy is taught by professors of chemistry, physics, and gymnastics, as well as by professors of political economy. Let the *alma mater* be ever so circumspect, her children will not escape contamination. Just as in the early pre-aseptic days hospitals were more dangerous than slums or battle fields, so to-day you are as likely to catch new ideas in a trust-endowed university as in a factory or a tenement house. Despite itself, the plutocracy subsidizes discontent and revolt. The plutocracy teaches more than it knows.

The issue is not yet decided, but as we review the field, it seems as though the plutocracy's assault upon public opinion, like its assault upon politics, invites its own failure by invoking a redoubled defense. The plutocracy strives for the possession of derelict newspapers and magazines; the popular mind strives for self-possession. The price of intellectual liberty and intactness is not only intellectual development, but eternal vigilance.

It is because of this vigilance, because of a constant, though casual, relation which the people maintain towards the organs of public opinion, that the plutocracy's control of the public mind is by no means complete. After all, the newspaper, the magazine, and the printed book are merely *organs* of public opinion. They are not public opinion itself. Back of them all lies the mind of the nation, fed by sights, sounds, conversations; a mind more or less excitable and transient in its manifestations, but maintaining itself for the most part with a certain tenacious sanity. Not all the combined organs of public opinion can convert the population to lies too gross and palpable, nor to truths too unpleasant, and a thousand "special articles" cannot prove that the shoe does not pinch. Bruises and pains teach as well as sermons, and a butcher's bill may be more edifying than an eloquent editorial.

The growing wisdom of the people is the final and irrefutable answer to the plutocracy's attempts to corner the intellectual market. More and more the people insist upon doing some of their own thinking.

Now the voice of the people, the adage to the contrary, is not necessarily the voice of God. In some lands and at some times it is but a babbling, obscene, and intolerant clamor. Public opinion may either be, as Sir Robert Peel defined it, a "great compound of folly, weakness, prejudice, wrong feeling, right feeling, obstinacy, and newspaper paragraphs," or it may be the temperate, slowly formed, and definitely formulated consensus of a free and resolute people. In countries used to its rule, it is more responsible and intelligent than in lands where it is violent because repressed. Public opinion in Switzerland, the home of the referendum, is very different from public opinion in Nicaragua or Liberia.

In the United States, despite racial and territorial cleavages (which are bound to be wide on a continent settled by immigrants), we have a broad and fairly coherent public opinion. This is in part due to our comparative freedom of speech and press, our political and religious tolerance, our varied facilities for interchanging ideas and manifolding words, our relative intelligence, our diffused prosperity, and our possession of formal political rights. "In no country," says Mr. Bryce, "is public opinion so powerful as in the United States."

This public opinion is at times still confused and self-contradictory, or else uninformed, dwarfed, and hysterical, and occasionally it degenerates into mob opinion, and for brief moments whirls in dangerous, ineffectual eddies. Nevertheless no one can fairly study its manifestations during the generation since Mr. Bryce wrote without being convinced that it is daily becoming more powerful and beneficent. It sweeps over opposition, brushes aside legal technicalities, and, attaching itself to democratic leaders, backs them up against great odds. This public opinion emancipates itself even from the newspaper by widening the field of intellectual supply. The average city man now takes two newspapers. He also reads one or two magazines. He comes in hourly contact with men who derive their information from still other sources. Like his country neighbor, he is less stereotyped than was his father. He is also more wisely skeptical.

To-day public opinion is seeking to become the ruling power in America. No overt opposition can withstand it. It cannot be bribed. It cannot be stifled. To overcome it, the people must be fooled, and, year by year, it is becoming more difficult to fool them.

In the end, therefore, the plutocracy must rest its case on the solid ground of truth. The body of doctrine which it pours into press, pulpit, and university is retarding,— but that is all. Evasions, appeals to prejudice, artfully induced misconceptions, half-truths, quarter-truths, and plain lies all have their day, as have lurid exaggerations, acrid personalities, and vague, sensational charges. Abuse does not last. You can drown a single individual in printer's ink, but great causes and solemn charges somehow survive leaded columns and italicized ridicule. When the whirl of apologies, charges, and countercharges subsides, as it always does subside, the result is a clearing of the field and a joining of the plain issue, whether the nation will be ruled politically by industrial despots, or whether it will stumble forward to both political and industrial democracy. The plutocracy brought before the court of highest instance is at last compelled formally to plead.

CHAPTER X

PLUTOCRACY AND EFFICIENCY

THE plutocracy rests its defense upon the ground of historical necessity. It has come to be because it was the fittest to be. It survives because it meets our national needs. What though it be ugly, smoky, noisy, parsimonious, murderous, if, all things considered, the plutocracy is the most economical form of national organization, then it will live. It can cure itself of minor ills. It can outgrow youthful immoderations, for the plutocracy, it must be remembered, is still very young. The plutocracy believes that the American will not exchange an effective for an ineffective business organization. He will not quarrel with his bread and butter.

The plutocracy claims to be a progressive, upbuilding force. It denies that it is reactionary, as was the oligarchic slave power, to which it has been likened. While, politically, our plutocracy is on a lower level than was the slave power (because depending on bribery and corruption), it is indubitably in the van of one form of economic progress. Our business princes develop territories, resuscitate industries, create new by-products.

The plutocracy cites many pages of statistics to prove (what is already evident) that during its domination we have been growing stupendously wealthy. One cannot read our government bulletins or the files of technical journals; one cannot glance over the daily paper or walk through the streets, without realizing that in everything which pertains to material progress we are moving at a giant's pace. The trust puts an end to the waste and brutality of an unregulated business war. The trust imposes peace. It may be the peace of industrial despotism. But it is peace.[1]

The plutocracy admits that in the conflict with competitive business the trust often won illegally. But illegality was equally the weapon of its rivals, and a too scrupulous respect for the law was never a condition of the contest. Even without such illegalities the trust would have been eventually victorious,[2] for its being was decreed by the law of business evolution. Even trusts burdened by an excessive capitalization survived and prospered, because they gave a greater profit than their constituent companies had done. Combination, where possible, made competition impossible, and, if combination resulted in monopoly and

[1] A comparison might be drawn between our trusts and the political despotisms which grew up with the nations in the fifteenth, sixteenth, and seventeenth centuries. These despotisms represented politically the budding national consciousness; the trusts represent, in the same despotic way, the national unity of business. The absolute monarch of the sixteenth century put down the feudal lords with a high hand. He either attainted the nobles, and confiscated their estates, or, by compelling their attendance at court, divorced them from their followers. In a similar manner our industrial despot crushes his competitors and confiscates their businesses. Or he buys them out and compels their attendance at directors' meetings. Even the personalities of some of the old nation builders illustrate the temper of our trust builders. We have among us to-day the craft and subtlety of a Louis the Eleventh of France, the narrow intensity of a Philip the Second of Spain; the avariciousness of a Henry the Seventh of England; the intensely ambitious *bonhomie* of a Henry of Navarre; the overweening self-consciousness of a "grand monarch" who could boast "*L'État c'est moi.*" Finally, before we leave this comparison, which is, of course, merely illustrative, our despotic plutocracy, after vanquishing the business leaders, finds itself face to face with the broader masses of the people, just as the Bourbons, having at last made France one, found themselves on a certain summer day of 1789 face to face with an awakened French nation.

[2] Had the Standard Oil Company not secured a practical monopoly of the oil business through railroad rebates in the seventies and eighties, it is highly probable that either that company, or some other, would have been formed in 1901 (or earlier) for the purpose of securing control of the entire oil business.

extortion, these were, after all, goals to which each competitor of the trust had secretly aspired.

Because of its alleged efficiency, the plutocracy claims remission of past sins and indulgence for future transgressions. We forgave the pioneer his crudity, recklessness, and exaggerated individualism, because *for his time* he made the most effective use of the still unconquered continent. We then sent gentlemen to Congress whom we should now send to jail, and we then rewarded with fortunes men who might to-day end in almshouses. At the present time, on this argument, our toleration of the old individualist should descend to the equally typical representatives of a new economic development. The overwhelming of the citizens at the polls and in the primaries, the rise of a more subtle and ramified political corruption, the evolution of a powerful boss, were but the political expression of a contemporaneous economic evolution, the rise of the trust. And this stupendous development, the plutocracy insists, was but a step in a progress from chaos to order; a step towards a wiser, and longer-viewed exploitation of the continent.

Not only does the plutocracy assert that this end justifies the means, but it also claims that, because of its higher industrial organization, it has a broader ethical basis and a wider program of social reform than had the competitive business which preceded it. Not being so hard pressed as were its forerunners, the plutocracy can afford a little virtue. Or, rather, it cannot afford *not* to have a little virtue, for our growing business concentration has changed the incidence of certain industrial evils, so that they who cause the damage occasionally suffer from it. From considerations of policy as well as because of its acknowledged leadership of industry, the plutocracy has been obliged to accept certain industrial responsibilities, and has thus developed its own code of social morality.

Under the old *régime*, competitors did not mind any conceivable waste of natural resources or human lives. The community paid. Jekyll could not afford philanthropy in competition with Hyde. With increasing concentration of business control, however, it is becoming wiser to mitigate certain evils of unregulated employment, and make the additional cost a fixed charge to customers, rather than let things go and pay the cost of negligence in taxes. The growing popularity of company-paid pensions to employees, of welfare work, even of reductions in hours — although these have another side — is indicative of a certain rudimentary sense of responsibility on the part of big business. That this broader ethical view is largely determined by the desire for profits does not detract from its social beneficence.

More and more, though as yet only partially and grudgingly, the ruling plutocracy gives up its petty business corruption, as a man puts away childish things. It finds that it does not pay to rob its own cash drawer. The mere progress of big business means the abolition of the worst evils of little business. Under a plutocracy, as under a democracy, we should gradually end petty adulterations, small cheatings, "truck stores," "company houses," and the most flagrant abuses of patent medicine fakirs, ticket speculators, and bucket-shop keepers, just as we are gradually eliminating the burglar and the bruiser in favor of more refined members of an antisocial class. Paramount among all considerations is the welfare of big business, of the super-financier. Big business is zealous to "reform" little business out of the running.[1] Even the dullest of our business princes are beginning to see that to a certain extent humanity is the best policy, and that honesty pays where

[1] An election appeal to the ten commandments may mean an attack upon the little business of vice by the political allies of the big business of franchise stealing. The man who takes thousands may be relegated to an innocuous and law-abiding existence by the taker or holder of millions.

it is obvious to all. The improved *morale* of the huge department store, with its ostentatious *noblesse oblige* towards customers, indicates the general trend.

Even apart from an improved business *morale* due to the greater publicity and extension of business, the plutocracy has its own program of social reform, which aims to reconcile it to the judgment of the nation. The plutocracy's code of reform includes a charity designed to widen the eye of the needle. It is a business charity, with organization and prevention of waste; with efficiency and by-products. It is a charity which has evolved (following industrial changes) from the instinctive, soul-saving giving of the Middle Ages, through a competitive, shrieking, advertising charity, to a well-organized, far-seeing charity on a trust basis. The plutocracy believes in the prevention of non-economic causes of poverty in so far as such prevention does not interfere with business arrangements. It believes in special institutions for the blind, halt, insane, feeble-minded. It believes in laws against child beating, and, with reservations, in laws against child labor. It believes in welfare work for employees. It assists many forms of ameliorative social work.

Other ideals of the plutocracy are of larger import. The plutocracy believes, as does the democracy, in an increase of national productivity. It therefore recognizes the advantages of education, especially of a technical education, which makes the nation a more effective industrial group. It desires more railroads and better railroads, improved technical processes, irrigation of deserts, filling in of swamps. It usually desires peace, social security, and general well-being. It is opposed to an unprofitable waste of things which cost money. It desires a healthy community in which all men can work, and it essays the extirpation of contagious diseases, which social barriers cannot exclude from the homes of the rich. It desires the governmental development of such national resources as cannot be profitably exploited by individuals, and it encourages unremunerative public activities, translatable into private profits. Finally, the plutocracy is imbued with certain humanitarian, artistic, and educational ideals, in no direct way undermining the influence or lessening the welfare of the group.

This program of the plutocracy, halting though it be, is as much superior to the negative social program of the earlier individualist as is the organization of the Standard Oil Company to that of the little companies which have been superseded. If the plutocracy were attacked by individualists alone, its arguments would avail, and its social program, like its industrial labors, would justify its existence.

But the plutocracy is also assailed by men who desire, not a return to individualism, but a progress toward democratic socialization. These opponents of the plutocracy point out its wastes, inefficiencies, and injustices, and accuse it of standing in the way of a complete harmonization of our industrial organization with our political and social aspirations.

The plutocracy's argument from prosperity is turned against itself. Who gets the prosperity? Why, after the wastes of production have been so largely eliminated, do we still suffer from overwork, child labor, sweating, industrial disease, preventable accident, slums, poverty, wretchedness? Why do wages remain low after the plutocracy has established a little order in industry? Why does an increasing inequality accompany an improved utilization of the resources of the continent?

In lessening the wastes of production, the plutocracy has increased many of the wastes of consumption. By improving industrial processes it has drawn attention to heightened inequalities of distribution. Our senseless inequalities of distribution, from our new point of view, are poor economy and low efficiency, because a gross inequality means a lessened pleasure in the consumption of wealth. A masterpiece of art in a private gallery, seen by a hundred people, gives less pleasure than would the same masterpiece in a public gallery seen by a million people. A million dollars of commodities consumed by one overrich man gives less pleasure than would the same sum added to the expenditure of ten thousand people. If the plutocracy's wiser utilization of our national resources leads only to an increasing inequality of wealth and income, the net gain to the people may be dubious.

It is exactly as though the plutocracy, with its brand-new tool, the trust, had trebled our production of coal, but had distributed the fuel so badly, overstoking some boilers and understoking others, that the total production of heat was no greater than before. It is as though the plutocracy, boasting of its trebled production of coal, and exulting in its increased output of smoke and ashes, had failed to realize that a shivering people was demanding, not more coal, not more smoke, not more ashes, but more heat. What the people want is not wealth, but distributed wealth; not a statistical increase in the national income, but more economic satisfactions, more widely distributed.

Our new economic thought emphasizes as the industrial goal of nations, not wealth in the sense of objective values, but economic pleasures or satisfactions. The older conception measured value in terms of toil or pain involved in production, or the sheer scarcity of a desired article. If potatoes became twice as hard to get, they became twice as valuable. In this sense, our American forests are more valuable to-day, are worth more, than they were thirty years ago, because we have fewer forests and they are more easily monopolized. If to-day we could increase our deposits of coal one hundred fold, the nation (according to the earlier economics) would be poorer *because* it had more to enjoy. Much that we count as wealth is, from the point of view of the economic satisfactions of the community, not wealth at all, but its exact opposite.

Our crassly unequal distribution means not only a less effective production, but, what is worse, a comparatively pleasureless consumption of wealth.[1] A bad distribution of wealth means a wasting of vast quantities of labor in the manufacture of unprofitable articles, and the rendering of unnecessary services. A full-grown footman devoting himself to the cultivated wants of a gold-collared puppy as clearly illustrates wasted social labor as does a man manufacturing nails by hand after machinery has been introduced, or as does a man employed in a small, ill-equipped workshop at labor which can better be done in a large, well-equipped factory.

The Achilles-heel of the Plutocratic Economy, as of the economy which preceded it, is this individualistic and objective conception of wealth. It makes the goal of our national economy the increase in articles, possessed by certain citizens and demanded by others, instead of an increase in the economic pleasure derived from a more universal, varied, and harmonious consumption. The plutocratic conception identifies wealth with gain, with the individualistic accumulation of scarce things. The plutocracy stands for "business," which is concerned uniquely with profits, and not, like industry, with production. Business means gaining money, not making things. Business destroys, when it pays to destroy, as it upbuilds when it pays to upbuild.

[1] In earlier ages, when population pressed sharply upon the means of subsistence, inequalities of wealth were often the truest national economy. Wealth more evenly divided would simply have meant more babies. The opulent class served the valuable function of depositors and protectors of the social surplus. They were the useful fat cells of the social body. To-day, however, a nearer approach to an equality of wealth and income would undoubtedly mean a vast increase in the sum total of economic satisfactions of the more advanced nations.

Whether profits are secured through monopoly, adulteration, advertised poisoning, or the making of good bread and good shoes at fair prices, the end of business is the same — the maximum of profits.

For the individual man, in business against competitors, this goal of profits (within bounds of law and decency) is legitimate. For a nation the conception is self-destructive.[1]

The social program of the plutocracy is tainted by this individualistic conception. That program is too profit-cramped, and consequently too pedantically restrained, to gain general approbation. The man on the street, though astounded at the magnitude of certain benefactions, is seldom with any deep sense of gratitude. He vaguely feels that the social program even of philanthropists is for the most part second-hand. He suspects that it comes from an outside intellectual and moral pressure, or even from an abiding sense of avertible evils to come.

These suspicions are perhaps unfounded. Yet the social ethics of the plutocracy sit somewhat awkwardly upon the victors in the great game of American profit-seeking. It is an ethic which, acknowledging no evils, proceeds to cure them; which, finding the economic world theoretically perfect in all its parts, proceeds to patch it up. The plutocrat does not come by his good intentions honestly. He is a man who instinctively worships the *status quo;* who instinctively lauds the conditions of which he is the product; who inevitably attributes the failures of others to those others' failings. If he becomes a philanthropist, or a social and political reformer, it is not so much by virtue of his philosophy as because he has a sense of order and dislikes

[1] The plutocracy, like the individualists before it, exalts the instinct for gain as the one redeeming economic virtue of a humanity, otherwise immersed in slothfulness. Protestants against the plutocracy condemn this instinct as the original irrepressible economic sin. Actually the instinct of individual gain (including herein wages) is individually an end, but socially, only a means.

waste. Moreover, city life and the newspaper bring home to us — and, through us, to him — poverty, illness, cruelty, and a festering wretchedness; and to all these things a growing general comfort and an increasing national wealth have made us — and him — most painfully sensitive. The cramping of the plutocratic philanthropy, however, consists herein, that the huge benefactions of multimillionaires are seldom *intentionally* and consciously directed towards the equalization of incomes, the prevention of future inequalities, the democratization of government, or the extension of popular control over industries now given over to private exploitation. The profits of the plutocracy, even when directed to social reform, are seldom intentionally enlisted in a war against profits.

The very qualities of the plutocracy have this inevitable defect, this prenatal taint. Our business magnates, though perhaps the greatest industrial organizers in the world, are in many respects reactionary. They demand free access to the spoils of the continent. They claim the privilege (as price of their leadership) of levying a legalized tribute. By arbitrarily identifying their interests with those of the community at large, they subtly exalt their own demands above those of other social groups. They believe in docile labor. They favor business secrecy, financial absolutism, liberty of action to the industrially strong. They wish, for the sake of private profits, to rule despotically in the business field.

Because of this inability to rise above the conception of individual profits, the plutocracy finds that its own arguments, used so effectively against the individualist, are now directed against its own pretensions. As the old individualist, so, in its turn, the trust was necessary, and was tolerated. The pioneer period could not lead immediately into the period of democratic socialization, because neither we nor our businesses or governments were adjusted to such a transition. Our industry was too detailed, inchoate, multiform; our government was too amorphous; our individualism too confident and dogmatic. Before a democracy was possible, the house must be set in order, the house industrial, political, and socio-psychological. The cleaner appointed for this necessary task of preparing the house for the owner's occupancy was our resplendent, unpremeditated plutocracy.

The task of cleaning, however, is a temporary one, and the more efficiently the cleaners work, the sooner they may be paid off and dismissed. The rapidity with which our trust builders, financiers, business engineers, and long-distance organizers are unifying our national businesses hastens their own supersession through the creation of conditions which make a still more efficient *régime* possible. The more rapidly our plutocracy, acting under the stimulus of profits, introduces the coöperative element into our businesses, the sooner will the democracy be able to adapt this coöperative element to the socialization of industry. The function of the plutocracy is to reduce chaos to order. But order is the very rock upon which democratic socialization is built. When the plutocracy shall have finished its task, it must take its booty and go.[1]

The new democracy accepts the plutocracy's theory of the survival of the fittest civilization. It recognizes that the efficient utilization of our national resources means the wealth, bread, life of the people, and that all political aspirations must conform to this underlying economic factor. The democracy, however, instructed by its wants, interprets the word utilization in a new sense. Where the plutocracy means the greatest wealth, the democracy means

[1] That is, it must go as a group especially favored in an economic sense. Under any practicable *régime* of industry there would be an acute demand for the well-recompensed services of men with the trainings, abilities, and intuitions of our great trust builders.

the widest range of economic satisfactions. Where the plutocracy thinks of profits, the democracy thinks of recreation, leisure, a wise expenditure, and a healthful toil. Where the plutocracy emphasizes a saving in wages, the democracy emphasizes a saving in labor.

The democracy does not believe that a nation is rich because the majority owes the minority money and labor. The democracy does not wish the nation to possess that "wealth" which is merely the capitalized value of an economic rent due from the people to monopolists, but it does desire meat, potatoes, school books, public parks, and surcease from excessive toil. The democracy interprets utilization as such a production, distribution, and consumption of wealth as will give the highest excess of economic pleasure over economic pain to the largest number of people for the longest possible time. Upon this end all the industrial, political, social, and ethical ideals of the democracy converge.

These two conceptions of efficiency conflict in many problems. The plutocracy, where it pays in the long run, will usually reduce hours of labor, let us say, from twelve to ten a day, as distinguished from the early individualist or our present parasitic industries, which have no time to consider the long run. The democracy, however, will demand a still further reduction of the working day, if such reduction is to the *net ultimate advantage of the whole community*, and *whether or not* it lessens production and profits.[1]

[1] At this point a senile argument comes doddering to the rescue. Even before it opens its mouth, you hear the question: "If eight hours, why not four, two, or one? If you leave the safe ground of supply and demand in regulating the length of the working day, why work over ten minutes a day?" The obvious answer is that from the social point of view the hours of labor should be so regulated that the final increment of work should not mean more loss in fatigue or in abstention from recreation than it means in the pleasure from increased wages or output. It is a subjective analysis, more difficult to explain than to make, as are many of our everyday determinations.

Similarly the question of the "speeding up" of labor *versus* the "restriction of output," the problems of unrestricted *versus* restricted child labor often (though not always) involve the choice between an individualistic utilization in terms of profits or even of production and a social utilization in terms of life. Many trade union demands are to-day misunderstood because we are largely under the dominion of ancient ideas identifying the best utilization of our resources with a maximum of production and profits.

The conflict between the plutocracy and the democracy thus becomes a contest between rival methods, purposes, and beneficiaries of the exploitation of the continent. It is not, and never has been (and probably no social conflict ever was), a mere contest between bad men and good men. To our trust builders are sometimes applied such indecent epithets as "vampires" and "bloodsuckers," while their victims, the common people, are represented as meek and humble citizens, who would rather suffer injury than inflict it. This ethical contrast, so solacing to honest poverty, does not, however, quite square with the facts. In actual life, affability, honesty, courage, and other virtues have a way of dividing themselves rather equally between men who favor and men who oppose social progress. Rogues are often exemplars of all the gentle domestic virtues. Our transcendent and incomprehensible money-makers, after breaking laws faster and more scientifically than legislators make them, decline into philanthropy and scatter their vertiginous fortunes to libraries and hospitals, while an imitating horde of lesser magnates — mere inconspicuous millionaires — unostentatiously give time and money to correct the minor iniquities of our industrial life. Our plutocrats are not wicked men.

What is perhaps more significant, they are obsolete. The very qualities which fitted our plutocracy for establishing efficiency unfit it for establishing a democracy, which, as far as the people are concerned, is but a higher form of efficiency. The democracy is learning that the elimination of waste means the elimination as well of the present-day trust. Just as the trust builder taught the old pioneer that, without a change in industrial organization, the conquered wilderness would relapse into a social wilderness, so our new democrats are teaching that, without a readjustment in the distribution and consumption of wealth, improvements in production will be of no permanent advantage. The mere accumulation of wealth will be but an aggravation of poverty.

All of which the plutocracy does not understand. It does not in truth comprehend this fascinating industrial world, which in a certain sense is its own creation. It cannot conceive how a society growing in wealth can simultaneously grow in discontent, and it regards all subterranean rancor as a lack of gratitude. The plutocracy listens astounded to men who once spoke of patriotism and national consciousness, but now speak of socialization and class consciousness, and it views with bewilderment the precedence which Labor Day parades and speeches seem to be taking over Fourth of July parades and speeches. The plutocracy does not understand all this "sectionalism," "demagoguery," and "incitement to class hatred."

The plutocracy would like to issue an injunction, not only against the new spirit, but equally against the new and unconsecrated uses attached to the plutocracy's English. It had always interpreted the phrase "economic freedom" in the good, old, simple, juridical sense, according to which a poor Roumanian, consumptive widow, half-supporting her children by sewing, is a "free agent" enjoying "economic freedom," as is also the recently landed Italian day laborer, party of the first part, who enters into a wage agreement (through the padrone) with the party of the second part, a trans-continental railroad corporation. The new democracy is putting a new meaning into the old phrase, and is insisting on a real, economic (as well as a legal) equality between bargainers; upon a real, economic (as well as a legal) freedom. All of which is revolutionary, and, what is worse, confusing. The plutocracy, which is far from subtle when removed from the countinghouse, does not understand.

When the plutocracy is attacked, as it often is, by the uncompromising class-conscious socialist, it answers his unanswerable attacks by equally unanswerable attacks upon the socialist. The trust builder, not knowing how to reply, not understanding even the terminology of his opponent, leaves his own position defenseless and invades and lays waste the enemy's country. To the socialist's arguments that the plutocratic (and capitalistic) system creates and preserves poverty, the trust builder answers nothing. But he does prove, or believes that he proves, that the coöperative commonwealth cannot be created by any forces now existing in society, that it could not be maintained without the desire for profits, and that, if established, it would disappoint its creators and would founder on the rock of a residual egotism. To the argument that plutocratic rule is no longer possible, the trust builder replies that the cooperative commonwealth will never be possible. Thus each contestant, without meeting the other, gains over him a splendid logical victory.

To the proponent of a new, socialized, and plenary democracy, the plutocracy opposes a similar argument. Against such a democracy he pleads as a devil's advocate. He describes the Demos as an ignorant, self-satisfied, rapacious, and violent brute; as a brute which must be caged. In his eyes "the people" is a Thing far lower than its constituent individuals; it is a mob, with a mob's insolence and a mob's cowardice. The plutocrat recalls many foibles, errors, and crimes of a stumbling, half-seeing democracy. He believes that the masses are always wrong; that all progress comes from the few. Democracy, he asserts, will let loose the original, ineradicable perversity of the mass. The human herd, set free from the leash of subordination, possessed with the mad, evil spirit of self-rule, will run violently down a steep place into the sea, and will perish in the waters.

Against such democrats, the plutocracy opposes what it claims are the best traditions of Americanism. The plutocracy honestly regards itself as merely the old American individualist, a trifle rejuvenesced,—the individualist trying to make an honest living by developing the country. It believes that it is the true representative of our sterling American qualities of initiative and self-reliance.

In this interested attachment to old ideals, as in the very humbleness of its merely pecuniary ambitions, lie the strength of the plutocracy's appeal to public opinion and the menace that it may corrode our national morals, or at least tend to maintain them on a low level. What is so transcendently perilous in our present conditions of industrial success and failure is not our inequality of wealth with its evil effect upon the consumption of the nation's goods, nor even the subtle corruption of our politics — although both are evil — but rather the echo of the rich spoiler's ambition in the soul of the average men. Our real plutocrats are not all rich. Doubtless, in the army of King Charles, the stableboys, most ardent despisers of equality, were *plus royalistes que le Roi*. To-day in America, just as the standard of democracy is borne aloft by some men of fortune, so, on the other hand, wealthy plutocrats are backed up by millions of like-minded poor men, *penniless plutocrats, dream-millionaires*. The men of great fortunes give resplendency to the ideals which unite rich and poor fortune seekers.

Secure in the adherence of its humble millions of imitators and admirers, the plutocracy looks forward to many generations of peaceful control of the labor, votes, and thoughts of the American people. It relies upon its enormous wealth, and its strong position in industry, politics, and the machines of public expression. It believes that it still possesses a mission, and it cannot conceive of the possibility of any alternative social organization. The plutocracy hopes, by a self-directed curbing of its own worst impulses, to live many years in uncontested rule of the American nation.

But this very program, which is the final appeal of the plutocracy for the suffrages of the people, is but the dwarfed expression of the new spirit; is but the shadow, cast before, of the coming democracy. When the plutocracy could not understand the minds or interpret the motives of the increasing numbers of earnest men opposed to it, it should have begun to suspect that, despite its resplendency, something was already radically wrong with it. The plutocracy, which denies the possibility of a democratic revolt, is making such a revolt inevitable. It is furnishing a common point of attack to diverse assailants. In opposition to the plutocracy, insurgent Americans are developing vague, large programs, in the execution of which the elimination of the plutocracy is but a first step. Just as the demand for an American nation was born, not of a common positive ideal, but of a concerted opposition to petty British aggressions; just as "the old nationalism" found its highest expression in opposition to an ethically dead slavery, — so in a common antagonism to a towering, menacing plutocracy, men imbued with new ideals and new hopes are uniting to establish in America a full, free, socialized democracy.

CHAPTER XI

THE NEW SOCIAL SPIRIT

THERE are men who believe that the plutocracy is undying, like one of its favorite 999-years' leases. They believe that, as the years pass, the noise and fury of the battle against the trusts will die down; the chants of victory will be sung; the returning heroes will be crowned, while quietly the unscathed trusts will emerge from the conflict. Thereafter a wiser race of business princes will rule America through vassals, retainers, and mercenaries, while granting bread and circuses to a light-hearted populace. Through speciously democratic constitutions these rulers will fasten their hold upon a hunger-driven or pleasure-lured people. The Declaration of Independence will end in government by check book. Democracy will become the equality of underlings, dominated by pomp-shunning dictators.

A completely triumphant plutocracy would be no new thing under the sun. In many ages we have had a rule of the wealthy, a gilding of the state and of the laws. Plutocracies have shown vigor, skill, and martial quality.

There is reason, however, to believe that the trend in America is not towards a perpetuation of plutocratic rule nor towards a subversion of democratic sentiment, which would be its intellectual accompaniment. We Americans, it is true, have surrendered some of our former aggressive egalitarianism. We have borrowed some of the class distinctions of Europe, and have evolved some upon our own account. The "hired girl" is now the servant, sitting at the servant's table; the tradesman enters by the tradesman's door; policemen, firemen, conductors, letter carriers, "submit" to uniforms;[1] and an increasing number of persons accept the subordinate status involved in the receipt of tips and gratuities. But these facts, while they undoubtedly show stratification and the beginnings of caste, do not constitute an argument that we are forever to be ruled by a sovereign wealthy class. The plutocracy is still far from the attainment of a separate legal status or from a recognized economic sovereignty. As it grows in power, opposing forces grow equally. The plutocracy is not always on the offensive. Nor is its defense impervious. It has no glamour, no traditions, no superabundance of intelligence. It does not even possess a monopoly of the community's wealth. Its pretensions, to avail, must combat the growing national consciousness and the new skeptical knowledge of the multitude.

There is a variant to the foregoing theory of a perpetual plutocracy. Some men believe that an eventual democracy — as much as is good for us — will come as a free gift from omnipotent millionaires, like the charter of a city granted by grace of an absolute monarch. The plutocracy will act as the faithful steward of our liberties. The golden calf, seeing a new light, will descend from his pedestal and mingle with the baser herd. This theory is idyllic. Unfortunately, however, the full program of the plutocracy, while it may carry us far along the line of social reform, will not bring us to democracy. Moreover, were we to become the sudden peaceful legatees of abdicating industrial despots, we should not know what to do with our easy heritage.[2]

[1] It is highly significant of the fierce egalitarianism of our grandfathers that the wearing of a uniform, even by a railroad conductor, was hotly repelled as unworthy of a free-born American.

[2] We have very few precedents of any real abdication of power by social groups or classes. In 1789 the French nobles, and in 1911 the British peers, made more or less graceful relinquishment of pretensions, but in

What we dimly see to-day is not the promise of a permanent plutocracy, nor democratic institutions graciously conceded by repentant money lords, but the native growth of a democratic spirit. At the moment when maturing forces culminate in the florescence of our powerful plutocracy, when the cleavage between Americans at the top and Americans at the bottom appears deepest, when millions seem doomed to an ambitionless, ignoble, precarious existence in a preëmpted land, the new social democracy is born.

Our hope of this democracy does not depend upon the chance of a sudden, causeless turn of the wheel. The motor reactions of society, like those of individuals, proceed only from prior accumulations of nervous energy. If we are now to move towards democracy, it is because we are already moving, or preparing to move, in that direction. Our conscious social actions are but a fulfillment, a sanction, an epilogue; the unconscious social strivings precede and prepare.

That this democratic evolution is already preparing is overlooked by him who runs. The development is too multiform and bewildering, and we are too near. If we fix our gaze at one point in progress, we conclude that results are small. If, however, we look over the field and note progress in a succession of social efforts, we are amazed at our advance. A democratic reform is instituted in one of our States with a blazon of trumpets. Thereafter we hear rumors of its working ill or well. Then silence. A dozen years later, we are surprised to learn that half the States have adopted the new institution, and soon we forget the evil conditions which preceded, and think of the reform no longer as an improvement, but as a thing upon which we are absurdly slow to improve.

It requires a historical perspective to make any com-

each case the action was induced by the expectant attitude of a none too patient heir.

parison of present and past. "The heirs of all the ages" are spoilt children, valuing only their very newest toys. An infant born a few generations ago might have been elated over the steam engine; a child born to-day will find the telephone, automobile, and X-ray commonplaces. He will no more think of aviation as progress than we regard plowing and arithmetic as valuable social acquisitions.

So great is the insistence of the immediate, that we find it well-nigh impossible to picture the state of, let us say, the workingman of a century ago — of the indentured servant, of the slave, of the man who sailed before the mast and was beaten, starved, and "hazed," of the workman arrested for debt, of the child without chance of education. A sunlit haze softens the outlines of the past, and inclines us to describe present evil conditions in words which in earlier times had a harsher significance. We sometimes apply to modern labor conditions the word "slavery," without realizing how inapposite is a comparison of our present conditions with the auction block, the forcible separation of families, the willful maiming of slaves, the prohibition of education, and other features of the Southern labor system of 1860.

Similarly, because we are so hypnotized by the glitter of our plutocracy, we fail to see the countervailing developments of the last twenty years in political, industrial, and social life. We overlook an evolution which in many States and cities has already given a larger popular control over government, which in one industry after another has subjected business to governmental supervision. We do not trace the new democratic movement in its innumerable ramifications; in ordinances, laws, judicial decisions, group actions, and individual labors. And yet, without knowing in detail this vast, multiform movement, we cannot escape its impelling spirit.

That spirit is still inchoate and speaks with many voices. To many men it means many things. It inspires the striker, who fights for "principles" even when the bread-and-butter balance is against him. It may also inspire an opposing employer, who, with more rudimentary a social sense, dreams of good houses, clean bath towels, and other welfare work for his employees. It inspires the city reformer fighting for "a city for the people"; the political insurgent rebelling against laming political traditions; the muckraker painfully hunting for "graft"; the inventor, engineer, bacteriologist, planning to remove physical barriers which impede a driven humanity. The new spirit is the language of social reformers, who, from being almsgivers and tract distributors, are becoming merciless, slow-speaking critics of social abuses. It inspires the philanthropic multimillionaire, who founds hospitals, libraries, universities, and research laboratories, as it inspires the revolutionary, who wishes to end both philanthropy and millionaires by reconstituting society on a basis of justice. The new message is heard in schools, churches, trade-unions, political meetings, social gatherings. One hears its echoes in the Pullman coach, the street car, on the "bleachers" at the baseball game.

The new spirit is not all new. Before this we have known these types, or, at least, their prototypes. But what has been small has grown great, and what has been still has become loud. There has been a change in emphasis, which makes the new spirit a something different from the crass, state-blind individualism of yesterday.

The new spirit is social. Its base is broad. It involves common action and a common lot. It emphasizes social rather than private ethics, social rather than individual responsibility.

This new spirit, which is marked by a social unrest, a new altruism, a changed patriotism, an uncomfortable sense of social guilt, was not born of any sudden enthusiasm or quickening revelation. It grew slowly in the dark places of men's minds out of the new conditions. The old individualism — carried to its logical sequence — would have meant impotence and social bankruptcy. Individualism struck its frontier when the pioneer struck his, and society, falling back upon itself, found itself. New problems arose, requiring for their solution slight amendments of our former canons of judgment and modes of action. In many spheres of economic life the individual began to find more profit in his undivided share of the common lot than in his chance of individual gain. On this foundation of an individual interest in the common lot, the new social spirit was laid. This egoistic interest, however, was shared by so many interdependent millions, that men passed insensibly from an ideal of reckless individual gaining to a new ideal, which urged the conservation and thrifty utilization of the patrimony of all in the interest of all.

In obedience to this new spirit we are slowly changing our perception and evaluation of the goods of life. We are freeing ourselves from the unique standard of pecuniary preeminence and are substituting new standards of excellence. We are ceasing solely to adore successful greed, and are evolving a tentative theory of the trusteeship of wealth. We are emphasizing the overlordship of the public over property and rights formerly held to be private. A new insistence is laid upon human life, upon human happiness. What is attainable by the majority — life, health, leisure, a share in our natural resources, a dignified existence in society — is contended for by the majority against the opposition of men who hold exorbitant claims upon the continent. The inner soul of our new democracy is not the unalienable rights, negatively and individualistically interpreted, but those same rights, "life, liberty, and the pursuit of happiness," extended and given a social interpretation.

It is this social interpretation of rights which characterizes the democracy coming into being, and makes it different in kind from the so-called individualistic democracy of Jefferson and Jackson. It is this social concept which is the common feature of many widely divergent democratic policies. The close of the merely expansive period of America showed that an individualistic democracy must end in its own negation, the subjection of the individual to an economically privileged class of rich men. The political weapons of our forefathers might avail against political despotism, but were farcically useless against economic aggression. The right of habeas corpus, the right to bear arms, the rights of free speech and free press could not secure a job to the gray-haired citizen, could not protect him against low wages or high prices, could not save him from a jail sentence for the crime of having no visible means of support. The force of our individualistic democracy might suffice to supplant one economic despot by another, but it could not prevent economic despotism.

To-day no democracy is possible in America except a socialized democracy, which conceives of society as a whole and not as a more or less adventitious assemblage of myriads of individuals. The old individualistic system pictured the individual freely bargaining with the state, not only in a mythical social contract, but in the everyday affairs of taxation and governmental expenditure. For so much protection the individual would pay the state so much taxes. "The subjects of every State," said the great economist Adam Smith, "ought to contribute to the support of the Government as nearly as possible in proportion to their respective abilities; that is, in proportion to the revenue which they respectively enjoy under the protection of the State. The expense of government to the individuals of a great nation is like the expense of management to the joint tenants of a great estate, who are all obliged to contribute in proportion to their respective interests in the estate."[1]

[1] "Wealth of Nations," Book V, Chap. 2. From an individualistic point of view, no theory could be juster. Our federal taxation to-day,

The individualistic point of view halts social development at every point. Why should the childless man pay in taxes for the education of other people's children? Why should the rich and innocent pay for better almshouses and better prisons for the poor and guilty? Why should those who do not use the public parks and public playgrounds pay for them in taxes? To the individualist taxation above what is absolutely necessary for the individual's welfare is an aggression upon his rights and a circumscription of his powers.

All the inspiring texts of democracy fall into nonsense or worse when given a strict individualistic interpretation. "Government should rest upon the consent of the governed" is a great political truth, if by "the governed" is meant the whole people, or an effective majority of the people; but if each individual governed retains the right at all times to withhold his consent, government and social union itself become impossible. So, too, the phrase "taxation without representation is tyranny," if interpreted strictly in an individualistic sense, leads to the theory that government should be in the hands of property owners, that they who pay the piper (in taxes) should set the tune, that they who are without "a stake in the country" should not participate, or at least not equally, in a government designed to raise money and to expend it.

In the socialized democracy towards which we are moving, all these conceptions will fall to the ground. It will be sought to make taxes conform more or less to the ability of each to pay; but the engine of taxation, like all other social engines, will be used to accomplish great social ends, among which will be the more equal distribution of wealth and income. The state will tax to improve education, health, recreation,

which falls with especial severity upon people of small and moderate means, is immeasurably below the standard set by Adam Smith five generations ago.

communication, "to provide for the common defense, and promote the general welfare," and from these taxes no social group will be immune because it fails to benefit in proportion to cost. The government of the nation, in the hands of the people, will establish its unquestioned sovereignty over the industry of the nation, so largely in the hands of individuals. The political liberties of the people will be supplemented by other provisions which will safeguard their industrial liberties.

To-day the chief restrictions upon liberty are economic, not legal, and the chief prerogatives desired are economic, not political. It is a curious, but not inexplicable, development, moreover, that our constitutional provisions, safeguarding our political liberties, are often used to deprive us of economic liberties. The constitutional provision that "no one shall be deprived of life, liberty, or property without due process of law" has seldom prevented an Alabama Negro from illegally being sent to the chain gang, but it has often prevented the people of a State from securing relief from great interstate corporations. The restraints upon the liberty of the poor are to-day economic. A law forbidding a woman to work in the textile mills at night is a law increasing rather than restricting *her* liberty, simply because it takes from the employer *his* former right to compel her through sheer economic pressure to work at night when she would prefer to work by day. So a law against adulteration of food products increases the economic liberty of food purchasers, as a tenement house law increases the liberty of tenement dwellers.

In two respects, the democracy towards which we are striving differs from that of to-day. Firstly, the democracy of to-morrow, being a real and not a merely formal democracy, does not content itself with the mere right to vote, with political immunities, and generalizations about the rights of men. Secondly, it is a plenary, socialized democracy, emphasizing social rather than merely individual aims, and carrying over its ideals from the political into the industrial and social fields.

Because of this wideness of its aims, the new spirit, in a curiously cautious, conservative way, is profoundly revolutionary. The mind of the people slowly awakens to the realization of the people's needs; the new social spirit gradually undermines the crust of inherited and promulgated ideas; the rising popular will overflows old barriers and converts former institutions to new uses. It is a deep-lying, potent, swelling movement. It is not noiseless, for rotten iron cracks with a great sound, and clamor accompanies the decay of profit-yielding privileges. It is not uncontested, for men, threatened with the loss of a tithe of their pretensions, sometimes fight harder than the wholly disinherited. It does not proceed everywhere at equal pace; the movement is not uniform nor uninterrupted. And yet, measured by decades, or even by years, the revolution grows.

This revolution is comparable in extent and content with the Protestant Revolution and with the revolts which drove James the Second and Louis the Sixteenth from their thrones. The social revolution of to-day is greater than those earlier revolutions, for, reaching further into the consciousness of nations, it stirs more men and stirs men more deeply. In the Protestant Revolution, the subjects of petty German rulers followed their princes in successive bewildering changes of faith. In the Revolutions of 1789 and 1830, the Paris workman fought for the Paris manufacturer, without knowing why. To-day, when education is almost universal, the revolution is in the perceived interest of classes still lower in the social hierarchy. It appeals to multitudes who sweat. It enrolls grimy, overworked democrats, men hitherto believed to lie outside the range of social consciousness.

I use the word "revolution," despite its fringe of misleading suggestion, because no other word so aptly designates the completeness of the transformation now in process. A social revolution, in the sense here implied, is a change, however gradual, peaceful, and evolutionary, which has for its cumulative effect a radical displacement of the center of gravity of society. Such a revolution is the substitution of a new for an old social equilibrium; a fundamental rearrangement of the relations subsisting between conflicting or allied social groups. It is a recrystallization of society on new planes. It is a new chemical union of constituent social molecules. A relatively more rapid growth of a single organ or of a single function of the social organism, a hypertrophy here, an atrophy there, may suffice to bring about a fundamental social overturn, such as we designate by the word "revolution."

This revolution, in the very midst of which we are, while believing that we stand firm on a firm earth, is a revolution not of blood and iron, but of votes, judicial decisions, and points of view. It does not smell of gunpowder or the bodies of slain men. It does not involve anything sudden, violent, cataclysmic. Like other revolutions, it is simply a quicker turn of the wheel *in the direction in which the wheel is already turning*. It is a revolution at once magnificent and commonplace. It is a revolution brought about by and through the common run of men, who abjure heroics, who sleep soundly and make merry, who "talk" politics and prize-fights, who obey alarm clocks, time-tables, and a thousand petty but revered social conventions. They do not know that they are revolutionists.

Nor do all these revolutionists comprehend that they are allies. One group in the community strives to end the exploitation of child labor. Other groups seek to extend and improve education, to combat tuberculosis, to reform housing conditions, to secure direct primaries, to obtain the referendum, to punish force and fraud at the polls, to secure governmental inspection of foods, to regulate railroad rates, to limit the issue of stocks and bonds of corporations doing an interstate business, to change the character and incidence of taxation, to protect and recreate our forests, to reserve and conserve our mines, to improve the lot of the farmer, to build up trade-unions among workingmen, to Americanize incoming immigrants, to humanize prisons and penal laws, to protect the community against penury caused by old age, accident, sickness, and invalidity, to prevent congestion in cities, to divert to the public a larger share of the unearned increment, to accomplish a thousand other results for the general welfare. Every day new projects are launched for political, industrial, and social amelioration, and below the level of the present lie the greater projects of the future. Reform is piecemeal and yet rapid. It is carried along divergent lines by people holding separate interests, and yet it moves towards a common end. It combines into a general movement toward a new democracy.

The world does not change at once, and a progressive action excites reactions, as it, in turn, is incited by them. There occur simultaneously violent antidemocratic revulsions. Industry seeks to obtain independence of the state; the popular control over government is resisted; industrial forces are allowed to work to the debasement and impoverishment of the citizens.

These two sets of forces, the democratic and the antidemocratic, meet on a million obscure battle grounds every hour, minute, and second. The contest is so wide, so uninterrupted, so infinitely split up into big, little, and microscopic encounters, that no one man can oversee the field. It is so multiform and so full of apparent exceptions that it is difficult to apply to this movement any large, consistent theory.

Nevertheless no visible social movement can proceed without our forming mental concepts, which seek to interpret it. We cannot play our full rôle in such a social movement without forming at least a vague conception of it and of our relation to it. What our interpretation will be depends upon our education, occupation, race, religion, traditions; upon the part of the movement that we see; upon the manner in which it affects our income and predilections, and the income and predilections of our relatives, neighbors, and friends. Our interpretation is a combination-personal-group-class interpretation, for when John Doe conceives of the universe his conception always contains more of John Doe than of the universe. And group interpretations are but blurred, composite photographs of all these individual interpretations.

The interpretations of our present democratic struggle and adjustment, although many, may be reduced in substance to two, answering roughly to two differing temperaments and to two differing positions in the social structure. These interpretations may be called the theory of the social rebound and the theory of social expansion. Or, expressed somewhat differently, these interpretations may be called the theory of progress through poverty and the theory of progress through prosperity.

Of these theories the first is the older and the more instinctive. All through history we encounter the prophecy that worse evil must precede the good. The cup of bitterness must first be filled. The avenger must be hardened in his resentment. When the victim and the avenger are one, the theory is that of the crushed worm. The theory of the social rebound presupposes conflict; and conflict presupposes classes, with sharply defined and mutually antagonistic interests, since if opponents do not recognize themselves as opponents there can be no war. The theory of the social rebound thus finds its clearest expression in the doctrine according to which social classes are engaged in a bitter and inescapable class war, in which compromise and conciliation play the smallest possible rôle, and in which scant regard is paid by either class to traditions of social peace.

CHAPTER XII

DEMOCRACY AND THE CLASS WAR

THE theory that no real democracy can be attained except through a class war between capitalists and wage earners has been held in some form by almost all, if not all, socialist parties.

According to this theory, the class war is not a voluntary struggle, provoked by ambitious leaders, but is an inevitable result of "the economic development of industrial society." That development, it is claimed, depresses the city workmen, the small tradesmen, and the little agriculturalists (peasant proprietors) by producing "an increasing uncertainty of existence, increasing misery, oppression, servitude, degradation, and exploitation. Ever greater grows the mass of the proletariat, ever vaster the army of the unemployed, ever sharper the contrast between oppressors and oppressed, ever fiercer that war of classes between bourgeoisie and proletariat which divides modern society into two hostile camps, and is the common characteristic of every industrial country." [1]

This theory of a class war, which is applied to America, as to other "lands governed by capitalistic methods of production," conceives the state as a class-state, as an organ and a weapon of one economic class, and it conceives of society as merely a battle ground for classes, with interests antagonistic and irreconcilable. It underestimates those common interests of classes, those broad, unifying bonds in society which inspire certain national ideals and race pur-

[1] See the Erfurt (1891) Program of the German Social Democratic party.

poses. It postulates the ultimate reduction of all class antagonisms to one sharp, inevitable antagonism between the owners of the means of production and the wage earners.

In its earliest form, in the Communist Manifesto of 1848, the theory of the class struggle involved something of the idea of a servile revolution, with the impulsive ferocity of such an uprising. The revolutionary class was to be hardened to action by a progressive debasement. "The forcible overthrow of all existing social conditions" was to be attained by the united workingmen of all countries who had "*nothing to lose but their chains,*" and "a world to gain." "Let the ruling classes tremble at a Communistic revolution."

Not only the reactionary ruling classes of 1848, but all friends of civilization, might well have trembled at the prospect of such a "Communistic revolution." "There is a very great danger at hand," wrote Rodbertus in 1850, "lest a new barbarism, this time arising from the midst of society itself, lay waste the abodes of civilization and of wealth"; and the poet Heine thought with horror of "those dark iconoclasts," "who with horny hands would break the marble statues of beauty." In 1848 the workers of western Europe had not recovered from the shock of a Titanic economic disruption, which in the course of half a century had lowered real wages, had dislocated the old industrial system, had robbed the workman of the protection of old laws and ancient customs (without granting him new protection), and had thrown him defenseless into a new arena, in which there was no rule but free competition and no pity or remission of fate to the vanquished. Masses of the German workers, whom the Communist Manifesto seemed especially to hold in mind, were impoverished, overworked, often actually starving. They did not enjoy the primary rights of free speech, free press, free movement, or combination. They had no protectors in the futile German courts, nor in the churches, Lutheran and Catholic. They had no allies in the political parties. Beaten down by the machine and the competition of the English factory, the German workman was abject. So also, though to a less extent, were the English workers, who had borne the first brunt of machine production; and so, generally, were the working classes of all European countries. Men treated savagely respond savagely. Men denied the beauty of the world have small respect for the beauty of the world.

It was no accident that the doctrine of an inexorable class war, motived by an increasing impoverishment of the working classes, was born of the repression and intellectual ferment of "the hungry forties." There seemed at that time no other way out. Stated then most clearly and absolutely by Karl Marx and Friedrich Engels, men of Titanic intellectual stature, the theory imposed itself, by means of successive modifications, upon the minds of millions of men. Long after 1848, when the workmen were slowly achieving political and industrial democracy, socialists continued to write under the impress of those early barbarous conditions.

This socialism, which I shall call "absolute socialism," to distinguish it from the Utopian socialism which preceded it, and from the conditional socialism into which it seems now to be passing, was a dogmatic, uncompromising, and revolutionary philosophy. It was a system of absolutes, of right and wrong, of things necessary and unescapable; not of relatives, of more or less. It was the philosophy of wage earners who accepted what their employers gave them, and not of bargainers, traders, savers, owners. It did not strive, like trade-unionism, gradually to whittle away the employer's power, gradually to weaken his position, while recognizing it in trade agreements. Absolute socialism claimed for the workingman the full product of labor. Anything less, however little less, was exploitation.

Exploitation, however, could not be little. The share of

capital tended to absorb the whole product of labor above a despicable subsistence wage. It was not the employer's fault. However much he might be ridiculed and hated, the greatest capitalist of them all was recognized to be as much in the grip of the inevitable economic development as was the least of his employees. Because of this very inevitableness there could be no parleying between labor and capital; no joining of hands; no giving or asking of quarter; no softening of the conflict; and (in the early logical days of the doctrine) no preliminary betterment of the workman's lot. For the sake of his profits the manufacturer must allow his workmen to survive. For the overturn of capitalism nothing but this survival was necessary.

The framework of this absolute socialism was the factory. The new doctrine visualized the sharp conflict of interest within the factory between manufacturer and workman. It was impersonal, necessary. It was a philosophy of tool users, who understood and obeyed physical impersonal forces. It taught that social evolution was as natural and inevitable as the expansion of steam; as irresistible as the passage of hardened steel through a yielding metal.

Since private ownership of the means of production led automatically to "increasing misery, oppression, servitude, degradation, and exploitation," it followed, even without other assumptions, that private property must be expropriated and converted into public property. Such a philosophy of wholesale expropriation would, it was foreseen, antagonize all property owners, including tradesmen and farmers or peasants. But, it was assumed, the automatic progress of industry would expropriate these "rapidly sinking middle classes," who would then instinctively join hands with other proletarians. Finally the proletariat [1]

[1] Engels defines the proletariat as "the class of modern wage laborers who, having no means of production of their own, are reduced to selling their labor-power in order to live."

would come to represent practically all society, and would be aligned against a "comparatively small number of capitalists and great landowners." When that time came, the capitalistic system with all its exploitations and disharmonies would cease, and a new era would be born, in which economic, political, and social organization would be based on the common ownership of the means of production, and economic justice and human dignity would be attained.

The unifying value of such a philosophy and its strong emotional appeal to factory populations in the grip of evil conditions enormously aided conviction, and the doctrine soon became a cult and almost a religion. For, buttressed though it was by reasonings from science, absolute socialism remained in its appeal essentially religious. It taught the vicarious atonement of all our economic sins by one class which bears the cross. It foretold the advent of universal peace, and the end of poverty, hunger, vice, crime, and bitterness. It proclaimed a heaven on earth as opposed to a present hell. It presented to believers a choice as absolute as that between good and evil, thus saving them the intolerable travail of an appraisal of reforms and half measures. It shielded the future heaven from the gaze of the more skeptical devotees, assuring them that the inevitable social revolution would shape society in ways undreamed of — but with a visage benevolent. It was not a quietistic religion; it did not teach submission, but faith and works, solidarity and revolt. It was a religion, inspiring and solacing, a religion which enlisted the affections of millions, and was contended for fanatically and literally, and not without a measure of theological odium.

To-day men who were formerly convinced are escaping from the obsession of this imposing theory of absolute socialism. They are beginning to see that the predictions of Marx, based upon the conditions of an earlier and cruder era of machine production, run counter to the mass of evidence accumulated during the last fifty years. Lesser men possessed of later knowledge are learning to interpret otherwise the vast democratic reorganization of society which Marx foresaw.

In the first place, as Marx later saw, no progressive impoverishment of the working classes, no "increasing misery, oppression, servitude, degradation, and exploitation" has taken place. The workers have become, not poorer, but richer. While wages have not increased at a rate commensurate with the growth in social wealth; while the progress of workingmen has been everywhere slower than the ideals of our civilization imperatively demand and the resources of our civilization render possible; while the status of the unskilled laborer remains exceedingly low, still it is evident that in America, Germany, France, England, and elsewhere, progress has been continuous. Wages during the last half century have risen faster than prices,[1] hours of

[1] It is absolutely impossible within the compass of a note, or indeed of a whole book, to give even an outline of the vast body of evidence pointing to the rise in wages in the industrial nations of the world during the last sixty or seventy years. One can here refer to only a few of the various compilations made in the different countries. For a succinct statement of the rise of wages in Germany from 1871 to 1907, see the masses of statistics collated by Dr. R. R. Kuczynski, "Die Entwickelung der gewerblichen Löhne seit der Begründung des Deutschen Reiches," Berlin (Georg Reimer), 1909. For England, see Bowley (Arthur L.), "Wages in the United Kingdom in the Nineteenth Century," Cambridge (University Press), 1900. For France, see Lévasseur (Émile), "La Population Française," as also a later pamphlet, "Le Salariat" (1903). See also the report of the French *Office du Travail* showing the rise of wages in France from 1806 to 1900. For summaries of the course of wages in various occupations in Denmark, Norway, Germany, France, Austria, Hungary, etc., within recent decades, see the various tables in the Board of Trade (Labour Department), Fourth Abstract of Foreign Labour Statistics, London, 1911, pages 21–132 inclusive.

Any summary of figures so broad can have but a vague meaning, but it would appear that from 1840 to 1911, money wages have more than doubled in France and in England, and that the rate of increase during the last forty years has been more rapid in Germany than in England or France in the same period. These wages, it is true, are merely money or nominal

labor have been reduced, and factory conditions have been improved. Laws have set limits to the labor of women and children, have protected life, limb, and health of workers, and have provided for a recovery of damages in case of injury or death. In many countries (although not in America) the status of the workingman is improved by compulsory state insurance against old age, sickness, accident, and invalidity, and, in isolated places, even against unemployment. Trade-unions, growing to enormous national aggregations, greatly improve labor conditions. Through the spread of general educational facilities, through housing reform, health reform, and a progressive social policy, the status of workmen is further raised. In one country after another the workingman is enfranchised, and is protected from intimidation and fraud at the polls. The right to combine in trade-unions and to strike is generally acknowledged. Large sections of the working class are successively raised above the level of the unskilled, and fresh demands are constantly made by new industries for new grades of skill. While there are counteracting tendencies, while the increasing intensity and monotony of labor and the divorce of the worker from the plot of ground which he once owned work to his disadvantage, his continuous progress is indis-

wages, but after deduction has been made for the net increase in prices (including the enormous increase in city rents), there is apparently left a fairly wide margin of net gain. According to an estimate of Gide (Charles), "Cours d'Économie Politique" (Paris, 1911, p. 665), there has occurred in France, during the nineteenth century, an increase in the cost of living of not over one third, while money wages have more than doubled. This estimate does not take into account the relative amounts of unemployment at the beginning and at the end of the period, nor the rapid rise in prices during the years since 1900.

The masses of statistics, while they do not allow conclusions to be drawn as to the exact amount of the increase in real wages, do not permit doubt as to the reality of such a rise. For an "attempted explanation of the increase in wages during the last half of the nineteenth century," see Schmoller (Gustav), "Die historische Lohnbewegung von 1300–1900 und ihre Ursachen."

putable. The motive power of the workman's dissatisfaction and revolt is the enormous distance between his actual status and his increasing demands, rather than any hypothetical impoverishment.

Not only is the wage earner not becoming impoverished, but there is no likelihood, in America at least, of an absorption by this class of all other classes, and a reduction of all conflicts to one great class war. Although our factory population, recruited largely through immigration, is increasing at a stupendous rate, the other classes in the community maintain themselves. In America, as in Germany, France, and elsewhere, the non-wage-earning class is actually growing. Despite department stores and "chains of stores," the number of shopkeepers seems to increase; and even where these small tradesmen are more dependent than formerly upon the favor of an industrial overlord, they cannot be identified in interest with the wage-earning proletariat, and cannot be gathered upon a platform which calls for the social appropriation of the means of production.[1]

The independent farmer is not disappearing. He is not becoming a proletarian. The bonanza farms, far from killing off the little farms (as had been predicted), are themselves succumbing; and the tendency, in America as in most countries, is away from any concentration of farm ownership. In 1900 there were four times as many American farms as in 1850. The average size of the farm was smaller in 1900 than in 1850 or 1870. The great estates of 1000 acres and more, while aggregating (in 1900) over 200,000,000 acres, are for the most part largely uncultivated areas or else cheap and arid tracts in the West, of which the cultivable portions are doomed to be speedily parceled out among an increasing number of farmers. Notwith-

[1] According to the census of 1900, the number of retail merchants and dealers in the United States increased in ten years from 660,239 to 790,886, a rate of increase slightly less than that of the population.

standing an increase in farm tenancy, both relative and absolute, the actual number of farmers owning and operating their own farms is greater than ever before; while, parenthetically, the tenants are for the most part not an entirely unpropertied class. The number of farm laborers (other than members of the farmer's family) remains small, aggregating only two such laborers to every five farms; while the chances of these laborers eventually to become farmers, although probably decreasing, are still good. A concentration of the land into a few hands is not microscopically probable. A proletarization of our property-owning farming class is impossible.

Nor are other small property owners being reduced to the position of proletarians. Like the wage earners, so also our small property owners are advancing in prosperity and are accumulating more property. That a violent concentration of wealth is taking place at the top is confoundingly patent, but it is almost equally evident, and is even more significant, that a wide diffusion of wealth is occurring simultaneously. Tens of millions of Americans own farms, houses, shops, businesses; or have bank accounts, life insurance interests, mortgages, bonds, stocks, or other property or evidences of property, individual or joint. In countries where there are income tax figures, a progressive diffusion of wealth can be statistically shown. In America the tendency is evident, although not equally capable of statistical demonstration.[1]

The Marxist theory of a successful revolution based upon the creation of two hostile classes, standing nakedly opposed in society, one, the superfluously wealthy possessors of the means of production, the other, a swelling mass of miserable,

[1] For European evidence, see Leroy-Beaulieu (Paul), "Le Collectivisme," Paris (Félix Alcan), 1909. See also the Socialist, Bernstein (Edward), "Evolutionary Socialism," New York (B. W. Huebsch), 1909. For the diffusion of French wealth, see Neymarck (Alfred), "French Savings and their Influence upon the Bank of France and upon French Banks." Senate Document, 61st Congress, 2d session, Document No. 494.

absolutely destitute proletarians, thus appears economically untenable. The proletariat advances; wealth becomes diffused; the small property holders increase in numbers. The theory is perhaps even more untenable on other grounds. For were a struggle between two such classes possible, its outcome might be very different from what Marx predicted.

In America there are men, who not only foresee, but actually *see* such a sharp and naked alignment of the two classes. For them there are but two groups — the very rich and the desperately poor. So completely is their canvas filled by sprawling, fatuous scions of multimillionaires on the one hand and overworked, unskilled laborers on the other, that they no longer see the average man, who keeps no servant and has but a one week's vacation, but who, judged by the standards of other nations and other times, is well-fed, well-housed, well-clothed, well-conditioned, with some leisure and recreation. They note only the melodramatic contrasts between excessive wealth and abysmal poverty, and they generalize and despair. For the extreme contrasts are glaring, and the rich seem so strong, so entrenched, so splendidly and brutally successful, while the very poor seem to lack all elements of defense or aggression, — without money, without education, without political traditions, without cohesion, or the common tongue upon which to build it.

A few years ago, Mr. Upton Sinclair, in a startling book called "The Jungle," described the horrible conditions of the Chicago stockyards. A Lithuanian laborer, named Jurgis, is exploited at every turn; his wife dies, his family is broken up; he himself is sent to jail. He passes from despair to vindictive hatred, only to be rescued by his conversion to socialism.

The book is not false in essentials, whatever its exaggerations in detail. We read accounts of almost equally brutal conditions in Pittsburg, Bethlehem, and in the sweatshops of a dozen American cities. We need not go beyond cautious and authoritative government reports to believe that organized anonymous cruelties are perpetrated for profit on hundreds of thousands of workmen and workwomen in the United States. It is murder veiled and impersonal, but it is still murder.

It is an error, however, in fixing our attention upon this menacing problem of the destruction of our very poor, mentally to carry over conditions such as existed in the Chicago stockyards to our whole industrial problem. America is not divided into Beef Trust magnates and Lithuanian helots. Jurgis, poor, ignorant, dumb, and bewildered, is no more typical than Armour, though both exist, and both are problems.

From the men at the very bottom (so long as they remain there) less perhaps is to be hoped than feared. Such men are not the standard bearers of revolt, nor the steady carriers of the torch of progress. They are the stuff of which bloody, unsuccessful uprisings might be made, but they are too poor, too ignorant, and, by their very economic dependences, too inconstant and fearsome, to lead or even effectively to participate in the tenacious, long-continued campaigns which must precede any revolutionary change in the bases of modern society. You can vote illiterate men more easily than literate. You can appeal with a "full dinner pail" to men on the verge of starvation. You can convert a mass of underfed, and, therefore, irresolute and credulous, men into engines of tyranny and reaction. The nobler men on the hunger line are full of generous aspirations, but they have not preëminent intellectual power nor the capacity for objective thinking and sustained action. These starved souls evolve religious, not political policies; they develop kingdoms in heaven, not materialized coöperative commonwealths.

That the most indigent among Americans are not the leaders of democracy may be seen from a consideration of the status of the Negro. Our ten million Negroes, considered as a whole, are the most exploited section of the community. To the burden of racial prejudice have been added severe industrial handicaps and a general disfranchisement. The race is too poor, weak, ignorant, and disunited to make effective protest. For the most part it constitutes — through fault of circumstance — an inert mass, which could perhaps be more readily used, both industrially and politically, for the prevention of democracy than for its attainment. While the Negro is rapidly progressing, while the future may well bring forth a prosperous, intelligent, united, and politically intrenched colored population, the rôle of the Negro in our progress towards democracy will for the time being remain wholly subordinate.

The same is true, to a less extent, of the most exploited of our recent immigrants. The newly arrived Italian day laborer is not so discontented, nor so effective a fighter for democracy, as is the richer immigrant who has been here a dozen years, or as is the son of the immigrant. Where the newcomer possesses a keen intelligence and an aggressive discontent, these qualities may make up for a low industrial status. Generally speaking, however, intense poverty, bearing the sordid fruits, pauperism, crime, vice, sickness, and premature death, does not make for democratic reform. A really effective discontent accompanies a larger income, a greater leisure, a fuller education, and a vision of better things.

The hope of society lies, not in the oppression of men to the verge of revolt, but in the continuous elimination of oppression. The hunger of the multitude is not the true motive of revolution. Hunger degenerates; insecurity of life leads to crime; and these, by enfeebling their victims, strengthen the oppressive bonds and make them perpetual. A man or a class, crushed to earth — is crushed to earth.[1]

What then remains of the early vigor of the theory of a successful class war between a swarming proletariat and a small machine-owing class? If the men who have "nothing to lose but their chains" are actually the weakest, most ignorant, and most disunited members of society; if those who have nothing are only a minority, gradually dwindling (and are opposed to an increasing majority who are indeed poor, but are growing steadily wealthier),— what hope is there that the smaller, weaker, declining class will overcome the opposition of the larger, stronger, growing class? If, on the other hand, the proletariat does not consist solely of the propertyless nor even of wage earners; if rising wages, savings, and the actual ownership of the means of production do not take a man out of the proletariat, where is the alignment of the class war?

These considerations have not been without their effect upon the defenders of the class war theory. In the writings of many socialists the conception of a class war has been so watered as completely to alter its original significance. In many countries there have been observable the beginnings of a change from an older, more abstract, absolute, and dogmatic socialism to a newer, more concrete, conditional, and conciliatory socialism. The tendency is especially apparent in countries which are democratically representative, and in which, therefore, a conciliatory policy is likely to secure a larger vote and a greater measure of

[1] Neither Marx nor Engels believed in the revolutionary qualities of paupers and criminals. "The 'dangerous class,' the social scum, that passively rotting mass thrown off by the lowest layers of old society, may, here and there, be swept into the movement by a proletarian revolution; its conditions of life, however, prepare it far more for the part of a bribed tool of reactionary intrigue." "Communist Manifesto." Authorized English Translation. Edited and annotated by Frederick Engels, Chicago (Kerr & Co.), p. 29.

immediate influence. It is less apparent in countries where political democracy is not so assured and where an uncompromising party must fight for preliminary political rights.

In Germany, where a reactionary feudal class still holds power, the Socialist party is the most effective democratic party, and many men who do not believe in the class struggle vote the Socialist ticket to express their preferences for immediate reforms or their protest against concrete evils. In more democratic countries, on the other hand, such as France, England, the United States, and Switzerland, the Socialist party is obliged to compete for the suffrages of the people with other democratic parties, with the result that not only is the vote smaller, but the movement tends gradually to lose something of its old class war characteristics. "Some of our Socialist comrades," recently said Jaurès, "interpret the class war in a sense much too simple, one-sided, and abstract." According to Sarraute, the class war is not "an absolute abstract principle" absorbing "the whole life of society." "As soon as the State is democratized, and equal rights are admitted for all, whether capitalists or proletarians, . . . it becomes contradictory and meaningless to talk of a class State."

The rise everywhere among Socialists of "possibilists," "opportunists," "revisionists," and "Fabians" emphasizes the attempt to adjust the old absolute theories not only to varying conditions in different countries, but also to those broad democratic impulses which are now sweeping through other classes besides the proletariat. The tendency is to change party policy from a merely critical and sweepingly destructive, to a constructive, and therefore more conciliatory, attitude, to moderate the demands, to broaden the appeal. The attempt to found a majority upon "the proletariat," upon the propertyless wage and salary workers, is being given up, and the appeal is now being made, not so much to "wage earners," as to "workers," "producers," and to the masses generally. In the effort to secure the adherence of farmers, even property owners are being addressed, a distinction being drawn between the means of production which exploit labor, and those means of production (the small farm) which are already in the hands of the producer, and are therefore, inferentially, not exploitative.[1] These non-exploiting means of production, moreover, seem likely long to remain innocuous. "One thing seems certain," says the American socialist, John Spargo, "namely, that farm ownership (in the United States) is not on the decline. It is not being supplanted by tenantry; the small farms are not being absorbed by large ones. . . . The small farmer will continue to be an important factor — indeed, the most important factor — in American agriculture for a long time to come, perhaps permanently. If the socialist movement is to succeed in America, it must recognize this fact in its propaganda."[2] In other words the Socialist party, to become effective, must secure the adherence, or allay the opposition, of this powerful property-owning class.

It can do this in one way only — through a surrender of doctrines. Tenets which alienate classes whose support is essential must of necessity be abandoned. Such doctrines may be bravely recanted or eloquently ignored, or by process of interpretation may be magically transformed into their opposites. But their change is inevitable, when the classes to which they were to appeal have changed.

The socialist believers in a class war between proletariat

[1] Such a distinction could be more easily made in practice than justified in theory. If it is not exploitation for a farmer to till his own farm, does it become exploitation when he hires his son, or his nephew, or, at harvest times, a single outside helper? An attempt to apply this distinction would result in a rough discrimination against large estates, which thereupon would be parceled out into small holdings. Such an agricultural decentralization, however, would be very far from the old socialistic ideal.

[2] Spargo, John, "Socialism, a Summary and Interpretation of Socialist Principles." New York (Macmillan), 1909, p. 134.

and bourgeoisie are in an uncomfortable dilemma. If the proletariat does not become the overwhelming majority of the nation, but remains a minority, it cannot hope to gain its ends unaided. If, on the other hand, the city proletariat seeks the permanent adherence of small farmers, of farm laborers (with the hope of becoming farmers), of small tradesmen with some little equity in their business, of other men with a little property, it must so mitigate the original rigor of its demands as to insure these potential allies against expropriation. The owner of a five-thousand-dollar farm, covered by a two-thousand-dollar mortgage, has still a precious equity of three thousand dollars in his land. Such a farmer may be vitally interested in the control of railroad rates, elevator charges, and trust prices, but he does not approve of any social reorganization, however ultimately beneficent, which will take from him his three thousand dollars, or his farm and his immediate livelihood, with or without compensation.

If, however, the private ownership of small and medium-sized farms, and of houses, live stock, and machinery on farms, be conceded, other demands for concessions will be inevitable. The small shopkeeper, with no aptitude for factory labor and with a consciousness of fulfilling a humble social service, will demand the retention of his business, which has a greater value to him than the money which it represents. Gradually the socialists will recognize that the hope of a radical industrial reorganization depends upon the assent of so large a section of the men with small property as to compel a readjustment of their social program.

Such a readjustment involves a complete surrender of the old idea of expropriation, which appeals only to the already completely expropriated. The Marxian theory of surplus value had given this demand for expropriation an ethical justification. But that theory has proved untenable. We can no longer argue deductively that private ownership automatically, inevitably, and always leads to exploitation. To prove that our present distribution of income is immoral, we must base the immorality inductively on the social consequences of such distribution. The whole problem of distribution ceases to be one of absolute right and becomes one of relative utility.

Moreover, just as the *extent* of the proposed expropriation must be limited by exceptions in favor of the little farm and other small properties, so the *quality* of expropriation is bound so to be changed as to make the very term "expropriation" inapposite. When social utility rather than abstract right becomes the guiding force of socialism, the problem will arise, whether a given property should be taken over or merely regulated and its profits limited; whether in another industry increased taxation, or perhaps the retention by the state of the future unearned increment, may not be more socially advantageous than collective ownership and operation. In short, the problem will become one of ways and means. The line of attack will become the line of least resistance and of greatest results. Society will seek to modify and socially utilize, rather than incontinently to destroy, our machinery of industrial organization (trusts, corporations, exchange, wage system, etc.). Progress will become adjustment by the gradual adaptation of production to social uses, rather than a complete overturn, either violent or peaceful, either rapid or slow, of our industrial habits and implements. This process will tend to become an attrition, a wasting away, a successive attenuation of "vested rights," rather than a naked expropriation. Finally this abrasion of rights will be compelled by an overwhelming flood of votes and an irresistible pressure of an enlightening public opinion, rather than by a class war, as the class war was formerly interpreted.

It is not assumed that this complete *volte-face* of the Socialist parties has already taken place. Even in countries with universal suffrage, popular institutions, improving labor conditions, and large classes of small property holders, the change in policy has only begun; and even the beginnings are resisted. Party leaders are usually narrow, formal, and conservative, seeking to emphasize distinctions, placing party organization and party claims above the general welfare. But parties, whether in power, opposition, or protest, tend to reflect the voter's perception of industrial changes; for a party without votes, however high its ideals, is not a party. The gradual *domestication* of the Socialist parties, if one may use that word, is thus compelled by the view, not of the leaders, but of the outside masses of potentially Socialist voters.[1]

[1] The National (1908) Program of the Socialist party reveals the extent to which the class war doctrine has been surrendered. The class war was originally an inevitable, universal, unique, and absolutely unconditional war between proletariat and bourgeoisie, between wage earners and capitalists, who, by the very fact of their being capitalists, were exploiters of labor. That war now becomes a softened conflict between "*the workers of the nation* and their allies and sympathizers of all classes" on the one side, and "a few capitalists, . . . permitted to control all the country's industrial resources," on the other. The party no longer appeals solely to men who sell their labor, but also to those who sell the products of their labor. It no longer appeals exclusively to the *wageworkers* or proletarians, but to the far vaguer and more inclusive groups of "workers" and "producers." A half appeal is made to "the small farmer, who is to-day exploited by *large capital*"; to the "small manufacturer and trader, who is engaged in a desperate and losing struggle" against "*concentrated capital*"; and to "even the capitalist himself (note here the meaning of "capitalist"), who is the slave of his wealth rather than its master." The goal of the party is the social ownership, not of the land and the means of production, but "of the land and the means of production *used for exploitation.*" "The Socialist party strives to prevent land from being used for the purpose of *exploitation and speculation.* It demands the collective possession, control, or management of land *to whatever extent may be necessary to attain that end.* It is not opposed to the occupation and possession of land by those using *it in a useful and bona-fide manner without exploitation.*" In these and other directions, logic and the traditions of socialism are sacrificed to new party ideals, and the class war theory, no longer necessary, is denied in the very process of affirmation.

If it be contended that the National Party Program does not represent

This incipient modification of the policy of the Socialist parties thus acquires a peculiar significance, because of the light it casts upon the tremendous, deep-lying changes in public opinion outside. That there will long remain a small group of Simon-pure, hard-shell, "stand pat" Socialist irreconcilables is as probable as that there will remain for decades groups of men hopeless of betterment. For the majority of avowed Socialists, however, to whom the general ideals, rather than the abstract philosophy or ultimate program of their party, appeal, a progressive *rapprochement* with other democratic elements of the population seems decreed by the logic of our development. What will be the name, badge, or token of the party, parties, or allied fragments of parties, which will result from such a union or absorption, is insignificant. The essential tendency, however, seems to be a progress of Socialist parties towards coalescence with other democratic movements, the socialists losing many of their separatist views, while infusing the democracy as a whole with broader concepts of industrial polity.

In America the old doctrine of a class war between two classes must of absolute necessity be given up by the Socialist party and must fail of adoption by other parties. The dogmatic absoluteness of the position appeals, because there is in all of us a certain primitive downrightness, which abhors gradations and qualifications and delights in sharp moral contrasts. But the facts are in flat contradiction with this oversimplified theory, and to propitiate these facts, one fat generalization after another is vainly offered up. "Capitalism" develops elasticity. Instead of dying of its own excesses, it shows wonderful recuperative and self-reforming power. Class hatred softens as the working class strengthens, and

the true attitude of socialists on the class war doctrine, the reader is referred to the debates in convention. See "Proceedings of the (1908) National Convention," edited by John M. Work, Chicago (Socialist Party), 1908. (The italics are my own.)

the impending clash between the classes is always delayed. The absolute socialist cries "War, War," when there is no war. If the owners of capital were fighting for life and were now, as is alleged, in power, they might at least be tempted to restrict suffrage, censor the press, raise armies for defense, close schools, lock out workmen, stop philanthropy, and generally carry the war into the proletarian camp. Either the capitalists are as deficient in class consciousness as are the workingmen, or else the class war is a less definite thing than we have been taught to believe.

What has happened is that the whole problem of the mutual relations of classes has moved from its old moorings, and we — all of us alike — have drifted into a new economic and, therefore, into a new psychological world. Just as the old liberalism was deaf and blind to the development which was to superimpose big business upon little business, and monopoly upon competition, so the old absolute socialism, with keener prevision, failed to realize the limitations and minor tendencies of the change, the persistence of the small farm, the survival and even the strengthening of a middle class, the material progress of the workingman, the possibility of alignments in the new society different from the alignment within the factory. The old *laissez-faire* liberal philosophy is done for, and the old absolute socialism is dying in the embrace of its dead adversary. To-day even conservatives unhesitatingly accept reforms which, a generation ago, would have been decried as socialistic, while socialists in good party standing propose alliances, concessions, and palliatives which would formerly have been called (and by the crassly logical are still called) subversive of socialistic doctrine and inimical to the emancipation of the proletariat.

The Socialist parties of to-day are caught in a bewildering transition, analogous to that of their opponents. (Indeed they scarcely realize now who *are* their opponents.) The aging, dogmatic revolutionaries, who for forty years have dreamed in the dark of the hoped-for flash of lightning, are both disappointed and dazzled by the sober light of social reform. The revisionists, while adapting their views to the changed conditions, still cling desperately to a verbal allegiance to the old cramping doctrine of class war in order to distinguish themselves from the so-called bourgeois social reformers — themselves no less confused — who have approached the same goal from a diametrically opposite direction. The socialist, who is beginning to lose his faith in the class war and the rigorous nationalization of the means of production, is adopting a theory of a democratic socialization of industry and of life; the old individualist, losing his faith in economic harmonies that do not harmonize, and in the beneficence of a competition which has gone lame, is approaching in a more tentative manner a similar theory of a democratic socialization of industry and of life. The men who were sharply sundered in interests and ideals by the conditions of the earlier machine production have been brought into partial accord by the conditions of a later machine era. The trust builder, the monopolizer, the new Titan of industry, has not only merged his factories, but united his opponents.[1]

In the decades to come — during the democratic socialization of America which has already begun — we shall hear less of this doctrine of the class war. There will be wide-ranging conflicts between coalitions of classes, but

[1] There is a naïve theory that the so-called "menace of socialism" will disappear once its doctrines are demolished. Prove that Marx's analysis of surplus value is erroneous, or that his predictions concerning agricultural concentration are false, and lo, the repentant hosts of socialism will rally about the old standards. Unfortunately for its proponents, this soothing theory contravenes the most elemental facts of social life. Heretics do not so much depend upon heresies as vice versa. Men do not become discontented because they have theories, but have theories because they are discontented.

there will also be adjustments and unions for the attainment of common aims and for a succession of compromises rendered possible by an enormous increase in the social product to be distributed. Democratic civilization will progress even more through adjustment and education than through a war which aids one class and injures another. Political power in the state will not change from one class to its opponent, like a reversible top or an overweighted balance, for the state is not, and will not be, absolutely the representative of a single class. What will happen will be a relative increase of influence by certain classes through the nearer attainment of the rule of the majority. There will be an infiltration, a permeation of the state by elements more and more democratic. We shall *grow* into democracy.

CHAPTER XIII

DEMOCRACY AND THE SOCIAL SURPLUS

OPPOSED to the theory that democracy is to be attained through a class war is the theory that the attainment of democracy will result from a national adjustment. Opposed to the theory of democratic progress through impoverishment is the theory of progress through prosperity.

It is the increasing wealth of America, not the growing poverty of any class, upon which the hope of a full democracy must be based. It is this wealth which makes democracy possible and solvent, for democracy, like civilization, costs money. Finally it is this social surplus, our clear gain in wealth after the year's business is over, our excess of social product over social effort, which renders ignorance, poverty, and minority rule anachronistic, and gives to our democratic strivings a moral impulse and a moral sanction.

The surplus of society, which thus overrides all our traditions and shapes all our philosophies, is a phenomenon of transcendent importance. It is a new factor in man's career. During all history, prior to the last few centuries, poverty, pain, and deficit ruled the world.[1] Back of every society, simple or complex, lay the fateful force of human fecundity. The increasing population pressed upon the

[1] For the original statement of the transition from a pain economy to a pleasure economy, see the brilliant book of Professor Simon N. Patten, "The Theory of Social Forces," Philadelphia (American Academy of Political and Social Science), 1896. Without wishing in any way to fasten responsibility upon Professor Patten for any of the statements in this present book, the author desires gratefully to make the fullest possible acknowledgment of his deep indebtedness to that great teacher.

means of subsistence. The babe pushed his parents into the grave. For every man killed by disease, famine, war, overwork, a child was born.

During certain periods of this long reign of poverty there were "Golden Ages," in which cities of brick were transformed into cities of marble. But this prosperity was only relative. The social surplus sufficed to create a lavish court, to build pyramids, palaces, and cathedrals, to maintain harems and armies, to furnish to the few a suicidal sensuality; but it could not give ample bread and leisure to the swarming people. Wretchedly poor were the hewers of wood and the drawers of water. The toilers who built the wonderful edifices of antiquity, the men who lived in the astonishing cities, even the Roman populace, fed by doles from the tribute takers of the world, were for the most part miserably fed, clad, and conditioned. As for the slaves, the serfs, the peasants of the world, they were on the lowest floor of human life. Production was limited by the narrow bounds of muscle power and simple tools. It was limited by the contraction of the market, for commerce was largely the exchange of luxuries. An ultimate prosperity for all did not seem conceivable. The very Utopias of ancient times were based upon slavery.

The political equivalent of this early poverty was despotism. When men produce barely enough to permit a miserable existence (whatever the system of distribution), there is small need for political rights. Men do not vote, just as they do not fight, unless there is something to vote or fight for. If through revolt the poor were to gain temporary control, there was still not enough to go round. The scant social surplus was held by great lords and military chiefs, who defended it against fecund, restless peoples, descending from barren lands and pressing hungrily upon the warm southern empires. Overpopulation meant chronic, uninterrupted war. Fighting, in turn, made for despotic government. From the extra-hazardous occupation of politics, an occupation largely compounded of flattery and assassination, the lowly were excluded.

The intellectual equivalent of this early world poverty was passivity, ignorance. Oriental fatalism was a product of poverty, and of its accompaniments, pain, hunger, death. For the unnumbered human worms who lived and died, there was no need of education. The art of life was traditional. The race persisted through force of a hard-shell conservatism, crystallized into an instinct, which took the place of intelligence and innovation.

During all those thousands of years, while empires rose and fell, and rose and fell again, the masses of the people remained abject. A servile revolt was but a demand for straw with which to make bricks, for a little more food, for an abrogation, not of evils, but of unaccustomed evils. These revolts were futile. Even though for a moment the hand of the exploiter relaxed, inevitably the people sank to their former evil state. Religion, philosophy, superstition, folk-lore; the sword, lash, wheel, gibbet, torture chamber, — all these but reënforced a submission which social poverty imposed.

Without an excess of wealth no democracy on a large scale was possible, however much men might dream dreams or voices cry aloud in the wilderness. The bases for such a surplus were not laid until the economic and political revolutions of the fifteenth and sixteenth centuries destroyed the decentralized feudal structure and called forth nations and a national economy. With the demolition of local customs barriers, commerce grew, the market was widened, and division of labor was rendered possible. The exploitation of American silver mines and the rounding of the Cape of Good Hope hastened the growth of wealth. It was not, however, until the eighteenth and nineteenth centuries that steam and machinery brought forth the industrial revolution, and created a social surplus in comparison with which all prior accumulations were insignificant.[1]

For the first time there was a "stake" for the people, enough, if properly held, to provide a livable life for all the populations. The denial to the people of wealth and rights, which had found its moral justification in the early poverty of society, became ethically untenable. Democracy became ultimately inevitable. For in final analysis, however it may be clothed in legal rights and political immunities, democracy means material goods and the moral goods based thereon. It means the things that are Cæsar's, the objectivized desires of men — the chances of wealth, recreation, leisure, culture. All these things, the product of the social surplus, have been multiplied almost *ad infinitum* by machine process. The opportunities of life in our new world of surplus exceed the opportunities of life in the old world of deficit and pain as the thousand copies of the printed book exceed the solitary illuminated manuscript.

When the things that are Cæsar's were provided, a new Cæsar came into being. It was the people. The people, once servile, ignorant, and satisfied, had eaten of the fruit of the tree. The people no longer cringed. They glowered at the bright new wares in the windows; they angrily broke the new machines which poured forth masses of wealth in which the workers could not share. The people, realizing that they were hungry (now that there was something to eat), began to question all the revered traditions which had made eating (by the vulgar) a sin, crime, and economic absurdity, and which had exalted abstinence as a peculiarly amiable popular virtue. When the people saw that the

[1] It is a curious but explicable fact that the theory which explains the poverty of the ancient world, the theory of population, did not receive authoritative expression until the age was already passing. When, in 1798, Malthus made his famous generalizations, his conclusions, so largely true of the past, were already being falsified by a stupendous increase in productiveness and wealth.

new wealth did not descend the factory chimney of a Christmas morn; when they saw that the new wealth did not grow spontaneously in the garden of the "bread giver"; when they traced the wonderful new wealth to the farms, workshops, and grimy factories, where very common folk worked, — the people began to question the morality and social efficiency of all historic distributions of wealth. The social surplus not only excited the desires but stimulated the intelligences of the people.

The creation of a social surplus, however, does not automatically or immediately give rise to a socialized democracy. It creates merely the opportunity for such a democracy. The new wealth does not distribute itself spontaneously according to the needs of the population, and, for a time, an increase in the social product may mean an actual lessening of the share of the masses.

In the beginning of the era of a great social surplus, which we may approximately date from 1760 in England and from 1789 in France, the fruits of the revolutionizing discoveries were largely monopolized by acquisitive men. Had these wealthy manufacturers, themselves revolutionists and upstarts, been able to conserve their sudden new wealth side by side with a general wretchedness, ignorance, and subjection, the masses would have secured a share of wealth and rights, had they secured it at all, only after the bloodiest of revolutions.

Fortunately, the rising middle classes, finding themselves held down by a reactionary class, were compelled to appeal to the lowest classes. The manufacturers needed the pikes, guns, and clamor of the mob to overcome Swiss guards, an arrogant nobility, and a courtier clergy. To loosen the grip of the feudal fist upon their own purses, the manufacturers were compelled to hold out promises to the "lower orders."

Other rights were indispensable to business, which, as

we are gradually learning, is the core of our social arrangements. To "entice" laborers from the stiff old agriculturalists, it was necessary to give workers freedom of movement and of contract. Freedom of contract, sooner or later, meant the right to strike. Striking meant higher wages, shorter hours, and better conditions of work. As communication improved, men widely separated in distance came into contact, and as business became concentrated, workmen gathered in factories and learned more from each other in the lunch hour than they had learned from pastor or school-teacher. Schools, too, were necessary, for the new machines could not be run by blockheads. Gradually, through strikes, violence, threats, through an unrest which was bad for business, the workers gained an extension of the suffrage. The majority had the vote.

Popular suffrage does not end group struggles, but merely lifts them to a higher plane. A minority which has long ruled by its own right soon learns to rule as the theoretical representative of the majority. Certain forms of economic and intellectual pressure may make universal suffrage harmless to the minority.

Back of all political institutions, although themselves important, lie always the essential status and character of the population, its wealth, intelligence, coherence, and traditions, and the essential character of the dominating group. Through industrial changes, through political battles, through, above all, an intellectual war *à outrance*, the great changes in the balance of power within the community take place.

The vast social wealth, however, which went on accumulating in a geometrical ratio during more than a century, not only now makes democracy possible, by providing the wherewithal, but it also furnishes the weapon with which the democracy may be attained. That weapon is a moral idea. The possession by society of a great wealth invests the desire of the people for a fuller life with an ethical sanction. Society can no longer interpose a *non possumus*.

The increasing social wealth shifts the basis of social morality from a mere war ethics, from the old tribal instinct of group survival, to a new ethics which demands a full life for all members of society. Just as, during the last few millenniums, we have evolved a theory of the sanctity of human life, by which the saving of life becomes theoretically more important than even the saving of property (although the facts often flatly contradict this assumption), so to-day we are developing a theory of the dignity of human life, by which society, because of its greater wealth, becomes morally responsible, not only for the mere physical survival of the individual, but equally for the provision of facilities by which the highest physical, intellectual, moral, and social capacities of all citizens, born and to be born, may best be secured. The old morality, it is true, still survives. The clash between the old and the new is seen in the struggle between imperialism and industrial democracy, between battleships and libraries, between the old poverty ethics of survival and the new wealth ethics of social improvement.

The motive force of our modern ethics of social improvement reveals itself in a sense of disequilibrium between social wealth and a residual misery of large sections of the population. Two centuries ago, when population still pressed narrowly upon wealth, statesmen could look callously upon starvation, imprisonment for debt, and the hanging of vulgar rogues who stole a shilling and a penny. If fifty per cent and, in some years, seventy-five per cent of London babies died in the year, were there not too many people anyway? But to-day our surplus has made us as sensitive to misery, preventable death, sickness, hunger, and deprivation as is a photographic plate to light. The disequilibrium between social surplus and social misery colors all our thoughts. It is the basis of our social unrest. It causes the stirrings of uneasy social consciences.

It is also responsible for a more sober and searching social analysis. A salient fact about our modern social thinking is that we no longer so light-heartedly attribute to a personal delinquency the residual, persistent poverty of great masses of the population. We no longer so often hear the *dictum* that any one who wants a job can get one; that no man need be idle; that all men can save against the rainy day, when they may be injured by industrial accident or discharged because of middle age. We have become more temperate in our social judgments and our social admonitions. The beautiful industrial idyls of half a century ago, the charming inculcation of thrift to the desperately poor, the stories of the astounding progress of the newsboy and the grocer's clerk (who inevitably marries the daughter of his employer), have given way to somber investigations of the real conditions of newsboys, messenger boys, grocers' clerks, *et al.*, and to a very wide bookshelf on the influence of evil industrial conditions upon the virtues and vices of the industrial classes.

The disequilibrium between social surplus and social misery is weighing like a great moral incubus upon thousands of the beneficiaries of present arrangements. To-day there are many rich men who lie awake nights, and not through fear. These men are not bound by narrow class ethics, but echo distinctly the moral feelings of the mass, from which they have so recently risen, as a man on the fringe of a crowd may still be subject to its radiated will. The philanthropist (the rich man with a conscience) speaks of social "maladjustment" and strives for "social betterment." Such a man, far from desiring the impoverishment and brutalization of the mass (were that now possible), is compelled by an ethical imperative to demand, in the interest of the general community, reforms by no means in harmony with the special interests of favored classes.

Upon the wide democratic masses, the social disequilibrium exercises a far more direct and potent influence. With these classes, the theory that social wealth should be devoted to social uses — in ways to be determined by society — becomes axiomatic. It becomes a fixed idea. This impelling idea is all-conquering. By creating this idea, the growth of the social surplus lends to the democratic masses a vast new impetus to action.

For, fundamentally, it is ideas, born of conditions, which rule the world. Without an idea to back it, force is not permanently effective. Without an idea, men will not risk their lives or fortunes, will not take off their easy slippers and comfortable smoking jackets, will not spend long evenings on dreary committees. The idea which animates a great group, which holds it together in defeat and delay, is something different from the sudden, angry mob spirit. Ideas are mortal. They are vulnerable to argument. If a popular idea therefore survives in the struggle of all ideas for the possession of men's minds, if it survives to be effective and to leaven the mass, it is only because it closely corresponds, not perhaps to social facts, but to social needs and aspirations. Such an idea, slowly formed in the minds of millions by the deposition of myriads of impressions, slowly hardened by resistance to other ideas and molded by adjustment to new facts, gradually accumulates sufficient force to arouse multitudes and to convert them to a flaming ideal. What incites every manifestation of social power is this idea, bred of social conditions and social needs.

This idea of the social disequilibrium is a conception based on actuality and corresponding to the needs of the most numerous and potentially most powerful elements of the community. It is the instinct of a fuller life for the mass. It is a turning of the people to the great social surplus, a movement as spontaneous and resistless as the advance of a hungry horde upon a fertile, life-giving plain. It is a new version of the life-old quest of food.

To-day a progressive, though slow, diffusion of wealth already gives to all a foretaste of the civilized life which it can create. Once the giving of bread and fishes to the multitude was a miracle, for there were in all the world not bread enough and fishes enough to go around. To-day food and material and moral goods for all being provided, a fairer distribution has become an imperative ethical demand. Out of the ever-growing disproportion between social surplus and social misery, there evolves the doctrine of exploitation, a doctrine as yet vague and illogical, but slowly crystallizing into a sentiment which identifies social injustice with excessive claims upon the surplus.

About this demand for a full life for all the people cluster a host of ethical ideas — clear or confused. The right of the laborer to the entire product of labor; the right of the community to the social value created by the community — to the unearned increment; the belief in society as the ultimate inventor of all inventions and the ultimate designer of all improvements, — are all by-products of the hopes excited by the social surplus. The possibility of giving a full life to all the people has remolded our religion, changed the basis of our ethics, and revolutionized our historical conceptions. It has put down the mighty "great man," who once obsessed history, and has exalted those of low degree, the unnamed multitude. It has caused the individual to shrink; it has wonderfully expanded the hitherto dumb crowd. It is gradually destroying all ideals of prerogative and privilege, God-given, law-given, wealth-given, and is reducing all inequalities to the one inequality of heredity. It has shifted the burden of proof to the shoulders of those who are satisfied with present social conditions.

The gradually increasing share of the people in the social surplus has not only strengthened these conceptions (since the appetite for life grows with the larger life it feeds on), but it gives to the success of the popular struggle for the rest of the surplus a certain sense of inevitableness. The fundamental belief in the ultimate success of the people rests in final analysis upon the success hitherto attained. The economic determinism which makes laws, ethics, political institutions, and social theories largely the reflex of changing economic conditions seems itself to be a reflex of the past success of the mass in securing a larger share of the surplus. Since the masses have grown in wealth, they have become confident of ultimate victory. The best augury of the coming democracy is its first fruits.

To America this social surplus promises more than to other nations. Never in history has there been a social surplus equal to that of America to-day, or at all comparable with the surplus which the still undeveloped resources of the scarred continent are to bring forth. Of all the children of the Industrial Revolution, America — one of the youngest — is the most favored.[1]

This incomparable wealth present, and above all prospective, gives to the democratic movement in this country a tone different from that of England, Germany, France, or Belgium. It makes our past blunders seem mere youthful pranks. It makes us preëminently the heirs of science and invention. Science, more mobile even than money, goes where money is; and America, because her wealth is greater, profits in greater measure than other nations from the inventions of those nations.

It is our future wealth, due to the fact that we still occupy a continent, preëmpted but still fertile, that enlarges our

[1] England, which is the great creditor nation of the world, has a larger per capita wealth than has the United States, but its total wealth (or that of the United Kingdom) is much less than that of this country. In America, moreover, wealth is increasing far more rapidly, both relatively and absolutely, than elsewhere.

hopes. Under a perfect system of production and distribution, the average Italian would not be so well off as is to-day the average American under our most imperfect system.[1] The bitterness of group struggles in Belgium, Italy, Austria, is born of their relative poverty. In those lands intelligence and energy constantly push forward their frontiers — but, at best, they are not continents.[2]

There are exalted and impatient souls who pay no heed to tales of mere material progress. They believe that the geniuses — the Shakespeares, Beethovens, Botticellis, Kants, Darwins — do not arise in the pork-and-pig-iron-producing nations; that a full belly means an empty mind; and that they who wax fat kick against the Lord. They are willing, with Renan, to give up America and all her future for medieval Florence; and, like Carlyle, they have no patience with a boundless land, which produces only dollars and bores. In the eyes of such men America's wealth is her weakness.

Nevertheless a palpable nexus exists between a modicum of national wealth and the elements of democracy and civilization. Intellectual and moral progress cost money as do steam engines and Dreadnoughts. Money — though only a part — is necessary for education, sanitation, leisure, and the amenities of life; for schools, universities, libra-

[1] According to the estimate of Pantaleoni, made in 1889, the wealth of Italy was 55 milliards of francs (less than eleven thousand million dollars). In 1902 Nitti estimated this wealth as being not less than 65 milliards, "*troppo poco senza dubbio,*" for a country of about thirty-three million inhabitants. Nitti, Francesco S., "Lezioni di Scienza delle Finanze," Naples, 1902, pp. 110, 111.

[2] That America is so wealthy in prospect is due to no inherent superiority of Americans. We cannot claim exceptional virtues, marking us off from less favored breeds. We had the one virtue of adapting ourselves — for better and for worse — to an entirely new environment, but what we have accomplished must be attributed primarily to that favoring environment. A vigorous, intelligent, and enterprising people (of which there are many) found itself in surprised possession of almost illimitable resources.

ries, research institutes, art galleries, hospitals, museums, theaters, conservatories, magazines, books, parks, improved houses, better factories, clothing, shelter, recreation, and the endowment and production of what is good and worth while. Eight hundred million dollars intelligently spent on education is better than four hundred millions. The growth of two bales of cotton, or two bushels of wheat, where one grew before, may make the difference between a besotted, superstitious, and reactionary people and an intelligent, cultured, and progressive people. Until the material problems which beset mankind are solved; until misery, disease, crime, insanity, drunkenness, degeneration, ignorance, and greed — which are the offspring (as also the parents) of poverty — are removed (and their removal costs money), humanity will not be able to essay the problems of mind and of social intercourse. Our chance in America of an eventual civilization rising above the demand for daily bread and more money depends upon our wise utilization of our national resources and our national earnings. However spiritual a structure civilization is, it is nevertheless built upon wheat, pork, steel, money, wealth.

Our wealth is already so gigantic as to be almost incomprehensible. A billion dollars exceeds the fortune of any individual since the world began. It is like a "light-year" or some other convenient but unimaginable astronomical term. Yet in 1904 our national wealth was estimated by the census authorities at 107 of these billions of dollars. The present estimated wealth of New York State is twice the entire estimated wealth of the United States in 1850. We would sell under the hammer for fifteen times as much as we would have done a little over half a century ago.[1]

[1] This comparison is, of course, only rudely approximate. The possessions enumerated by the census are actual material things (property, not deeds, mortgages, or paper evidence of ownership). But the conception of property changes. Valuable slaves in 1860 ceased to be property in 1865, and forms of wealth exist in 1911 which did not exist in 1850. Moreover,

The wealth of America, moreover, is not a secret hoard to which new billions are brought and added. It is a living thing, which grows at a stupendous rate as new millions of men pour into the land, and new machines, new scientific processes, new methods of organization, lay the continent wider open. From 1870 to 1900 our wealth increased at the rate of almost two billions a year; from 1900 to 1904 it recorded an apparent increase of almost five billions a year. During every eighteen months of those four years there was added to our possessions an *increment* greater than the whole estimated wealth of the country in 1850.

Everywhere are signs of a stupendous productiveness. The number of our horses, sheep, mules, swine increases; our production of wheat, corn, cotton, rice, has enormously grown. So also our mineral production. In 1840 we produced less than two million long tons of coal; in 1909 we produced four hundred and eleven millions. The mere increase in coal production in 1907 over that of the preceding year was about equal to the entire output of all the country's mines during the eighty-five years from the Declaration of Independence to the outbreak of the Civil War.

In 1870 we produced three million long tons of iron ore; in 1909, fifty-one millions. Our pig iron production, which never amounted to a million long tons before 1864, increased to almost twenty-seven millions in 1910. The production of steel, which remained below one million tons until 1880, rose to twenty-four millions in 1909. Enormously rapid, also, has been the increase in our output of gold, aluminium, cement, copper, lead, salt, stone, and zinc; while our production of petroleum, which averaged about a hundred million gallons a year during the Civil War, rose in 1909 to over seven and one half billions of gallons.

the standard of value changes and money does not go so far to-day as when Washington threw the silver dollar across the Potomac. Nevertheless, an enormous increase in the real wealth of the country is indisputable.

Our American agriculture has not only fed our growing population, but it still permits vast exportations of grain, flour, and meat products. Moreover, it has been carried on by a steadily lessening proportion of the capital and labor of the country. There has been simultaneously an almost bewildering increase in our manufacturing industries.

When we try to visualize the statistics of our American railroads, the mind sinks exhausted under the effort. The traffic increases incessantly and enormously. While our population has not quite doubled in thirty-three years, our railroad passenger and freight traffics have more than doubled in nine years. In 1909 our railroad freight mileage was equivalent to the work of our ninety-two millions of inhabitants carrying each a load of over four hundred pounds a distance of over thirty miles each day. This enormous traffic, like the tremendously increasing water carriage on the Great Lakes, reveals the actual and potential power of the machine-aided American nation.

It is figures like these, almost inconceivable in their totals, which give to Americans their abiding sense in the infinite potentialities of the continent. From the beginning the continent poured forth new millions, and later new billions, of wealth. An invention which netted the discoverer a few thousands or hundreds of thousands brought to the nation hundreds of millions of dollars. Better methods, improved machinery, a more scientific and effective organization of industry, combined to increase our stupendous productiveness. Our national resources were enormously increased by discoveries of new foods, by new uses to which the land might be put.

So much for the wonders of the past. But they are wonders only so long as we think solely in terms of the past. Actually our utilization of the continent has hardly begun. It has hardly begun to begin.

When we regard the vast domain of the United States as a business man regards his plant, from the point of view of maximum possibilities, we realize how far we are from a reasonable exploitation of our resources. Our total farm production is almost nine billions of dollars (or almost five hundred dollars for every family in America), and yet we usually average less than fifteen bushels of wheat per acre and less than two fifths of a bale of cotton per acre. We have cotton farmers planting the small seed, using the worst methods, wasting the most fertile lands. When we compare the worst, or even the average, production in America (in agriculture, mining, manufacturing, transportation, and everything else) with the best; when we remember that our present stupendous wealth is based upon an ignorant, wasteful, and inefficient exploitation of resources,—we begin to arrive at some vague conception of what, under a proper social and industrial polity, could be made of our continent, of this vast physical substratum of our hoped-for American democracy.

Even to-day, with a poor national economy, we do not owe our worst evils to any corporate poverty. Even to-day we could, with a better distribution, provide a livable life for many more millions than our present population. Already the most stupendous social undertakings are carried out with the greatest ease. Our billion-and-a-half-dollar Congresses of to-day hardly cost us as much as the twenty-million-dollar Congresses cost the Americans of 1810. A century ago the nation found it more difficult to pay fifteen million dollars for Louisiana than to-day to pay twenty-five times that much for the Panama Canal. The more than a third of a billion of dollars which that canal represents about equals one month's accretion to the national wealth.

A great social surplus, however, does not mean that a democracy is attained, but only that it is attainable. Without social wealth, a real democracy is not possible; with it, it is not inevitable.

The masses of the people, if they are to secure a democracy, must not fall or remain below the three levels of democratic striving. Below the economic level of democratic striving, men are for the most part too ill-fed, ill-clad, ill-conditioned, too depressed by want or sickness, too harassed by debt or insecurity, too brutalized by child labor or overwork, or too demoralized by recurring unemployment to maintain the *morale* required for the attainment of democracy. Below the intellectual level of democratic striving, most men are too credulous, too suspicious, too immersed in petty preoccupations, too narrow-viewed to perceive their individual interest in the wider interest of group or nation, and they are too near-minded to value the larger social gain of the future above the smaller social or personal gain of the moment. Below the political level of democratic striving, men are too unused to political weapons, or too removed from them, to be able effectively to translate their economic and intellectual powers into political facts. To achieve a real popular sovereignty, the masses of the people must rise or remain above all of these levels.

Of these three levels the economic and the intellectual are the more important, for a voteless people with economic and intellectual resources can better secure political representation than can an impoverished and ignorant people in full possession of political rights. All these three levels are in a sense connected and all are related to the social surplus. It is the social surplus which permits the economic advance of the people, which in turn facilitates their intellectual enfranchisement, which in turn tends strongly in the direction of political representation. The lack of complete parallelism between these three levels results in many of the worst abuses of our pseudo-democratic government of to-day. The possession of the vote by ignorant masses below the poverty line leads to sluggish, reckless, or perverse legislation and seems to justify the most hopeful fears of interested reactionaries. But the true remedy for these evils is not what the reactionaries desire, a change in the political level, but, on the contrary, a raising of the people to a higher economic and intellectual level. Illiterates should not be obliged to stay away from the voting booth, but voters should be obliged to learn their letters, in much the same way that we compel incarcerated tramps to submit to an initial bath. The parallelism between these three levels should be maintained by the steady rise of larger and larger sections of the people above all three levels, to a position in which the economic, intellectual, and political weapons of the people may be effectively used in their common interest.

Thus, though the accumulations of the great industrial nations render democracy possible, and furnish a stake, motive, and ethical justification to democrats; though in America this social wealth is so stupendously growing as to place, *beyond even the possibility of doubt*, our ability, present and future, to pay for such a democracy, — still, whether or not we shall achieve democracy depends upon these other factors, upon the character of our population, upon its mean position above or below the levels of democratic striving. Given the energizing moral impulse of the startling disequilibrium between our social wealth and our abiding poverty, it is still essential that the mass of the population have sufficient wealth or income, sufficient intelligence and clearness of perception, sufficient political power, political experience, and political wisdom (as well as a high enough capacity for joint action), to permit them unitedly to do their part in wresting a democracy from men who have an interested attachment to present conditions. The attainment of democracy depends upon the all-of-us, upon the qualities and resources of the potentially overwhelming democratic masses.

CHAPTER XIV

THE LEVELS OF DEMOCRATIC STRIVING

IT is difficult to translate the economic level of democratic striving from the field of theory to the field of practice. It is difficult to say of any group what sum of wealth or what annual income will divide its members into two sections, of which the upper is likely, and the lower is unlikely, to become a prime factor in the attainment of democracy. Like the blurred line which we seek to draw between the conceptions of luxuries and necessities, of skilled labor and unskilled labor, of interest and usury, like many other conceptions of economic science, that of the level which separates the economically emerged from the economically submerged is wavering, indistinct, changing. The level is not uniform for all countries, nor for all sections, classes, and industrial groups within a country. It is not invariable, but changes from decade to decade with changes in the cost of living and the cost of education and communication. A wage or income which in a New Hampshire town provides leisure, education, and an ambitious discontent may in New York City compel a resort to charity, and an income which might have sufficed a dozen years ago might to-day depress a group below the economic level. Whether four hundred, six hundred, or nine hundred dollars a year establishes the limit of family earnings, below which economic pressure and degradation will prevent men from taking a wide view of group and national interests, is a question depending upon a large group of changing factors.

One thing, however, seems certain. The economic level of democratic striving is above what has been called the "poverty line." That line, which may be called the level of mere physicial efficiency, is exceedingly low. "Let us clearly understand," says B. Seebohm Rowntree,[1] in speaking of the great masses of the English poor, "what 'merely physical efficiency' means. A family living upon the scale allowed for in this estimate must never spend a penny on railway fare or omnibus. They must never go into the country unless they walk. They must never purchase a halfpenny newspaper or spend a penny to buy a ticket for a popular concert. They must write no letters to absent children, for they cannot afford to pay the postage. They must never contribute anything to their church or chapel, or give any help to neighbor which costs them money. They cannot save, nor can they join sick club or Trade Union, because they cannot pay the necessary subscriptions. The children must have no pocket money for dolls, marbles, or sweets. The father must smoke no tobacco, and must drink no beer. The mother must never buy any pretty clothes for herself or for her children, the character of the family wardrobe as for the family diet being governed by the regulation, 'Nothing must be bought but that which is absolutely necessary for the maintenance of physical health, and what is bought must be of the plainest and most economical description.' Should a child fall ill, it must be attended by the parish doctor; should it die, it must be buried by the parish. Finally, the wage earner must never be absent from his work for a single day."

Even above the line of "merely physical efficiency," even above the so-called poverty line, the demoralizing effects of insufficient income affect large groups of the population.

That the average citizen is advancing in wealth and income seems equally probable from general observations and from

[1] "Poverty. A Study of Town Life," London (Macmillan & Co.), 1901, pp. 133, 134.

a study of statistics. It is not contended that the common run of us have as large a proportion of the national wealth as formerly, since a larger amount and a larger proportion of that wealth are being progressively absorbed by a relatively small minority of the population. It is at least probable, if not certain, however, that, leaving out of account this wealthy minority, the remainder of the ninety-two millions of Americans to-day are far more prosperous than were the fifty millions of 1880, the twenty-three millions of 1850, or the five millions of 1800. No one can travel through the country districts of America, or through the streets of our cities, without noting evidences of a widespread prosperity, small when compared with realizable ideals, but enormous when compared with that of the average Englishman, Frenchman, German, or Italian, or with that of the average American of a generation, or two, or three ago.

The farmer has undoubtedly improved his status. It must be remembered, of course, that the farmer is a composite, not a simple type, and that there is as wide a distinction between the economic status of farmers and of farmers as there is between that of lawyers and of lawyers. The Negro tenant of Mississippi has as little in common with the large dairy farmer of Iowa as the small proprietor in the Catskills or Berkshires has with the ranch owner of Texas or the fruit grower of Southern California. Not all farming districts started equally, and not all have progressed equally.

The better farms of to-day are far better than were those of 1860. The farmhouses, barns, stock, and farm implements are improved. The food on the farmer's table, the carpet on his floor, the curtains in his window, the pictures on his walls, the books and magazines on his shelf, everything which he eats, wears, or lives in, show a change. Labor-saving devices enter his house and farm. His school is better. Often a trolley car passes his door. The rural free delivery brings him into touch with the thought and business life of the city, while the rural telephone connects him with the farmers of the vicinity. What the farmer buys — furniture, ornaments, carriages, bicycles, occasionally even automobiles — as well as the enormous exodus from the farm to the State university, indicates a revolutionary rise in standards of living. The farmer's savings in banks and insurance companies, his investments in village business enterprises and in the capital of local banks, show plainly that he is emerging from his former money poverty. He is changing otherwise. The typical farmer of caricature — the credulous, inquisitive, hard-fisted, straw-chewing hayseed — disappears. The farmer who visits Chicago is not distinguishable among its citizens. The farmer is no longer isolated. He is not a serf attached by habit and poverty to his land. The farmer of to-day has one foot in the city.[1]

A similar rise in the standard of living in the cities is revealed by general visual impressions. The citizens, as judged by their clothes, shoes, gloves, underwear, houses, bathtubs, recreation, travel, and a hundred other everyday things, are better off. The shops patronized by the poorer classes have a greater variety and a better quality of wares. The cities, with few exceptions, have rapidly expanded, and cheap new houses have arisen everywhere. The housing conditions of Philadelphians, Chicagoans, and Bostonians are hardly to be compared with the far inferior accommodations of a generation ago. Gas, electricity, gas ranges, more rooms, better furniture, and more sanitary toilet accommoda-

[1] Our agriculturalists, during the three centuries of white settlement in America, always maintained a certain level of rude comfort, having ample wheat bread, corn, pork, milk, butter, chickens, eggs, firewood, and home-spun clothing. For the greater part of our national existence our farmers, who lived not far differently from their laborers, and, in certain portions of the Southern frontier, not far differently from their slaves, secured by much labor ample quantities of coarse food and such necessaries and comforts as could be made on the farm or bought in the up-growing cities.

tions evidence a complete revolution in standards. The food of working people has improved in quality, increased in quantity, and been extended in variety. An increase is shown in the quantity, quality, and variety of the clothing, furniture, and similar articles of use. The old joke about the maidservant outdressing her mistress has almost ceased to be a joke and become a social phenomenon. Nowhere in the world is there so lavish (and often so misdirected and perverse) an expenditure upon clothing, food, furniture, etc., as in the United States to-day.

The enormous expansion in the use of electric cars, telephones, tobacco, beer, coffee, sugar, fresh fruits, fresh vegetables, canned goods, etc., indicates this change. There is much waste. Men and women are to-day breaking and wasting in kitchen and drawing-room with the insane disproportionate lavishness of the pioneer who slashed and burned and wasted in the wilderness. We buy more for display and less for solid comfort than ever before. Nevertheless our new standards of living show not only present prosperity, but also (because of the weight which wealth gives to numbers) the potentiality of a still better life for the million.[1]

Fortunately we are not dependent upon mere visual impressions for our belief that the material power of the mass of Americans is on the increase. Our statistics point the same way. They throw at least a reflected light upon wealth, wages, savings, and standards of living.

That the wealth of the farming population is widely diffused may be gathered from a consideration of the statistics of the value and size of farms. From 1850 to 1900 the value of farm property increased 415 per cent as compared with

[1] A succession of foreign observers visiting America have come to the conclusion that the working classes in America are as well fed, as well clothed, and as well housed as are the lower middle classes of Europe.

an increase of 226 per cent in population and of 149 per cent in rural population.[1] The value of farms and farm property (including cash and sundry live capital in the hands of farmers) amounted in 1905 to a total of twenty-seven and a half billions of dollars, a huge capital which, though not evenly distributed, represents a decentralized and widely owned industry, with a large annual surplus, owned and secured by large sections of the community.

It is of course true that we have great farms. But our estates of over one thousand acres formed in 1900 less than 8 per cent of the value of all farm property, while over 86 per cent of the value of American farms were in properties of less than five hundred acres, and over 71 per cent in farms of less than two hundred and sixty acres.[2] Despite the fact that the great American farm, with its 841,000,000 acres (in 1900), has always been the goose that laid the golden egg (which golden egg has rolled off to the city, instead of waiting on the farm to be assessed by the census enumerator), the increase in the value of farms held outright by the cultivator or his neighbor has increased enormously. In 1900 there were 5,700,000 farms (not farm owners) worth an average of $3550 per farm. An enormous majority of these farms were valued at from $1000 to $8000.

It is scarcely possible within the limits of a chapter to indicate (to say nothing of proving) the great material progress of the mass of the population. Our farm statistics show that our distribution of wealth and income is not as grotesquely unequal as many writers claim, nor as unequal

[1] A part of this increased value is probably to be accounted for by changes in the value of money.

[2] In 1900 our 5,211,842 farms of less than two hundred and sixty acres had an average value of a little over $2800, while all farms of two hundred and sixty acres and over had an average value of a little over eleven thousand dollars. For the basis of these calculations, see Twelfth Census of the United States, Volume V.

as in several countries of Europe. Our wage statistics show a level of industrial remuneration greatly in excess of that in any country of Europe, and still rising, though at a slackened rate.

It is exceedingly difficult to give in statistical form the difference between wages in America and Europe. Real wages depend not only upon what is in the weekly pay envelope, but also upon the prices of ordinary articles of consumption, upon the amount of seasonal interruption and of unemployment for other causes, upon the length of the trade life, upon the provision of governmental insurance, and upon other factors. The real difference in favor of the American workman is less than the apparent difference. The weekly wages of bricklayers in American cities is from two and a half to three times the wages of bricklayers in the cities of the United Kingdom, but the actual superiority of the American bricklayers is smaller. From various official reports and analyses of wages in the United States, the United Kingdom, and Germany, however, it would appear that, all deductions made, there remains a substantial advantage to the American workingman, an advantage which, for the chief trades, cannot be estimated at less than from 50 to 80 per cent. In other words, were the English or German workman to earn American wages and pay American prices for articles and services generally similar to those which he now consumes, he would be able to save an amount equal to from 50 to 80 per cent of his present wages.

There are many outstanding facts which point to the superior economic status of the workman in America. One of these is our enormous and increasing immigration, although it must here be borne in mind that the source of our immigration has shifted from countries with higher, to countries with lower, scales of industrial remuneration. Another, though a less distinct, indication is afforded by our far smaller use of the labor of women, and especially of married women, than is made in other industrial countries.[1] A third indication is found in the relative wages of certain groups, — the wages of agricultural laborers, of clerks, of women generally, of domestic servants, etc.

If we fix our eyes neither upon the advance scouts nor upon the stragglers in the industrial army, but upon the rank and file, we find, despite a constant immigration of workers from countries upon a lower economic level, a general status far above that of the leading industrial nations of Europe. This better condition is revealed in the consumption of wealth. "The American (workman)," writes an English observer, "having the control of a larger income, has developed a wider range of tastes and wants. . . . He dresses better, eats more varied and expensive food, travels more, and reads more."

When we consider not only the urban worker, but the great masses of the community with average or small incomes, our statistics of consumption acquire a new relevance. When we endeavor to see who actually consumes our annual production of goods and services, we are reënforced in our belief

[1] In the United States the proportion of gainfully employed females to the whole number of persons gainfully employed was 18.20 per cent. In France (1901) the proportion was 34.52 per cent; in Germany (1907), 33.79 per cent; in Austria (1900), 42.18; in Hungary (1900), 29.68 per cent; in Italy (1901), 32.47 per cent; in Belgium (1900), 29.20 per cent. See the Fourth Abstract of Foreign Labor Statistics, Board of Trade (U. K.), London, 1911, on pages 4 and 5 of which is given a statement of the original German, French, Austrian, Hungarian, Belgian, Italian, and American sources from which these comparative results have been obtained. The value of the comparison is conditioned by the fact that the various statistical authorities do not exactly agree in determining the meaning of gainful employment. A comparison of the relative numbers of men and women employed respectively in the United States and in Great Britain in a number of trades, cotton manufactures, wool and worsted, carpets, tailoring, etc., bears out the same relation. In 1901, 29.07 per cent of all persons gainfully employed in the United Kingdom were females.

as to the overwhelming aggregate economic power of the great mass of the population.

For whose benefit, for whose ultimate consumption, is our vast annual production?

In the year 1909, according to the estimate of the United States Department of Agriculture, we had a wealth production upon our farms of eight and three quarter billions of dollars, or of almost five hundred dollars for every American family. Disregarding articles exported (and duplications), who ate the wheat, the corn, the oats, the potatoes, the sugar, the milk, the butter, the cheese, the chickens? Who consumed the cotton, hay, tobacco? The production of food is almost entirely a production for the great mass. Olives, *patés de foie gras*, champagne, do not weigh in the balance with bread and sausage and pork. We hear occasionally of a fifty-dollar-a-plate dinner. We hear less often of the 250,000,000 simpler meals which are taken daily in the United States.

The same is true of our manufactured articles. In 1905 we produced roughly $320,000,000 worth of boots and shoes and $70,000,000 of rubber boots and shoes. How many of these did the rich consume? Who ate $270,000,000 worth of bakers' bread? Who ate those five billion loaves? Who consumed the $78,000,000 of canned goods, the $602,000,000 of men's and women's clothing; the $450,000,000 of cotton goods; the $713,000,000 of flour and grist mill products; the $298,000,000 of malt liquors; the $801,000,000 of slaughtering and meat packing (wholesale) the $277,000,000 of sugar and molasses? Who consumed the lumber, the paper, the glass, the hardware, the hats, the leather goods, the linen, the marble, the oil, the lead pencils? Who ate the $29,000,000 of pickles? or smoked the $331,000,000 of tobacco, cigars, and cigarettes?

Everywhere it is the great mass which buys, the men with incomes from $500 to $5000; and not the few great spenders with incomes in the tens of thousands. Our houses are in the aggregate the houses of the poor and of the middle classes. The million-dollar palace does not begin to compare in the aggregate with the three-thousand-dollar house, which the people own or rent. Steam yachts are built for the rich. How much of the wealth of the country goes into steam yachts compared with that which goes into trolley cars for the use of the people? Automobiles, beginning with the rich, have come down to the moderately wealthy, to small business men and farmers. Yet compare them with the farmers' wagons. Who, rich or poor, buys the harvesters, plows, agricultural machinery? Who buys the books, the magazines, the newspapers?[1]

The enormous consumption every year is a consumption by the average American, by the comfortable, and especially by the poor, by the people who must work to live. If each poor and middle class family had an average income of only one dollar per day (twenty cents per person), it would mean a total expenditure of well over six billions of dollars a year. An added expenditure of one cent per day per person on luxuries aggregates a total of three hundred and thirty-five millions of dollars per year.

We are singularly neglectful of such facts and curiously oblivious of our vast new expenditures, which signify so complete a revolution in popular standards of living. Every week Americans travel 550,000,000 miles upon trains. Every year they spend $564,000,000 on railroad tickets.

[1] In simple uncommercial communities (as in Europe during the Middle Ages) the wealthy did not directly consume great masses of commodities, but hired servants to eat for them and to wear out clothes for them. We have no statistics of our modern retinues of servants, and we do not know the number of domestic servants in families keeping, let us say, over one servant. The number, however, is probably not great. Even our richest families set limits to the numbers of their idle retainers, and "vicarious consumption" by servants is not so popular an ostentation as it was in simpler days, when there was no other equally spectacular way of spending money.

It means a new national habit. To-day there are over three and one half million telephone subscribers and over one connection daily for every family in the United States. Street car riding for pleasure, city pleasure parks, summer vacations, the purchase of books, magazines, and newspapers, the enormous extension of the five-cent cigar, the democratization of watches, bicycles, cameras, carpets, etc., signify a change within the last half a century of the farthest-reaching proportions.[1]

Nor do individual purchases measure the increased economic power of the average man. To-day we are spending far more through our national, State, and local governments than ever before. In 1870 we spent less than $8 per family on our public schools; to-day we are spending well over $22. No one can study the branching social activities of cities like New York, Chicago, Philadelphia, St. Louis, and smaller places without realizing the enormously increased spending power of the masses of the community.

This spending does not exhaust the earnings of the average American. It is no longer contended that all deposits in savings banks are made by workingmen or even by poor men; and, indeed, it is widely known that quite wealthy men often have deposits in various savings banks. Nevertheless, as an indication of the saving capacity of the average mass, the increase in savings bank deposits is not without significance. Until 1858 these deposits never amounted to one hundred million dollars. In 1870 they amounted to

[1] A highly significant indication of the increased spending power of the masses is furnished by the vast sums devoted both to cheap and to more expensive amusements. In the course of a generation the salaries of actors, vaudeville artists, baseball players, etc., has enormously increased as a result of the flood of wealth pouring from the pockets of the people. Mr. Keith (a great vaudeville promoter) has recently said, "It is not uncommon now for artists to receive as high as $2500 a week in vaudeville, and it is a fact in high-priced houses in the East and West, the average show, which used to cost $500 to $600 a week, now costs from $3000 to $4500." The *New York Review*, quoted in the *Literary Digest*, October 7, 1911.

five; in 1880, to eight; in 1890, to fifteen; and in 1910, to forty hundreds of millions. The amount of ordinary life insurance policies in force increased from less than 70 millions in 1850 to 12,513 millions in 1909; industrial insurance increased from twenty millions in 1880 to 2967 millions in 1908; while a simultaneous increase is recorded in the amounts of money invested in building and loan associations. Any one who will study the investment advertisements of penny newspapers and of five and ten cent magazines, who will examine the machinery for the sale of bonds and stocks to people of very small incomes; any one who observes the flood of gold which pours from thousands of obscure sources to any plausible swindler, — will realize the tremendously wide diffusion of wealth in America.[1]

It is claimed by some writers that the decline in individual house ownership in the United States proves that the masses of the American people are becoming less, and not more, prosperous. It is undoubtedly true that to-day a smaller proportion of Americans own houses in which they dwell than formerly, and this significant fact must be set off against other evidences of saving. What the increasing non-ownership of one's dwelling house proves, however, is not a decline in general prosperity, but a change in the unit of investment in houses and in the methods of general investment. It is no longer an invariable custom even among people of means to own their homes; and so far are we from any direct relation between poverty and non-ownership, that it is precisely in the poorer rural districts that men mostly own their homes, while in the richer cities ownership is less usual.[2]

[1] Note, for instance, the "financial" advertisements appearing in certain non-English journals, appealing to the very poorest of our recent immigrants. Note also the magnitude of the operations of the little immigrant banks, appealing to the same class. See the statistics of money forwarded to Europe by recent immigrants. See the Report of the Commission on Immigration of the State of New York, Albany, 1909.

[2] In Manhattan, which is an island of tenement and apartment houses,

Even with the increase of non-ownership, the vast sums of money invested in individual houses and lots and in building and loan associations are another evidence of a wide diffusion of property. So too is the wealth invested in hundreds of thousands of small manufacturing and mercantile establishments, ranging in value from a few hundreds to a few tens of thousands of dollars.

It is not to be contended that the increasing prosperity of the masses has been universal. Economic stress and distress are probably greater to-day than ever before among the free populations of America. There is more uncertainty. Our slums are greater.[1] There are sections of the rural community which have been depressed by our economic development, and in certain isolated places there has been a marked deterioration in the status and outlook of small communities. During the last dozen years, moreover, great masses of our working classes, especially among the unskilled workers, have been subjected to the pressure of increasing prices, and only with great difficulty have they secured wage increases superior, or even equal, to the rise in the cost of living.[2]

it is becoming impossible under present systems of ownership for men individually to own their homes.

[1] Our poverty has changed, as has our country, from a rural to an urban variety; from a poverty more dependent upon personal incapacity, to one more dependent upon economic maladjustments. Our later poverty is unrelieved by the presence of free land. To-day when the poor have the advantages of city sanitation, free schools, dispensary and hospital service, better water, cleaner streets, freer legal advice, free libraries, etc., a larger mass of men and women tremble on the verge of crime or dependence than ever before. We have established higher standards of success, and those who fall below these standards, whether through mischance, lack of training, inebriety, or physical or mental weakness, are more miserable than they would have been in a cruder society, in which an inefficient man could always secure *some* sort of a job. Despite the rise of the mass of our population, an empty stomach in America is as empty as in Russia or India.

[2] According to the Reports of the Bureau of Labor, based upon the records of 4034 establishments in the principal manufacturing and mechan-

Nor is it claimed that this general rise during the last half century, or the rise, where it has occurred, during the last ten years, is at all commensurate with the reasonable anticipations of the masses of the community. Content with what has been gained is the very worst way of retaining what has been gained. The question here considered has not been whether Americans as a whole should be satisfied with what

ical industries in the United States, full time weekly wages in 1907 were 22.4 per cent higher than the average for the years 1890–1899 inclusive, while hourly wages were 28.8 per cent higher. During the same period, however, the rise in the retail prices of food, weighted according to the consumption of the average workingman's family (and based upon data taken from the records of 993 retail merchants), was no less than 20.6 per cent. In purchasing power, therefore, full time weekly wages rose only 1.5 per cent from 1890–1899 to 1907, although hourly wages rose 6.8 per cent.

A recent investigation made by the New York (State) Department of Labor arrives at somewhat similar results. "The result shown by this investigation is that a workingman's living of a given standard cost 22 per cent more in 1907 than it did in 1897 in New York City, and averaged 21.5 per cent more in four other cities, so that 22 per cent may be taken as about the proportion of increase in workmen's cost of living at the same standard in this State. By reference to the foregoing pages it will be seen that the increase in average per diem earnings of Union members in the same period was found to be 22.9 per cent. The indication is, therefore, that cost of living has risen as much as wage rates in the leading trades. But owing to increasing steadiness of employment it was found that the half-yearly income of Union workmen in the principal trades had risen 31.2 per cent in the decade, or considerably more than the cost of living."

If with these figures we compare, for purely illustrative purposes, the crude averages of wages paid to 4,715,023 workers (men, women, and children) in 1900 and to 5,470,321 workers in 1905, we arrive at a somewhat similar result, viz. to an increase of 12 per cent in wages during a period in which the retail prices of food rose 11.2 per cent. (Summary of Manufactures. Reports of the Bureau of the Census. Department of Commerce and Labor.)

Similarly among steam railroad employees, while the wages of enginemen, firemen, conductors, other trainmen, and machinists (as given by the Reports of the Interstate Commerce Commission) increased from 1892 to 1907 faster, and in some cases much faster, than did the retail prices of food during the same period (as given by the Reports of the Bureau of Labor), the rise in wages among other classes was but little greater, and usually was actually less than the rise in the prices of food.

has fallen from the table, but whether the increasing prosperity of the general population has, or has not, placed it in an economic position where it is better able to take part in the work of securing industrial reform and industrial reconstruction.

It is not, however, by wealth alone that the masses secure industrial supremacy. We need not, it is true, fear either in America or elsewhere that the masses will ever attain to such a superfluity of possessions as to lame their future ambitions. The more a people possess above the mere absolute minimum necessary to life, the farther, other things being equal, are they removed from that hell of lethargic contentment to which moralists during so many centuries have consigned the populations that waxed fat. But wealth, without education, furnishes no sufficient motive power to democratic movements. It is possible that the German masses are to-day a more capable democratic group than are the English, because the Germans, though perhaps poorer, and with fewer political rights, are better educated.

An increased diffusion of wealth, however, tends towards the ultimate securing of education, just as it tends towards the acquisition by the masses of political rights and of a sense of corporate power and worth. They who laud the blessings of poverty (to others) fail to realize the enormous development of individuality made possible in modern society by an income above the level of existence. A man with a thousand dollars a year may have ten times as many educative social contacts as has the man with five hundred. A population the majority of whom have a surplus of income above necessary expenditure is enormously stronger than a population upon a lower earning line.

To-day the mass of Americans, grown in wealth, are a power in industry, education, and the state. They are not abject, "respectful" helots. They do not look up to superiors. They themselves, in their collectivity, feel their own superiority. They are aggressive, impolite, and socially irreverent.

There is perhaps a certain harshness to this emerging "common man," who with a little money and a little knowledge is beginning to feel his collective importance. He knows that he cannot be ignored by trust builder or political magnate. His custom must be appealed to; his prejudices must be respected. He can not be "voted," for his vote is worth as much to himself as to the briber. He need not vote for a "full dinner pail," but may canvass alternatives. He fears neither landlord nor employer. He has his preferences in clothes, books, newspapers, schools, and laws, and he has the material prosperity to back his choice.

The diffused wealth of the people is readily transmuted into intellectual influence. A poverty-stricken class will not have its interests represented by an able periodical press because (among other reasons) it cannot pay for it. To support a paper or magazine a social class must not only pay its pennies in circulation, but must spend its dollars on the wares advertised. There can be no better proof of the rise in wealth of the great mass than the enormous growth of five and ten cent magazines, supporting themselves by advertising soaps, razors, and breakfast foods.

The average man — finding money in his purse — determines to educate himself. Often this education is delayed a generation and is acquired vicariously by son or daughter. Sometimes it is desired because supposed to pay in dollars and cents, or in positions of more unquestioned "gentility." Behind this, however, there is a far more vital and general motive. It is the American instinct for education.

That instinct is perhaps rather crude, undiscriminating, and still intent upon quantity rather than quality. Much of our education is superficial and perfunctory, and some is absolutely noxious. Our schools have been as anarchic as our factories. We still maintain woefully underpaid and undertrained teachers, appointed in some towns and cities under a spoils system. We still have miserable schoolrooms, antiquated textbooks, and an incredible mass of tenacious incompetence and pedagogical perversity. And yet the American instinct for education — like so many popular instincts — is astoundingly true. It is perhaps our most fundamental appreciation of democracy.

A diffused education, like a diffused prosperity, is necessary to democracy. In a democracy, the government can hardly rise above the intellectual level of the mass. Where, as in America, the majority are but little inclined to submit their opinions to the judgment of a special intellectual class, it is absolutely essential that the mass of the people be intelligent — politically and otherwise.

Never before was education so necessary. Even in our personal affairs we are overwhelmed with an embarrassment of choices and a superfluity of theories. We must decide hourly a thousand questions — what to eat and drink and wear and buy; when to sleep; how to raise the baby; how to furnish the house; how to obtain money; what attitude to adopt towards germs. Our new science prevents us from falling back upon routine, as our new ethics forbid us to depend upon traditions. Even our religion is laicized, and most of us choose (and direct) our spiritual advisers, as we choose our public servants, newspapers, and patent medicines. Our laws against fraud do not quite relieve the intellectual strain. Pure food and corporation laws tell us whether there is alum in the baking powder or water in the trust, but it remains for us to determine whether we will take our baking powder and trusts that way.

Our public problems involve even a greater intellectual effort. In no democracy do the intellectually assembled people make all decisions. The people decide the broad issues, but delegate to legislators and administrators the power to prepare ways and means, reserving, at best, a potential veto. Despite this latency of democracy, however, the people, if ignorant, are powerless, however wide the vote or sensitive the political system. They are like a giant with occluded brain; a giant beating his own breast. Sovereignty tends to approach the intellectual (as it tends to approach the economic) center of gravity of society. If knowledge is concentrated at the top, society tends to become politically — as well as intellectually — top-heavy.

Wealth means education. Even in countries with free and universal education, the illiterates are, on the whole, the very poor, while the better-to-do classes have the higher education. Even where tuition is free, the ability to go to school depends upon the possession of money to support the pupil during these years of preparation. As the wealth of the average citizen increases, the school year lengthens, and the age at which children may legally leave school is raised.

Literacy is not learning, and learning is not intelligence. A sanity of judgment is often found among men without their letters, while, at the other end of the ladder, recipients of learned degrees often suffer through life from intellectual stodginess. Our intellectual measurements are arbitrary.

Nevertheless, the ability to read and write is the best single standard of education that we possess, for to-day, more than ever before, printer's ink rules the world, and literacy is indispensable to communication. To-day social knowledge requires a recourse, not to memory, but to the accumulated intellectual stores buried in print. Modern government makes literacy essential. The old direct democracy, as represented in the town meeting, broke down when the community grew so large that a man's voice could not carry. A political babel ensued, and there arose a representative government, which always tended to become a more or less unrepresentative government by a special class. To-day, when final decisions are again thrown back upon the people, when representatives are tending to become political automata, the old problem of direct government, that of making a man's voice carry, reappears. Through the printed word one can reach a hundred million literate auditors.

Illiteracy in the United States is not nearly so low as in Germany, Norway, Sweden, France, or Great Britain. We have still a heavy burden of Negro illiteracy inherited from slavery, and to-day a large proportion of our immigrants come from illiterate populations. While no less than one in ten (10.7 per cent) of all Americans ten years of age and over [1] are unable to write, the proportion of such illiterates among Negroes is 44.5 per cent, among our foreign-born is 12.9 per cent, and among our native white population is 4.6 per cent. Even this smaller percentage of illiteracy of native whites is largely due to the poverty, dispersion of population, and special racial problems of the South. Excepting Maine (which has a large French Canadian population) no State above the old Mason and Dixon line has an illiteracy of 2 per cent. In eighteen States the illiterates form less than 1 per cent of the population of the age of ten and over.

American illiteracy is slowly disappearing. In 1880, 17.0 per cent of Americans ten years of age and over were unable to write as compared with 10.7 per cent in 1900, and during the first decade of the twentieth century the percentage probably fell again. Negro illiteracy, almost universal in 1865, has fallen rapidly. As for the immigrants, their children (largely because city dwellers) are more literate than the children of native Americans. To-day illiteracy is practically a phenomenon of the South, and with the growth in Southern wealth and enterprise it is bound to dwindle.

A literate population may remain ignorant and socially impotent.[2] Although the ability to read is more important

[1] Census of 1900.

[2] Much of what has been called a deterioration of our newspapers and of our fugitive literature, generally, has in reality been caused, not by a

than any single, subsequent step towards the attainment of knowledge, mere literacy will not suffice for the attainment of democracy, to say nothing of the proper working of democratic institutions once attained. The intellectual level of democratic striving is above the literacy line, just as the economic level is above the poverty line.

Like the economic, so also the intellectual level of democratic striving is difficult precisely to determine. It varies among different nations and different sections and groups of a nation. It rises with the growing complexity of industrial and political arrangements and with the increased subtlety and *finesse* of antidemocratic maneuvers. The average citizen need not be as cunning as a counterfeiter to put a counterfeiter in jail by due process of law. He need not be a political economist, constitutional lawyer, and sanitarian combined ("like Cerberus, three gentlemen in one") to appreciate the social need of such experts, but he must be wise enough to care and wise enough to elect men who know. The irreducible intellectual minimum, necessary for the attainment of democracy, includes some form of social consciousness above the cruder manifestations of mere jingoism, some measure of group-consciousness, some appreciation of the importance of public developments, some recognition of the necessity of united action, some realization of the ordinary means of attaining common ends, a tempered confidence in leaders, and a capacity for distinguishing larger from smaller and more immediate ends. The citizen must have a certain social sense and sensitiveness. What is neces-

decline in the intelligence of the population but by the increasing literacy of the uneducated. Newspapers catering to these more ignorant elements of the population have a wide latitude of suggestion and statement, because their readers are satisfied with broad appeals to their corporate vanity and with general but misdirected denunciations, instead of demanding an effective expression of their views. Ignorant readers do not secure much real representation in public opinion, just as ignorant voters do not secure real representation in political action.

sary is not only the alphabet (that open sesame to the books of the world), but also a wide, deep popular education through the school, the public press, the city, the factory, and a myriad of social contacts.

American education has always encountered tremendous difficulties. During the colonial period the settlers were too scattered and busy to have much opportunity for study. The Revolutionary War dislocated the school system, and left the colonists impoverished. The second war with Great Britain, the drain of young men to the West, and the general dispersal of the population further retarded the educational development. As late as 1837 one third of all children in Massachusetts were without any school advantages whatsoever, and a large proportion of the remainder attended school only two or three months in winter or a few weeks in summer.

In the South the difficulties were even greater. The system of large plantations, the absence of township government, the sparseness of population, the institution of slavery, the aristocratic traditions and the parish schools of the Church of England, barred the way to the public school for almost two centuries. In the West, despite a great zeal for education, it was difficult to secure more than its rudiments. The little red schoolhouse was often an aspiration rather than a pedagogical accomplishment.

During the last three generations, however, a complete revolution has taken place in American instruction, and the free public school has been elevated to the first place in the democracy. By 1850 public elementary education, supported by taxation, had been established with varying degrees of completeness in all parts of the country, and its subsequent history has been one of rapid development. It is impossible here to sketch even in vaguest outline the stupendous changes which have taken place in pedagogical methods, in the character of textbooks, in the development of curricula, in the spirit of the school. Mere external figures are perhaps more convincing. To-day (1909) we have seventeen and a half million boys and girls enrolled in the public schools, with an average daily attendance of over twelve and a half millions. We have over half a million public school teachers, on whose salaries $237,000,000 are annually spent. Not only does the proportion of enrolled school children continually increase; not only do the children enrolled attend more frequently and for longer terms, but the number of teachers, the salaries of teachers, and the sums spent upon public education increase even more rapidly.[1]

The zeal, one might almost say the abandon, with which America is giving herself up to education is revealed by the increasing appropriations for public schools. Especially rapid has been the increase in our secondary education, the number of pupils in the secondary grades having increased 124 per cent in the fourteen years 1890 to 1904. The progress during the same period both in the quantity and quality of our college and university education has been even more startling. According to Mr. Bryce, writing in 1905, "there has been within these last thirty-five years a development of the higher education in the United States perhaps without a parallel in the world." [2]

Year by year, American education becomes broader, deeper, and more differentiated. We are rapidly developing special education for special classes, for special ages, for special aptitudes. The education of women has taken enor-

[1] While the population between the ages of 5 and 18 increased during the period 1870 and 1909 from 12,055,443 to 24,239,820, or 101.1 per cent, the number of pupils enrolled in the public schools increased 154.8 per cent (6,871,522 to 17,506,175) and the average daily attendance increased 211.1 per cent (4,077,347 to 12,684,837). During the same period the number of teachers increased 152.4 per cent (200,515 to 506,040); the salaries of superintendents and teachers increased over sixfold ($37,832,566 to $237,013,913); and the total expenditure for the public schools also increased over sixfold ($63,396,666 to $401,397,747).

[2] "America Revisited," *The Outlook*, March, 1905.

mous steps forward. Our professional schools, although many of them are still archaic and vicious, are being reformed. Our kindergartens, our manual training schools, etc., are enormously in advance of anything in America a generation ago.

Even more stupendous has been the effect of our recent library development upon the intellectual development of the broad masses of the people. Nowhere during the last twenty years has there been a development of the public library on anything approaching the American scale. The strengthening alliance between schools and public libraries, the deposit of book collections in schools, the widespread system of traveling libraries, the creation of special reading rooms for children, the specialization of libraries for the blind and other groups, the growing list of private benefactions to libraries, and the enormous extension in the use of libraries have been parts of a development which has brought books of all kinds to the masses of the people. Simultaneously there has been so stupendous a growth of the newspaper [1] and the magazine, and so keen a stimulation to general reading, that to-day one finds everywhere in the cities that men are much — if not well — informed. There was never a time in the history of the world when so many minds, uniting to form public opinion, were so stirred.

The mind of the nation is becoming not only more inquisitive into all things, but intelligence is spreading out over an ever wider area. The newspaper and the magazine, aided by the rural free delivery, now invade country districts,

[1] In 1775 there was not a single daily paper published in the colonies; by 1820 there were 27 dailies, with an annual circulation of 22,321,000. By 1828 this circulation had trebled; by 1871 it had increased 67 fold to the enormous total of 1,500,000,000 copies. Since then the development has been even more remarkable. In 1907–1908 there were published in the United States and Canada 22,487 periodicals (of which 21,320 were published in the United States). Of these 22,487 periodicals, 16,067 were weekly, 2681 monthly, 2494 daily, 269 semimonthly, 618 semiweekly, 190 quarterly, 49 biweekly; 57 triweekly, and 73 bimonthly.

hitherto inaccessible. Everywhere the links of thought are drawn closer. The mails, the telegraph, and the telephone spread intelligence with enormous rapidity. The statistics of the post office indicate the wide spread of intelligence through letters and newspapers. During the forty years ending in 1910, the population, according to the census statistics, increased 139 per cent, while the number of ordinary postage stamps issued increased 1806 per cent. The telegraph development, though rapid, has been stunted by the high rates for messages, but an enormous expansion of telephone communication is even now taking place.[1]

In the city, as in the country, a public opinion based upon many sources of information is steadily forming. Here the means of communication have been so perfected that the danger lies not in an under- but almost in an overstimulation of the mind. Men, separated by only a few blocks or a few miles, are united by the telephone and the street car. The spirit of the city is association, and in the growing cities of America are found the *nuclei* of vast associative efforts with the object of political, social, and industrial betterment. In the city, where a man may not know his neighbor, most men can find their like-minded fellows, and here — even more than in the country districts — is being created that associative and coöperative intelligence, public opinion.

This growing intelligence of the American masses,[2] like

[1] From January 1, 1904, to January 1, 1910, the number of exchanges and branch offices of the American Telephone and Telegraph Company, and of the operating companies associated with it, increased from 3740 to 4968; the number of subscribers increased from 1,525,167 to 3,588,247 or 111 per cent, the number of daily exchange connections from 9,876,402 to 19,925,194 or 101.7 per cent, while the population of the country increased less than 13 per cent.

[2] Twenty years ago, Mr. Bryce said ("American Commonwealth," Vol. II, pp. 867–869): "Nowhere in the world is there growing up such a vast multitude of intelligent, cultivated, and curious readers. It is true that of the whole population a majority of the men read little but news-

their growing wealth and income, is a vital fact in the achievement of political and industrial democracy. Just as the feudal *régime* began to totter when the bullet of the common soldier pierced the steel armor of the knight, so our *régime* of pecuniary and industrial privilege begins to crumble when its pretensions are riddled by the questions of the straight-thinking masses. The constantly greater drawing upon new and old agencies of education, from the trade union to the university, and from the Grange to the moving picture; the ever widening circle of influence of our education; in short, our gradual creation of an intellectual republic, while a consequence of our more diffused wealth, is in turn a cause of it. More money for the people means more education, and more education means more money.

To-day the American people are gradually attaining a wide diffusion of wealth and intelligence. They have already attained formal political rights.[1] There is growing up an enormous mass of people who not only possess the vote, but also sufficient money and sufficient intelligence not to be coerced or too often deluded. This mass of citizens, if they can unite, should be able to secure control of government and of industry and to reconstitute America according to the wishes of the majority.

The question remains, "Can they unite?" Have they interests in common? Are they part of an organic whole?

papers, and many of the women little but novels. Yet there remains a number to be counted by millions, who enjoy and are moved by the higher products of thought and imagination; and it must be that as this number continues to grow, each generation rising somewhat above the level of its predecessors, history and science, and even poetry, will exert a power such as they have never yet exerted over the masses of any country."

[1] As the economic level of democratic striving lies above the poverty line, and the intellectual level lies above the literary line, so the political level runs above the suffrage line. The ballot is a key which opens all political closets, but it is only a key — useless if unused. Besides the right and habit of voting, the average citizen must be cognizant of some of the present limitations and some of the future potentialities of the ballot.

A rope of sand, though it be composed of ninety million or of ninety quadrillion grains, is but a rope of sand. Is there an internal cohesion of the people? Is there a solidarity? Is there a mass to oppose to the privileges and pretensions of a class?

CHAPTER XV

THE GATHERING FORCES OF THE DEMOCRACY

THE solidarity of the masses above the three levels of democratic striving may not be arbitrarily assumed. Just as the visible lands above sea level differ from the submerged lands and yet equally differ among each other in altitude, latitude, and structure, so the emerged masses, though on a different plane from the submerged, are split into classes, groups, and sub-groups by the action of race, religion, tradition, occupation, and income.

This very broadness and vagueness of the democratic masses, of the masses above the level of democratic striving, is of the very essence of the problem. It is easy, by a logical *tour de force,* to divide society into two simple, antagonistic groups, each of which is supposed to be united by a single quality or condition and to be animated by a single purpose. Such a doctrinaire alignment of social classes, an alignment like that between proletariat and non-proletariat, or between the propertied and the absolutely unpropertied, has the advantage of clearness and literalness, but, interpreted clearly and literally, it does not represent actual divisions in society.

The more complex society is (and it becomes more complex yearly), the greater is the difficulty in dividing the community into two mutually exclusive groups, with clear-cut, antagonistic philosophies. The ideals of men tend more or less to coincide with their industrial interests, but the result is affected by prejudices, antipathies, sympathies, and traditions; and prepossession is nine points of belief. Nor are industrial interests themselves so simple or easily classifiable. *Special* group interests conflict with *general* group interests, as when the locomotive engineer sides with the railroad stockholder against the Negro or Italian track-layer. Subsidiary economic interests affect the result, as when the workingman is also a small investor or even a direct employer of other men's labor. Family bonds create cross-lines of interest. The stone mason's son may be traveling salesman for a trust; the daughter of a grocer may be a school-teacher or milliner; the brother of an obsequious butler may be a walking delegate, a village minister, a bucket-shop keeper, a tenant farmer, or a small pharmacist.

Here, as elsewhere in sociology, we must sacrifice a fictitious simplicity to the greater complexity and vagueness of the truth. The real facts of our economic life are too bewilderingly intricate to be covered exactly by any rigid formula, however necessary such formulæ may be. In depicting social cleavages we may profitably use with mental reservations such facile current phrases as "the public," "the common people." But who are "the common people," as distinguished from other members of society? It is easy to think abstractly of "the masses" and "the classes" as two distinct, antagonistic groups. When, however, we review the actual people in our block, city, or township, we encounter insuperable difficulties of classification. Take the milkman, the college professor, the locomotive engineer, the dentist, the eight hundred-dollar-a-year minister, the briefless attorney, the saloon keeper, the manufacturer of carpets, the importer of dolls, the semi-successful novelist, the chorus girl, the little pawnbroker, the truck-gardener, the city policeman, the penniless pickpocket, the farmer with a two-thousand dollar farm, the sweated employer of sweatshop labor, the bricklayer with one thousand dollars in the bank, the life insurance general agent, the four-thousand dollar-a-year designer for a cloak factory, the buyer for a big department store, — take these, and determine in each case whether the man or woman belongs to the masses or to the classes. Anticipate, without further knowledge, how the man will "line up" for or against democratic institutions. Take the farmer alone. How big a farm or how big a mortgage puts a man in one group or the other?

We must apply our standards modestly. Only roughly and inaccurately can we determine in practice what elements in the population constitute the democratic masses, the impelling force of democracy. We cannot designate individuals, just as in statistics, though we can predict how many men and maids will marry next year, we cannot foretell whether John Doe or Jane Roe will marry. Any classification will involve millions of exceptions, and groups, favoring certain extensions of democracy, will be opposed to other extensions.

It is only when we attempt to apply the levels of democratic striving to our extremely differentiated population that we realize the vastness of the social spaces which separate groups which must be united in the bonds of solidarity. From the point of view of wealth the bulk of the democratic mass (bearing in mind the multitude of exceptions) do not stand either at the top or at the very bottom of Fortune's ladder. This mass excludes a majority of our business princes with dependents and hangers-on, as well as other men, who have no affiliation with the plutocracy other than a common lawlessness. The democratic mass also excludes a majority of men below the poverty line, the abjectly poor, who are also largely the defectives, dependents, delinquents, the illiterate, and the disfranchised. The democratic mass represents a residue of the population, after a majority of the very rich and of the abjectly poor have been drawn off. This residue seems to constitute or to be about to constitute a vast majority. If in the total absence of statistics or even of a statistical classification which would be applicable, we arbitrarily estimate at twenty millions the people who are debarred through excessive wealth or excessive poverty, ignorance, or political impotence from effectively willing a large measure of democratic reorganization, there would still remain of our ninety millions of people some seventy millions who may perhaps have the material, intellectual, and political means to strive for the attainment of a democratic civilization, and who have a perceivable interest in its achievement.

It is from the very conditions of the problem impossible to say just what proportion of these assumed seventy millions [1] are actively interested in democratic reform generally, or in any specific reform. For the most part, the active proponents or opponents of any change, industrial, political, or social, are extremely few, and the great mass simply have their thumbs up or down. Many are counted who have not decided, and many vote who do not know what the voting is about.

Nevertheless, bearing still in mind the multitude of exceptions, we may speak of a potentially democratic mass, which though possessed of common attributes (some earning power, some intellectual ability, and some power to affect elections), is still a highly heterogeneous group of groups. This mass probably includes a majority of farmers and of farm laborers, especially in the more prosperous sections of the country. It includes a majority of men and women in professional service (actors, architects, designers, artists, clergymen, dentists, electricians, engineers, lawyers, journalists, authors, government officials, physicians, surgeons, teachers, and professors). It includes the majority of skilled workmen in all trades and a large proportion of unskilled men, employed with reasonable regularity. It includes many specialized domestic servants. It includes the major-

[1] To avoid misunderstandings, I wish to disclaim any even approximate accuracy for this number, which depends naturally upon the interpretation given to inevitably loose terms. What I wish by the somewhat arbitrary figure to emphasize is the largeness and looseness of the groups to be appealed to in any fundamental democratic movement.

ity of men in all grades of the railroad service, except common laborers, and an unknown proportion of the latter. It includes a majority of merchants and dealers, retail and wholesale; a majority of agents and brokers, bookkeepers, accountants, clerks, and stenographers, and a doubtful proportion of hucksters and peddlers. In certain trades it includes a larger proportion of workers than in others. The proportion is larger in certain States, cities, or wards than in others. The whole mass is fluctuating, ill-defined, composite, heterogeneous. But it is precisely of this large, not exactly definable, section that we speak; a section which may include a prosperous Montana farmer, a Baltimore grocer, a Maine lumberjack, a San Francisco bricklayer, an Atlanta cotton factor, a Schenectady drill-hand, a saving Polish miner in Wilkes-Barre, a Negro lawyer in Philadelphia, a Jewish peddler in San Antonio, and an Irish or a German saloon keeper in New York. This composite, with thousands of subtypes, is the American common people, the fount of the confused American public opinion, the potentially directive force of American life.

But the question which presented itself at the beginning presents itself anew and with redoubled force. "Can these potentially democratic masses unite?" Will the Maine lumberjack, the Negro lawyer, the German saloon keeper, the Montana farmer — men of different race, religion, and language; of different political traditions, of different economic status, of different social outlook, — will these think alike and vote together? Can a group with widely diverse interests so compromise conflicting claims within the group as to unite an effective majority, and thus compel a permanent victory?

This task of compromising conflicting interests, and conflicting sentiments and outlooks, is the more difficult because of our manifold differences of race, color, language, religion, class, and local environment. America is the world's melting pot, but the melting is not over. Unification is not complete. The striking Hungarian coal miner, who is a white man, a Catholic, and an immigrant, hates a native, Protestant, Negro strikebreaker for a wide variety of reasons. The constitution and by-laws of one of our American trade-unions is printed in nineteen languages. In many of our cities the attempts to solve the allied problems of Sunday liquor-selling and of police corruption are frustrated by a deadlock of sentiment between two well-intentioned, but opposed, racial sections of the community. The Negro problem still overrides all other problems in the South, and many Southern democrats would look askance upon any project of democratic reform which seemed even remotely to threaten the political, industrial, or social supremacy of the white race. The creation of a democratic solidarity is halted by this multiplicity of cleavages.

In some respects the democratic masses are as much divided among themselves as are the distracted races of the Austro-Hungarian Empire, and the task of creating a solidarity and of formulating a democratic program without excessive internal friction is at times comparable in difficulty with the delicate statesmanship which holds together, in a tolerably successful union, Germans, Magyars, Bohemians, Slovaks, Poles, Ruthenians, Servians, Italians, Roumanians, and Croats. The democratic masses are not uniform *automata* with a *tabula rasa* for a brain, but men of the widest-varying prepossessions and the most divided allegiances. It is essential at all times to unite, in permanent bonds of union, a majority of these unlike-minded men.

In other respects Americans are more inclined to an ultimate solidarity than are the peoples of certain European lands. Our various languages, unlike those of Switzerland and of Austro-Hungary, tend to disappear in the all-absorbing English tongue. Our religious differences are not exacerbated by religious intolerance, and are mollified by a separation of state and church. We have no aristocratic traditions, and we were, until recently at least, what one might style a middle-class nation; a nation, the majority of which enjoyed an earning power and possessed an outlook upon life comparable to those of the middle classes of the leading European nations. While our color antagonism does not seem to abate, while the cleavage of classes maintains itself with the growth of ever larger factory populations, there are gradually discovered bases upon which a partial solidarity of the people may be erected.

No absolute solidarity, moreover, is necessary nor, for that matter, conceivable. We often hear the word solidarity used in a sense as absolute as that of the terms of physical science, and we might almost be led to believe that a class attains solidarity, as a liquid attains solidity, at a definite, predetermined social temperature. But solidarity, though the word is used so trippingly, is itself a distractingly complex conception. Whether or not men can unite depends upon the issue upon which they are supposed to unite. There is a certain broad religious solidarity among the Christians of the world, but among them are also the sharpest of religious cleavages. Our economic congregations are equally split up into sects. The class-consciousness of the socialists does not preserve them from internal conflicts over principles and policies; and as for the so-called class-conscious capitalists — their solidarity is that of Yahoos. The solidarity of trade-unionists, although indisputable, does not avert jurisdictional disputes. Solidarity strengthens as the group narrows, and weakens as the group widens. Solidarity strengthens as the issue narrows, and weakens as the issue widens. Solidarity is effected more easily for ideals than for the means to attain those ideals, more easily for the general goal than for the specific plan. Solidarity is not a thing constant and invariable. It is a resultant of attracting and repelling forces. It is a fluctuating quality depending upon fundamental causes and upon transient phenomena. Solidarity exists, and its existence is the vital fact of social life, but nowhere in the world is there an absolute solidarity, or an absolute lack of solidarity. Solidarity grows and declines, flows and ebbs, becomes greater and smaller. Solidarity is relative, not absolute.

Were the solidarity of the plutocracy greater than it is, that of the democracy would needs also be greater. In the matter of solidarity, the plutocracy has the dual advantage of being small and rich. Men unite more easily in a parlor than in an amphitheater, and money remains one of the most powerful of social cements. And yet the plutocracy is not, and never has been, a complete unit.

There are to-day cross-lines of interest in the plutocracy which make some of its constituent groups at most lukewarm adherents of rival groups. There is never a perfect "community of interest," never a final division of the field, never a stable equilibrium in our gigantic, dynamic national business. Controllers of hundreds of millions still fight with one another as two men may fight for a job. It was the mutual jealousy of two financial interests which let the cat out of the insurance bag, and stolen goods have more than once been returned by financial Titans who failed to get their share of the "swag." The plutocracy, like the democracy, is in process of becoming one. It is not yet one.

As wealth accumulates, moreover, a cleavage of sentiment widens between the men who are getting rich and the men who *are* rich. The old Cincinnati distinction between the "stick-'ems" (the actual pork-packers) and the rich "stuck-'ems" is to-day reflected in the difference between the retired millionaires of New York and the millionaires, in process or hope, of Cleveland, Portland, Los Angeles, or Denver. The gilt-edged millionaire bondholder of a standard railroad has only a partial sympathy with timber thieves, though his own fortune may have originated a few generations ago in railroad-wrecking or the slave and Jamaica rum trade; while the cultured descendants of cotton manufacturers resent the advent into their society of the man who has made his "pile" in the recent buying or selling of franchises. Once wealth is sanctified by hoary age — and in this mellowing process a score of years in America exceeds a cycle of Cathay — it tends to turn quite naturally against new and evil ways of wealth getting, the expedients of prospective social climbers. The old wealth is not a loyal ally in the battle for the plutocracy; it inclines, if not to democratic, at least to mildly reformatory, programs. The wealth of New York City — that final storage-house of certificates of ownership — trickles by the tens of millions into works of social progress. The "stuck-'ems" dull the edge of their animosity against democratic programs; the battle between the plutocracy and the democracy, which furiously rages in the cities where wealth is being actually fought for, becomes somewhat gentler in those cities where bodies of accumulated wealth exercise a moderating influence. Inheritance works in the same direction. Once wealth is separated from its original accumulator, it slackens its advocacy of its method of accumulation. The plutocracy ceases to be a unit in defense.[1]

Nor is the democracy, though many-minded, absolutely

[1] When we consider not groups but individuals, the solidarity of the plutocracy is even less perfect. In the broadest sense of the word, the recruiting ground of the democratic army is the entire population. No man is too rich or too poor, too good or too bad, to be absolutely and forever immune from this moral conscription. Although the main body of the democratic army comes (and will doubtless continue to come) from men intelligent enough to perceive their benefit (either as members of their group or as members of society) from proposed democratic changes, still there are always thousands of men and women who, though they profit by present inequalities and maladjustments, are opposed to their continuance. Ultra-wealthy men, taken to our financial mountain tops and shown the kingdoms of the world, cannot always be bribed to silence or connivance, however large their share of the social surplus. Occasionally a rich young man sells all that he has and becomes an agitator.

without unity. The various democratic groups have two chief elements of solidarity: a common antagonism to the plutocracy, and a common interest in the social surplus.

In intercourse among social groups, as in intercourse among men, a common antagonism may be the beginning of a mutual understanding. Groups repelling the same group tend to attract each other.

The plutocracy is the chief objective of our social agitation. It, and it alone, unites in opposition factory workers, farmers, shopkeepers, professional men. The plutocracy creates between the few and the many a cleavage which for the time being obscures all other divisions.[1]

Not all our antagonism to the plutocracy is based upon an intelligent study of causes. Much of it is merely an instinctive anger, not free from considerations on a low plane. Much is exaggerated, wrong-headed, puerile, even insincere. Envy, hatred, and uncharitableness walk arm in arm with a flaming altruism. Our antipathy is a curious compound of good and evil motives, of wisdom and ignorance. But society is not squeamish in its selection of methods; and as for wisdom, social groups, like individuals, allege the most foolish of reasons for the sanest of actions.

The most curious factor in this antagonism is that an increasing bitterness is felt by a majority which is not worse but better off than before. This majority suffers not an absolute decline but a relatively slower growth. It objects that the plutocracy grows too fast; that in growing so rapidly it squeezes its growing neighbors. Growth is right and proper, but there is, it is alleged, a rate of growth which is positively immoral.[2]

[1] There would to-day be a sharper antagonism between country and city over the prices of meat but for the Meat Trust, which, not unprofitably, acts as a buffer.

[2] This attitude of the people is not unlike that of Bill Lizard in "Alice in Wonderland."

It is urged against the plutocracy that, because of its growth, it subjects an increasing number of people to a pressure to which they are becoming increasingly sensitive.

This pressure is not for the most part the pang of hunger. Our society is too well padded for that. It is a subtler pressure on a higher economic plane. In the plutocratic edifice the ceiling is too low for the growing people.

To a considerable extent the plutocracy is hated not for what it does, but for what it is. Though there have been enough well-attested cases of tax-dodging, bribing, franchise-grabbing, and other sins of great corporations, the popular antagonism lies deeper than a condemnation of individual offenses. More and more the growing opposition attaches itself to "good" as well as "bad trusts," to the system which produces trusts, and to the conditions which produce the system, rather than to the men, good and bad, who are more or less fortuitously the representatives of the trust. After all, though some of our wisest political moralists proclaim that "sin is always personal," there exist, in many industries, conditions (hitherto permitted by us) which force men in certain positions either to sin or to surrender their places to men who will. In such cases it is the system that sins, or it is we who sin, rather than the individual who has been bribed by a high salary to risk a jail sentence. The American people are looking beyond the titular offender in the search for a greater anonymous culprit.

From a more personal point of view, it is the mere existence of a plutocracy, the mere "being" of our wealthy contemporaries, that is the main offense. Our over-moneyed neighbors cause a relative deflation of our personalities. Of course, in the consumption of wealth, as in its production, there exist "non-competitive groups," and a two-thousand-dollar-a-year man need not spend like a Gould or a Guggenheim. Everywhere, however, we meet the millionaire's good and evil works, and we seem to resent the one as much as the other. Our jogging horses are passed by their high-power automobiles. We are obliged to take their dust.[1]

By setting the pace for a frantic competitive consumption, our infinite gradations in wealth (with which gradations the plutocracy is inevitably associated) increase the general social friction and produce an acute social irritation. There was ostentatious spending before the plutocratic period, as there will be after, for display is an inveterate form of individuation, older than humanity. Our plutocracy, however, intent upon socially isolating itself and possessing no title to precedence other than the visible possession of money, makes of this competitive consumption a perennial handicap-race of spenders. We are developing new types of destitutes — the automobileless, the yachtless, the Newport-cottageless. The subtlest of luxuries become necessities, and their loss is bitterly resented. The discontent of to-day reaches very high in the social scale.

This competitive consumption is so graduated that it reaches down from group to group, and does much to decivilize our whole society. Not only do multimillionaires "buy away" the best commodities and services in the market (from January strawberries to French *chauffeurs*); not only do they, with their high tips and loose purses, "spoil Europe" (for groups, which are trying to "spoil Europe" for other groups, and so *ad infinitum*), but they start up similar, if more modest, ostentations on the social planes below. Everywhere people are buying articles which have the sole merit of being inimitable — but which are nevertheless imitated. Everywhere there is a war between "the observed" and "the observers," a war as ceaseless and as costly as that between

[1] The automobile, although in process of democratization, seems in a curious way typical of our plutocracy. This is perhaps because of its speed, power, noise, and dust; its clumsy ease, its shrieking modernity, its essential practicality, its calm assumption of the middle of the road.

armor plate and ordnance.[1] Extravagance becomes a cult; reasoned expenditure, an oddity; and industries thrive in useless ways, while the nation wastes more in a contest of spenders than would pay for the proper education of millions of Americans. The end of it all is vexation of spirit. The sheer juxtaposition of overdressed and underclad, of elegant and genteelly shabby, give to envy, emptiness, and a merely comparative poverty the force of a revolutionary impulse.

The plutocracy is called to account for many evil or uncomfortable conditions which might more fairly be attributed to our increasing population, our greater social density, and our more tightly interwoven industry. But the plutocracy — not without a certain show of right — is held to blame. The plutocracy is an expanding force against which we strike. It is a social obstacle which cannot but be hated by men who have been used only to natural obstacles. Moreover, the plutocracy is held responsible for our economic qualms, because it is the visibly directive force of society. It cannot escape the liability of leadership.

For this reason the plutocracy is charged with having ended our old-time equality. In actual fact we always had less equality than we now like to believe, and, in any case, the plutocracy is itself but the result of an economic evolution which independently produced our present inequalities. Our industrial development (of which the trust is but one phase) has been towards a sharpening of the angle of progression. Our eminences have become higher and more dazzling; the goal has been raised and narrowed. Although lawyers, doctors, engineers, architects, and professional men generally, make larger salaries than ever

[1] It was less a paradox than a social dissection when an American wit praised a certain New York hotel because it gave "exclusiveness" to the masses.

before, the earning of one hundred thousand dollars a year by one lawyer impoverishes by comparison the thousands of lawyers who scrape along on a thousand a year. The widening of the competitive field has widened the variation and has sharpened the contrast between success and failure, with a resulting inequality and discontent.

Americans have never worshiped a rigid equality of wealth. They have always been willing to condone any inequality which was measurable, which could be overcome in a lifetime, which represented, or might represent, superior attainments of the wealthier. But present inequalities differ so widely in degree from our old inequalities as to differ in kind. The rich are so rich that they can hardly help growing richer. A multimillionaire may be dissipated, lazy, imbecile, spendthrift, and yet automatically he gains more in a month than the average man earns in a lifetime. The very wealthy, irrespective of brains or manners, are sought out in business and social intercourse. They are able to grant favors, to wreak vengeance, to compel the adherence of other men They can even afford to have their crimes committed for them.

The forces which give rise to the plutocracy also give rise to a certain circumscription of industrial opportunity. The enterprising, individualistic American resents his inability to go into the steel or oil business "for himself," even though he may be better off as an employee of the Steel Corporation or the Standard Oil Company. Tradesmen attribute all their economic ills to department stores, mail-order houses, and big trusts. The small retailer is perhaps less injured by the competition of department stores than by the natural overcrowding of his business. If the United Cigar Stores were to retire from the retail tobacco business, their place would be immediately taken by thousands of new competitors, and the average cigar dealer would be but little better off, except as to his chance of ultimately going to the top. The retail tobacconist has suffered a reduction less in income than in outlook. His horizon has been narrowed. He may have as much money in the cash drawer, but he is poorer in hopes. The resulting discontent is leveled against the plutocracy, the visible beneficiary of the economic trend.

Thus the plutocracy is more and more opposed by an ever larger number of social groups and individuals, not only for what it does and for what it is, but for the deeper economic tendencies which it represents. Different men are arrayed against the plutocracy for different reasons. While, however, such common hostility is a sufficient stimulus to an aggressive campaign, it is not a basis broad enough for a constructive program. Unless the opponents of the plutocracy have some common positive aim, their antagonism will dissipate itself in abortive assaults and waste heat, without permanent influence upon social conditions.

There exists, however, such a common aim. This aim, which holds together the opponents of an intrenched plutocracy, is the attainment of a common share in the conquered continent, in the material and moral accumulations of a century. When the trust raises prices, obtains valuable franchises or public lands, escapes taxation, secures bounties, lowers wages, evades factory laws, or makes other profitable maneuvers, it is diverting a part of the social surplus from the general community to itself. The public pays the higher prices, loses the franchises or lands, pays higher taxes, suffers in wages (and pays for the ill effects of low wages), and generally makes up dollar for dollar for all such gains. In all these things the people have a perceivable interest. The great mass is injured in its capacity of wage earner, salary earner, taxpayer and consumer.

Of these capacities that of the consumer is the most universal, since even those who do not earn wages or pay direct taxes consume commodities. In America to-day the unifying economic force, about which a majority, hostile to the plutocracy, is forming, is the common interest of the citizen as a consumer of wealth, and incidentally as an owner of (undivided) national possessions. The producer (who is only the consumer in another rôle) is highly differentiated. He is banker, lawyer, soldier, tailor, farmer, shoeblack, messenger boy. He is capitalist, workman, money lender, money borrower, urban worker, rural worker. The consumer, on the other hand, is undifferentiated. All men, women, and children who buy shoes (except only the shoe manufacturer) are interested in cheap good shoes. The consumers of most articles are overwhelmingly superior in numbers to the producers.

Despite this overwhelming superiority in numbers, the consumer, finding it difficult to organize, has often been worsted in industrial battles. In our century-long tariff contests, a million inaudible consumers have often counted less than has a petty industry in a remote district. The consumer thought of himself as a producer, and he united only with men of his own productive group. For a time there was a certain reason for such an alignment. It was a period of falling prices, of severe competition, in which the whole organization of industry favored the consumer. In fact, the unorganized and ruthless consumer was blamed — and rightly blamed (as he is still rightly blamed to-day) — for many of the evils of industry. The curse of the sweatshop and of the starving seamstress, sewing by candlelight, was fairly brought to the doors of the bargain-hunting housewife. The consumer, though acting singly, felt himself secure.

Even when prices began to rise, consumers remained quiescent. There was greater difficulty in resisting price advances, because the loss to each individual from each increase was so infinitesimal. The reverse of the overwhelming numbers of the consumers was the small individual interest of each in each transaction. Wages affected a man far more sensibly than did prices. If a motorman's wages were reduced one cent an hour he might lose thirty dollars a year; a rise of ten cents in the price of shoes, on the other hand, meant a loss of, at most, two dollars a year. A man could not spend his lifetime fighting ten-cent-increases. The cure for high prices was high wages.

As prices continue to rise, however, as a result (among other causes [1]) of our gradually entering into a monopoly period, a new insistence is laid upon the rights of the consumer, and political unity is based upon him. Where formerly production seemed to be the sole governing economic fact of a man's life, to-day many producers have no direct interest in their product. It is a very attenuated interest which the Polish slag-worker has in the duty on steel billets, but the Polish slag-worker and the Boston salesgirl and the Oshkosh lawyer have a similar interest (and a common cause of discontent) as consumers of the national wealth. The universality of the rise of prices has begun to affect the consumer as though he were attacked by a million gnats. The chief offense of the trust becomes its capacity to injure the consumer. Therefore the consumer, disinterred from his grave, reappears in the political arena as the "common man," the "plain people," the "strap-hanger," "the man on the street," "the taxpayer," the "ultimate consumer." [2] Men who voted as producers are now voting as consumers.

[1] Among these other causes are the increasing pressure of our population upon our available natural resources, the increased cheapness of gold and, in individual cases, a better quality of goods, a more frequent and quicker delivery under more difficult conditions, and generally a better service required by more exigent consumers.

[2] It is significant that none of these phrases gives any inkling as to the man's trade, calling, or position in the world of production, whether farmer or factory hand, employer or employed.

We are now beginning to appeal to the "ultimate consumer," the man who actually eats, wears, or uses the article. A generation ago we legislated for the penultimate shopkeeper, or the ante-penultimate manufacturer. Our contest for railroad rate regulation was formerly waged in the interest of the producer or shipper, and not primarily in the interest of the consumer. The rates in question were freight, not passenger, rates,[1] and the great problem was not so much low freight rates (which more immediately benefited the consumer) as equal freight rates, in which the competing manufacturer was primarily interested.[2]

It is difficult for the consumer to act industrially in concert. The "rent strikes" on the East Side of New York have always been unsuccessful. The meat strikes have been equally without result. The work of the Consumers' Leagues has been chiefly a humanitarian labor for the benefit of producers, and we have never successfully developed in America great coöperative associations of workingmen consumers, like those of England, Belgium, France, and Germany. The appeal to the consumer has therefore been made on the political field.

To-day the consumer is represented on party platforms. It is in his interest that a "tariff revision downward" is demanded. Where one formerly heard in tariff discussions of the necessity of protecting the workingman from "the pauper labor of Europe," one now hears of the rights of the "ultimate consumer." Where, in discussions of land policy, one formerly heard of the need of giving the land to the actual settler (or producer), one now hears of pre-

[1] Passenger rates are usually paid immediately by the "ultimate consumer"; the freight rate is paid, in the first instance, by the manufacturer or shipper.

[2] Similarly, in the England of 1846, cheap corn was secured not primarily in the interests of the people who ate the corn, but in that of the manufacturers who paid the wages that bought the corn. The lowered price of bread meant simply a lower cost of manufacturing cottons and woolens.

venting trusts from monopolizing mines, forests, and water sites, and thus raising the prices (to the consumer) of coal, wood, light, heat, and power. Our municipal ownership is in the interest of joint consumers, and more and more our railroad regulation is aiming at cheaper transportation.

To secure their rights as consumers, as well as to secure other economic interests, less in common, the people unite as citizens to obtain a sensitive popular government. They attain to a certain political as well as economic solidarity. This solidarity is by no means a complete unification of interest. There remain differences in agreement and discords in harmony. The middle classes are as much opposed to the trade-union as are the trusts, and the professional man is as anxious to secure a docile and cheap housemaid as the farmer is desirous of getting high prices for his wheat and paying low wages to his farm laborer.

The elements of solidarity, however, being found in a common hostility to the plutocracy and a common interest in the social surplus, it becomes possible gradually so to compromise conflicting interests within the group as to secure a united front against a common enemy. The regulation of railroads in the interest of consumer and farmer may be extended to the protection of the railroad worker; the conservation of natural resources may be linked to a similar policy of human conservation, to a campaign against destitution, and to a progressive labor policy which will insure the health, safety, comfort, and leisure of all workers. By such internal adjustments within the wide democratic army the possibility of a sufficient, permanent solidarity is given.

There is no evidence that the great army of potential democrats agree upon a clear-cut policy with regard to the solution of our economic problems. There is no reason to believe that they will ever agree in detail. But in various tentative and semiconscious ways they have already begun, through political organizations, non-political organizations, and through expressions of public opinion, to unite in formulating progressive plans. This coalescence is expressed in many ways, by a vote, by a storm of newspaper criticism, by the popularity of a democratic leader. This solidarity in formation does not express itself always on the same subject, nor does it always express itself consistently, but gradually it approves, one after another, a series of projects which, pieced together, constitute a democratic program. The fact that democracy, in so far as it has been hitherto approximated in America, has been attained not at one stroke, nor by one policy, but by a series of gradual and not always logical approaches, makes it appear possible that out of the great inchoate democratic mass of the community, with enlistments from below and with defections to the class above, will come the motive force to revolutionize society, to displace our present duality of resplendent plutocracy and crude ineffective democracy with a single, broad, intelligent, socialized, and victorious democracy.

CHAPTER XVI

THE TACTICS OF THE DEMOCRACY

THREE primary factors determine in the main the tactics and methods of the American democracy. The first of these factors is the complex of traditions, descended to us from the pioneer period. The second is our growing social surplus. The third is the wide diversity among the groups striving for democracy.

Because of our American traditions, our democrats are more likely to proceed in a tentative, experimental, and rather illogical way; to sail forward by tacking; to break as little and as gradually as possible with our ingrained individualism. Americans are not abstract, uncompromising thinkers. They are not like the men of the French Revolution, who would have dared to abolish the universe and recreate it on the morrow. We shall probably seek our salvation, to the limited extent still possible, outside of the state, and we shall doubtless "try out" governmental novelties in a few Western commonwealths (our political experiment stations) before applying them in the grand manner to the whole nation. Because of our traditions, we are likely to make changes by indirection and to preserve the form while altering the substance.

Our wealth, actual and potential, reënforces these tendencies. We live in a civilization where political animosities are not exacerbated by the actual hunger of the main bodies of contestants. The struggle is not less intense (just as prize fighting is not less intense because gloves have taken the place of bare knuckles), but the improved, and above all the improvable, economic status of the masses, tends to make their action more confident, compromising, and pacific. Our economic development, by giving some little wealth to so large a majority, binds over all parties to keep the peace. It exacts hostages to social order. It removes the incitement to the worst forms of social recklessness. Without recklessness, because not without hope, with a status to be bettered and with political rights with which to better it, the people, growing in power and discontent, can move forward gradually and quietly against the intrenchments of the plutocracy.

The many-sidedness of the democratic masses exerts an identical influence. A movement backed up by a majority of the voters is far more likely to proceed along constitutional and legal lines (making its constitutions and laws as it goes) than would be a movement backed up only by the industrial wageworkers without property, and opposed by all other elements of the population. Such a majority, composed of diverse groups with varying interests, is more indirect, conciliatory, compromising, and evolutionary in action than would be a single homogeneous class, with clear-cut class interests.

As a result of all these causes, our democracy will probably not need to resort to violence, and our democratic transformations may be carried through without the taking of lives or the wholesale confiscation of property.

In all conflicts involving even the possibility of change in the social center of gravity, physical force still threatens to play its part. The state, resting on soldiers and policemen, themselves resting (in democratic communities) on the acquiescence of the people, itself embodies this element of force, which is used legally when the murderer is "hanged by the neck until he is dead," or illegally when soldiers are quartered upon a peaceful population, or policemen violently break up strikes under cover of preventing violence. In America an extra-legal physical force has often been appealed to. The North forcibly nullified the Fugitive Slave Law, as the South subsequently nullified the Fourteenth and Fifteenth Amendments. To-day lynching and other mobs set the law at naught. The greater the political corruption and the larger the rewards of violence, the more frequent is the appeal to force.

Fortunately, in all advanced nations the rule of brute force in the fixing of the balance of power is diminishing. As conditions become more settled, the physical force of the state becomes so superior to that of any group (not a majority) within the state as to render revolt on the plane of mere violence impracticable.

In well-organized states the day of sporadic uprisings, of impromptu revolutions, is probably over. The modern organization of warfare favors the *status quo*. Effective arms have become too costly and too difficult of concealment to be held by the unorganized people. Barricades are built of cobbles; the modern streets are built of asphalt. To-day the deadly, state-owned cannon would sweep through the wide, straight, unobstructed avenues, as the old cannon could not through the narrow, crooked, barricaded lanes of the olden city. The organized powers in the community hold the railroad, telegraph, and telephone. The state fights on inside lines. It can concentrate all loyal forces against a disaffected minority. It can mobilize millions in the briefest time.

It is becoming recognized, also, that violence is a clumsy, two-edged sword, which ultimately destroys him who wields it. A social group, compelled to use force against other sections of the community, finds itself a prey to the most violent of its own members. Violence is not constructive. It is ugly. It alienates supporters and unites opponents, for, after all, civilization, with all its residual brutality, is squeamish about the sight of blood. Finally, we are coming into an intellectual, statistical age, where men know beforehand when they are beaten; where potential force, or the show of force, takes the place of force itself. Physical force remains always in the background as the ultimate determinant — as the weapon which must be used when votes and ideas fail, when a people without rights are opposed, as in Russia to-day, by a clique without vision, conscience, or humanity. In civilized communities, however, and especially in communities already advancing in democracy, force becomes of less immediate moment.

Our national wealth, present and prospective, is our chief guarantee that the social problem will not needs be resolved by a thrust of the sword. The richer the community, the greater is the cost of internal strife, and the more futile any policy which drives men to arms. The vastness of the wealth to be conserved makes even our revolutionaries somewhat conservative, for there is small wisdom in laying waste a city in which the victors must forevermore dwell. The victorious socialists of Milwaukee, but recently dreaded as iconoclasts, turn out to be constructive, conciliatory, Chesterfieldian, and enormously effective. Our most possessing classes are equally afraid of violence, not because it is likely to be successful, but because of the damage which would be inflicted before the bull could be driven from the china shop. They are therefore willing (as they are also able) to insure against the utter recklessness of misery by allaying the worst evils of poverty; just as the democratic masses are willing (and able) to refrain from recklessness because of the counter-recklessness which it would provoke, and because of the injury to their ultimate possessions which it would inflict.

In America we can for the time being lay this specter of violence. What might happen if certain nation-debasing tendencies, now at work, were to overcome counteracting forces, what might happen if misery and oppression grew with the growth of wealth, is another question. For the day it is easier to vote and easier to get your vote counted than it is to fight, and curative forces are leading away from the sharp antagonism which would involve an appeal to naked force. To-day, when our soldiers under arms represent less than one per thousand of the population, when our militia are loosely and not undemocratically organized, our broader democratic movements will in all probability neither rely upon force nor be resisted by force.[1]

Not only is it probable (though not certain) that our democratic progress will be unaccompanied by a clash of armed men but the process is also more likely, because of our accumulated wealth, to be a social upbuilding from within rather than a demolition with a subsequent reconstruction. It is common to-day to see a vast railway station completely rebuilt, while, simultaneously, the traffic is carried on. So necessary is continuity when enormous interests are involved, that change, destruction, rebuilding do not interfere with the ordinary conduct of the business. Our social revolution must be consummated with a minimum of shock to our delicate industrial, political, and social machinery. Moreover, all progress must be built upon the foundations of our stored wealth. Just as the Christian churches were fashioned of the marble of pagan temples, so our new world must be built upon the accumulations of the past. Our social reconstruction must be effected during business hours. It must be ac-

[1] The above statement is, of course, only general, and is perfectly consistent with instances in the past and the future, of the use of force by strikers, by employers, and by the State or nation in the interest of employers. In Colorado the conflict between mine owners and mine laborers resulted in bribery, intimidation, assassination, and a state of affairs which might be likened to a labor war. There have been numerous instances of the use of police, armed detectives, private constabulary, the militia, and the federal troops, against strikers. It is probable, however, that the number of men killed and injured during all the labor conflicts since the Civil War is very much less than the number killed or maimed every six months in the ordinary legally murderous course of industry.

companied by preliminary plans, specifications, and estimates of cost. It must be gradual and quiet, though rapid.

Nor is it inevitable that the progress of democracy will involve a wholesale confiscation of the property of the rich. Where wealth is growing at a rapid rate, the multitude may be fed without breaking into the rich man's granary; the lowly may be exalted without a pecuniary abasement of those of high degree.

In the early days of poverty all conflicts meant the taking of some men's property by others. War was a business for profit, as were slave-raiding and piracy. The army lived on the spoils of the enemy or the lands of the people which it defended. A palace revolution, an attainder for treason, even a national struggle for religious supremacy, were influenced by the desire to secure the property of individuals or classes. A revolution faced the necessity of paying its way at the expense of the defeated.

To-day the rapid growth of the national wealth has cut the bond between social progress and confiscation. Our hope of a greater national wealth is a promise that we may enrich the whole population without impoverishing any one. Compared to the stupendous totals of our coming accumulations, the cost of progress is small. Had we in 1861 paid dollar for dollar for the slaves, we could within a decade have easily extinguished the resulting debt. If in 1880 New York City had bought a few hundred square miles of territory in her vicinity, or had Pennsylvania bought her coal mines, or Minnesota her ore beds, the operation would have redounded so enormously to the public benefit as to have rendered the alternative of confiscation unthinkable. If to-day the nation were to buy up its railroads and run them efficiently, the mere accretion in value during the next generation or two would make the purchase so profitable that the collective people could well afford to pay a fair price. So, generally, the stupendous present values of monoplies, which the nation may in the near future be compelled to take over, will seem ridiculously small fifty or a hundred years hence. What Belgium, Portugal, Italy, or Hungary,—nations with a lesser and a less sure future,—cannot afford to do, America is abundantly able to accomplish. The growing wealth of America is sufficient to permit our social transformations being carried through with a minimum of disappointment to the more moderate anticipations even of monopolists.

Social appropriation without confiscation, however, involves a transformation much less likely to be violently resisted and much more likely to be actively welcomed. The social surplus thus makes for social peace. In the last analysis, the wars of all the ages have been wars of poverty. The dream of peace between nations, and of peace within nations, did not flourish until society had the prospect of enough to go around.

Only to a certain extent is the evolution of democracy in America a social conflict. Partly this democracy will come automatically through growth and enlightenment; partly it will be willingly conceded; partly it will be contested inch by inch. Where the road to democracy runs through the wide fields of social harmony — those fertile fields where practically all social groups may be educated to acknowledge identical interests — no fighting is necessary. Only where the progress is one in which the gain of the democracy is the loss of a privileged, powerful class must there result a conflict, allayed by successive compromises, but ultimately fought out to a conclusion.

These three elements of democratic progress, conflict, growth, and education are not always separate, even in thought. Fighting may involve growth. On the other hand, a relatively more rapid growth and a consequent physical crowding out of rivals is one form of conflict between social groups, as between plants, animals, and nations. Japan had to defeat Russia in order to grow large enough in Korea to resist Russia. The United States, had she not bought Florida in 1819, would in the course of a century have so overgrown the sparse Spanish settlements as to have made a continuance of Spanish domination in that peninsula unthinkable. The overwhelming at the polls of obstructive forces is an instance of democratic progress through conflict, as are also industrial concessions extorted through strikes. On the other hand, we grow into democracy or are educated into democracy through uncontested victories, through sheer technical progresses, improved political and industrial education, through an increased capacity for combined activity, through an enlarged social consciousness, through a widened social outlook. The mere expansion of the trade-union movement in England, Germany, and America; the growth of the socialist party in Germany; the spread of the coöperative movement in Belgium; the popularization of education in the United States; the development in America of a spirit of insurgency against respectable and bepraised evils, are all steps toward the attainment of democracy, independently of the actual use of such movements in eventual social conflicts.

In a certain sense, these conflicts themselves constitute less a class struggle than a national adjustment. In this adjustment the mutual attractions and repulsions of social groups play their part, but so great is the potential overweight of the democratic mass — once a strong solidarity is achieved — that victory depends not on the people's ability to fight, but on their capacity to unite. What hampers the democracy is not the actual, visible power of an intrenched plutocracy, but the lack of an intellectual perception to unite divergent classes; the lack of an emotional appeal to overcome the divisive forces within the majority itself. The democracy is halted by its fear that it cannot run its own business; by its very own conservatism. It is this inherent, though curable, timorousness, this social paralysis, as well as a tendency to split up into its constituent groups, rather than any outside constraining force, which in the past has delayed our democratic progress and has confined us to the ruts of a traditional thinking and voting.

The internal adjustment of the democracy is a process of uniting groups, by no means agreed in the details of what constitutes progress. We have "semidemocrats," with "leanings" or tendencies toward certain democratic reforms, but opposed to others. For this reason (and it is an outstanding reason) we are forced to content ourselves with half-reforms, especially when the half-successes are the earnest of further successes. Men opposed to the regulation of corporations will support ballot reform and direct primaries, and men who would bitterly fight a progressive income tax will support a corporation law. All these "semidemocrats" are utilized by the advancing democratic movement. Democracy hitches on behind even when the wagon does not go the whole way.

The democracy proceeds along a middle path, which is the line of least resistance. It uses broad phrases, vague enough to attract by different hopes men who are dissatisfied with only the details of our national economy, as well as those who wish a basic change in business and politics. The democracy, seeking ever to appeal to a majority, recasts its doctrines to attain that majority. It does not favor confiscation, because its own majority has property.[1] But it *does* attack "swollen" fortunes (which belong to the minority), as it attacks the monopoly which

[1] There is, of course, no clear boundary line to confiscation, and it is a matter of degree and opinion where taxation, reasonable regulation, or fair payment end and confiscation begins. Our courts have been wholly unable to give any logical and universally applicable definition of confiscation.

leads to them, the "special privilege" which increases them, the unequal, or evaded, taxation which conserves them, and the business secrecy and business oligarchy which make them perpetual. The democracy does not permit the issue to become one between the propertied and the unpropertied, but distinguishes between property and privilege, between earned, and unearned, increment; between legitimate investment and promoters' profits.

By taking this line of least resistance, the democracy finds allies where a more uncompromising group would find enemies. Men who are dependent on an industry, workmen and stockholders alike, do not necessarily desire an autocratic rule within the industry. The policyholders of the great insurance companies — the real investors — are benefited, not injured, by an effective governmental control. In the same spirit the democracy stops short, at least temporarily, of doing more than the immediately necessary. The government regulates interstate railroad traffic and other businesses affected with a public interest, and, as the need becomes apparent, control by the nation becomes more complete. But the democracy is not so impracticable as to wish to regulate the tillage of the independent farmer, the hours of labor of the doctor or lawyer, the capitalization and profits of the corner grocery store. The goal of the democracy is a maximum of control with a minimum of regulation.

In other words, the democracy, not being slavishly bound to logic, would rather be successful than thorough. It does not tear up root and branch, but merely weeds out roughly, for social, like natural, evolution permits the survival of harmless rudiments. Just as the vestige of a prehuman tail survives in the human coccyx, so we have, and always will have, a social coccyx, a social vermiform appendix, and other reminders of a lower past. America will always be a jumble of old and new, of "Yankee notions" in government and business and the political junk of the seventeenth and eighteenth centuries. We need not immediately slough off social beliefs and institutions when they cease to be visibly useful, just as we may still speak of Thursday after ceasing to believe in the great god Thor.[1]

In its gradual and progressive adjustment, the compromising and conciliatory democracy enjoys the advantage of being opposed by a cautious plutocracy. Just as the most dangerous fencer is the novice whose feints and sallies are unpredictable, so the most dangerous social opponent is the class driven by ignorance and cowardice into the most desperate ventures.

Though the plutocracy is cautious and comfortable, it often acts the rôle of a hard-driven, desperate antagonist. The road to democracy is scarred with "last ditches." As the people advance, the receding plutocracy cries frantically, "Thus far shalt thou go and no farther," and occasionally when a particularly inexcusable attempt is made to subordinate the national business to the nation, the plutocracy, in the outraged dignity of a tragedy queen, cries out aloud, "Another step forward, and I die." In reality, the plutocracy never dies. The railroads do not cease running; the refineries do not cease refining; the public service corporation, "swearing she will ne'er consent," consents. If the railroads were to close up shop, they would take the bread and butter from the mouths of millions of American citizens. It would be a terrible example. But to whom?

The democracy in the course of its instructive victories and its equally instructive defeats learns that the surest

[1] The metempsychosis of kings from arrogant tyrants to domesticated national pets and, incidentally, democratic advisers, illustrates how skillfully a democracy can adapt an old form to a new end. A Henry the Seventh, a James the Second, even a George the Third, would be an unthinkable anachronism in the England of to-day, but a George the Fifth is a national asset, as the Lord Mayor or the Tower of London is an asset.

method of progress is to take one step after another. The first step, often uncontested (*because* it is only one step), leads inevitably to others. Democratic progress is successive, not simultaneous.

The steps once taken are progressively easy. For example, the retention and exploitation by the federal government of the resources of Alaska would disappoint only a small number of prospective millionaires, while it would not only give the government an immensely increased wealth, but might serve as an opening wedge for other wide-branching programs of reform. If the billions of potential wealth in Alaska were to be devoted — let us say — to the subsidy of our national education, we should be a wiser nation thirty years hence. So, a purely "voluntary" federal incorporation law would doubtless lead to an efficient *compulsory* incorporation law which would eventually insure a control over the most recondite operations of all great corporations. A minimum tax on inheritances contains the germ of a definite prohibition of insanely large accumulations. A merely nominal tax upon our coal reserves involves eventually the end of the forestalling of our natural resources. There are mineral lands worth, to-day, a few hundreds of millions, which fifty or a hundred years hence will be worth billions of dollars. If the nation could approach the owners of these lands with the sword of a gentle tax in the one hand and the olive branch of a fair purchase price in the other, there would soon be no fear of any monopoly of our mineral resources.

As the government can unobtrusively enter the tent of business, so the people without proclamations or fireworks can enter into control of the state. The time will come when the Constitution will be made easily amendable by the people. Until this is accomplished, however, the simplest way, whenever an alteration of the Constitution is essential to progress, is to persuade the people, who elect the President and the Senators, who choose the Supreme Court judges, that the proposed change is in the public interest, and therefore is in harmony with the putative intent of the framers of the document. If in the full swing and current of a victorious democratic movement a majority of judges, imbued with popular ideas, would interpret a single clause of the Constitution in a sense often contended for, but never as yet accepted by the courts, the door would be opened to a complete democratization of our whole political and economic system.[1] Political, like economic, reforms lead the way to others of the same kind. A voluntary and partial regulation of party primaries leads within a few years to a compulsory and state-wide direct primary. A restricted application of the principle of referendum and initiative leads to its universal and unrestricted adoption. Extra-legal arrangements, such as the direct election of United States Senators, completely alter our fundamental constitutional system, without touching the Constitution. It is progress step by step. It is progress by indirection. It is a successful flank movement, instead of a brave, but suicidal, frontal attack.

[1] The clause consists of the italicized words in the following sentence from the eighth section of the first article. "Congress shall have power: To lay and collect taxes, duties, imposts, and excises, *to pay the debts and provide for the common defense and general welfare of the United States.*" The courts have always interpreted these final words, not as an independent grant of power, but as a statement of purposes for the levying of taxes, and, as such, a condition or limitation of the grant, "to lay and collect taxes," etc. But the courts have, before this, changed their interpretations and forced new meanings upon old words. The grant to Congress of the right to "provide for the common defense and general welfare of the United States," coupled with the right "to make all laws which shall be necessary and proper for carrying into execution the foregoing powers," would wipe away practically all restrictions upon our federal legislative bodies. It is not here contended that such a judicial decision would be entirely desirable in the present state of public opinion and political capacity, but in the years to come, either this or some other interpretation having a similar broadening effect is more probable than is the attainment of the same end by direct amendments to the Constitution under our present system of amending.

By such indirect means, which, after all, are the means naturally adopted by the people, even a revolution may be "safe, sane, and conservative." We may change the very bases of our government, law, and business; we may jump the hurdles of the Constitution, and may circumvent the obstacles of a mass of antiquated judicial decisions, while walking along the paths of legality and constitutionalism, and abjuring all get-there-quick methods and all violent conflicts with our historic past. A wound, to kill a man, need not be "so deep as a well, nor so wide as a church door"; a pin thrust at the right spot will serve. So, if we are to end a long list of industrial and political evils, we need not attack property, which is to attack the majority. We need not evoke a class war, which is a war of the weak against the strong. We need not take all the unearned increment, which we may find in our own farms and in our own single shares of stock. We need not cure everything at once. We may take step by step, as the chance presents itself.

In the working out of such a policy of successive actions and of well-considered delays, time and technical progress often work on the side of the democracy. When electricity supplanted horses on the street cars, the cities, aided by the States, had an opportunity of practically retaking their old franchises by refusing to permit to the old lines the use of the new traction, while at the same time offering the companies a fair price for their rusty rails. So, to-day, when the rights of way into the center of cities have given certain railroads an enormous monopoly value,[1] a new opportunity is afforded to the city, State, or nation to secure an underground entrance for new railroads run under the city streets. In every generation our inventors discover a virgin continent, and the new vast resources,

[1] For example, the New York Central's route into New York, the Pennsylvania's into Philadelphia, and the Illinois Central's into Chicago.

thus thrown into the public's lap, may be utilized, wasted, or monopolized. Usually they are wasted or given to favorites. The occasional sparks of social prevision shine out in a black infinity of utter governmental thriftlessness "like a good deed in a naughty world." But we are slowly learning. In the future we shall better know how to lay our corporate hands upon the things which science and invention throw our way.

Our progress, though gradual, must be rapid. We dare not make a virtue of slowness, nor exalt the snail as the only true reformer. Just as they who surrender themselves to celestial Utopias cease to care for progress upon a too, too solid earth, so they who content themselves with walking, when they might run or fly, see the long years pass without worthy progress. In our political and industrial world, as in Looking Glass Land, you must run very fast indeed merely to remain where you are.

Democratic progress, moreover, must be coördinated, prepared, tested. It must consist of necessary links in an increasingly visible chain. The advantage of gradual reform is that it permits a sort of psychological acclimatization on the part of the reformed. But for a policy to be truly graduated, it must possess an inherent unity. It must not be a choppy, disjointed, and spasmodic succession of uncorrelated social efforts. It does not hurt a dog less to cut its tail off by inches, nor a corporation less to subject it *gradually* to a dozen successive criminal prosecutions. No merely sporadic action, whether it be an "exposure," a tirade, a punitive fine, or an exemplary jail sentence, can effect much permanent good, and a series of sporadic actions does not constitute a graduated reform. The democracy, though compromising in action, must be uncompromising in principle. Though conciliatory towards opponents, it must be constant to its fixed ideals. Though it tack with the wind, it must keep always in sight its general destination.

What the democracy needs is a consistent and constructive policy, changed from time to time as new exigencies or new interpretations of social facts require, but carried out unflinchingly, and realized as opportunities permit. A policy of single steps is desirable only when each step leads to other steps, not yet practicable, but at least dimly foreseeable.

Finally, the democracy, in its forward march, must keep a watchful eye to the rear. It must promote a constant cohesion within its ranks. It must abate internal strife. It must gather an ever increasing number of recruits from the still unawakened but potentially democratic masses.

Whatever else its tactics be, the democratic movement must keep pace with the masses of its probable supporters, marching just far enough ahead to be able to lead. To proceed at a much faster rate than the psychological development of the mass is to court a swift and powerful reaction. More than anything else the democratic movement must maintain harmony among its groups. Social coöperation, which is the goal of democracy, is also its weapon.

The goal of internal harmony is more easily recognized than attained, and it is often more difficult to conciliate an ally than to defeat an enemy. The various subgroups of democrats and semidemocrats have divergent, and even antagonistic, interests. The workman has his sharp conflict with his employer, and he cannot afford, in furthering his general interests (those which he has in common with the business man), to surrender his special claims. The social surplus, so largely monopolized by the plutocracy, is a splendid prize in itself, and herein the proletariat, like other groups, has "a world to gain." But in giving their adherence to the democratic alliance, the workingmen, like other social groups, are entitled to a *quid pro quo*.

Even more divisive than these divergent interests of subgroups are the varying philosophies and the often startling idiosyncrasies of rival democratic leaders. A witty abolitionist once declared that to free the slaves, an all-wise Providence had chosen as His instruments people whom *she* would not touch with a ten-foot pole. Among democrats — as also among Methodists, single-taxers, stammerers, and longshoremen — there are wise and foolish, temperate and fanatic. There is the Quixotic genius, who eats up his energy in friction, and through very excess of zeal is thrown off tangentially into the frigid void of indifference. There are others of a more lethargic temperament, who live in a quiet connubial commerce with their ideals, neither demanding much nor failing often. There are people immersed in the pettiest of preoccupations, who nevertheless "catch" democracy as they catch influenza, and who rise to the surface because of their low specific gravity. These constitutionally hostile people, though hating the same thing, do not always love each other, and many serious difficulties arise from temperamental misconceptions and from the lack of an emotional appeal or of an intellectual insight powerful enough to overturn these psychological barriers.

A still heavier burden upon the democratic movement is the residual inertness of the mass. In part this is a defect of education, for knowledge is desire, and men want when they *see*. Outside the groups of men who are always or generally on the side of democracy, however, there is that wide fringe of indifferent men and women, who lack the leisure, the education, or the social conscience to see public problems other than vaguely and intermittently, and who oppose a sluggish resistance to the realization even of their own perceived advantages. The men who are harried by the quest of bread and butter and automobiles; who are intellectually withered through brainless overwork; who are ground up between the millstones of a feverish money-getting and a feverish money-spending; the men who are immersed in the most transient and insignificant of events, tend to lose sight entirely of their share in large public matters.

In this respect, in its being compelled to carry the *impedimenta* of a long accumulated indifference, the wide democratic movement of to-day may be compared with the woman's suffrage movement, which is one of its symptoms. The movement for the political emancipation of women suffers less from active antagonism than from the inertness of many women to whom it should appeal. The movement, when successful, will but slightly affect the distribution of political and economic power, because the lines of social cleavage do not largely parallel sex lines, and men will gain much more than they will lose from this extension of the suffrage. In the same way, the antisuffragists, far from being the opponents, are the real, though innocent, coadjutors of the suffragists. The antisuffrage movement, though it wanders rather forlornly in alien thoroughfares, is, after all, like the suffrage movement, an unmistakable sign of an awakened social consciousness among women. The antisuffragists — those strident declaimers for quietude, those able defenders of women's most cherished disabilities — are sprung, after all, from the identical soil as their progressive sisters. The "anti's" will convince all that some women are politically capable, and that some are politically ambitious, and, even more effectively than the suffragists, they will prove that the bonds which have so long gagged and blinded and hobbled the half of humanity are being one by one and forever broken. The real opponents of woman's right to vote are not our energetic though somnambulistic "anti's," but the great sluggish mass of pleasant, politically unawakened women, the psychologically submerged.[1]

[1] Antagonism is often a more fertile field for propaganda than indifference, for the will to combat is not always so different from the will to be-

To unite those who are already acknowledged democrats, and to enlist those who do not yet know or care what they are, a long continued campaign of education is necessary. This education includes the learning of the schools and colleges and that also of the newspaper, magazine, book, play, sermon, factory, street, railroad, market, and city. It involves a breaking of the tablets of conservatism; a freeing of the mind from political and economic fetish worship, and the cultivation of a popular receptivity for new ideas.

Our old notions, not our corporeal enemies, enslave us. We must throw over the old cramping maxims of days of poverty. We must throw over our conceptions of cost and value (which measure wealth by effort) and must accept new ideas of utility (which measure wealth by pleasure and satisfaction). We must recognize that we have the social wealth to cure our social evils — and that until we have turned that social wealth against poverty, crime, vice, disease, incapacity, and ignorance, we have not begun to attain democracy. We must change our attitude towards government, towards business, towards reform, towards philanthropy, towards all the facts immediately or remotely affecting our industrial and political life. Such an education of its own members, present and prospective, must be a necessary part of a democratic campaign.

One might well fear for a democratic organization which contained so many diverse and conflicting elements; which comprised such irreconcilable personalities; which depended upon so inert an outside mass; and which was forced to educate to new and revolutionary concepts so many listless millions of traditionally-minded people. Without undue skepticism, one might fear that a movement which

lieve. There often seems more hope of radical action from a rabid reactionary than from a contented conservative, because the reactionary, though he moves backwards, at least *moves*.

is merely the resultant of constantly changing social forces might fail to eventuate, or might succumb to its obstacles.

Nevertheless, while people are proclaiming that democratic progress is impossible, it is already upon us. While we are being shown by diagram that the people cannot even tell what democracy is, we need only look out of our window to see them actually achieving democracy. Babies learn to eat before they know the muscles of the alimentary canal or the chemistry of the digestive juices, and men learn to unite without seeing or knowing their allies, and to march stolidly without clearly seeing their goal.

To-day the democratic army, united by the loosest bonds, and subjected to the most attenuated discipline, is moving along three wide roads to a common but not clearly perceived goal. These three roads are the democratization of government, the socialization of industry, and the civilization of the citizen. These roads meet and cross and interwine, and the various contingents join and separate, and again join and again separate, while, all the time, the army, stretching out far into the distance, approaches nearer to its goal. The men in the rear, marching partly through an inertia of motion, partly through imitation of the men ahead, occasionally desert and again reënlist. They see only vaguely the outlines of the country to which they are marching. But with each advance their view becomes clearer and with each new day the habit of marching and the instinct of fellowship with the men ahead increase. Occasionally great bodies, attracted by new leaders, branch off into side paths, which seem shorter and straighter, and some of these detachments are lost, and some, by occupying cross paths, obstruct the passage of the main army; while others, by still marching, once more strike the common road and thus rejoin their comrades. Gradually the army, though composed of many detachments led by many generals, becomes somewhat more unified. Gradually, as many men coming from many places converge on common points, the three broad roads of the march, the roads of democratic government, of socialized industry, and of a civilized people, become clearly marked highways.

CHAPTER XVII

THE INDUSTRIAL PROGRAM OF THE DEMOCRACY

THE industrial goal of the democracy is the socialization of industry. It is the attainment by the people of the largest possible industrial control and of the largest possible industrial dividend. The democracy seeks to attain these ends through government ownership of industry; through government regulation; through tax reform; through a moralization and reorganization of business in the interest of the industrially weak.

Everywhere we find evidences of industrial developments in the general direction of this goal. Government goes into business. The Post Office embarks upon the banking business and threatens to engage in the express business. The Forestry Bureau raises and sells timber. The Reclamation Service goes into many separate businesses in connection with the building of dams and the selling of water. In the construction of the Panama Canal, the government builds roads and railroads and conducts dozens of separate enterprises. At the same time, the States and cities greatly extend the sphere of their direct participation in business, and buy and manufacture and sell on an enlarging scale.

Government regulation grows simultaneously. It extends over more industries, and over more operations of industries. Railroad regulation, both by the nation and by some thirty States, becomes wider. Railroad rates, services, accounting come within the purview of State and national regulation. A corporation tax law marks the beginning of a wider investigation of all corporation actions. A Bureau of Corporations and a Tariff Board demand explicit information concerning manufacturing and selling concerns. Factory and labor laws regulate the internal economy of businesses. Pure food laws, postal laws, corporation laws, etc., regulate business from the points of view of consumer and investor. A federal incorporation law is proposed with the idea of subjecting all corporations doing an interstate business to the control of the federal government.

Still other developments reveal this democratic goal. Our public lands, mines, and water powers are reserved for the people instead of being indiscriminately given away, as formerly. A strongly antagonistic attitude towards "swollen fortunes" is revealed, and proposals are made to reduce these swellings by heavy taxes, and to use the powers of taxation generally to lessen economic inequalities. Trade-unions with tens of thousands of members claim a partial control of industry, and the general community asserts its right to participate in the settlement of industrial disputes. A new insistence is laid upon the social interest in all manifestations of our industrial life.

The broad outlines of the democracy's industrial program, so far as they have reached the general consciousness, are to be found in the promises and declamations of the platforms of our political parties. These platforms are for the most part insincere, but it is exactly their insincerity which gives them their evidential value. A platform does not show what the politician wants, but does show what that astute person believes that the people want. It is the tribute, often the sole tribute, which the candidate pays to the popular wish. The platform's ambiguities are equally enlightening. Nothing reveals more clearly the presence, and even the relative strength, of two opposed forces in society than do the platform's nicely balanced sentences, in which two warring clauses reduce each other to an innocuous meaninglessness.

The superlative value of the platform as evidence is due

to the fact that it is always addressed to a potential majority. All platforms (Republican, Democratic, Socialist, Prohibition) appeal to "the masses," to "the many," to "the people." Thus the 1909 tariff is denounced by the Democratic State (1910) platforms because it oppresses "the many for the benefit of the few" (Alabama); because "it plunders the many to enrich the few" (Michigan); because it imposes "added burdens upon the toiling and consuming masses" (Colorado), while building "up great fortunes for a favored few" (Connecticut); because it has made heavier "the burdens of the consuming masses" (Georgia); thus "involving remorseless exactions from the many to enrich the few" (Indiana), and so on through all the States. For the protection of the many against the few, the trusts are assailed, the conservation of natural resources is approved, and the adoption of the income tax amendment is urged. All of which solicitude for "the many" is explicable, since while "the favored few" often rule the party, it is "the many" who furnish the votes.[1]

The most characteristic feature of the industrial program of the democracy, as revealed in party platforms and in books, newspapers, and speeches, as well as in actual legislation, is the emphasis which is laid upon the state in industry. Government ownership and regulation—national, State, and local—are urged for more and more industries. The dividend from industry, which people are demanding, is more largely a joint than an individual dividend. It is a dividend which the individual citizen can obtain only

[1] "The two dominant political parties," says the New York State Socialist Platform of 1910, "pretend to stand for all the people; the so-called reform parties claim to speak for the good people; the Socialist party frankly acknowledges that it is concerned chiefly with the working people." Since, however, *all* the working people of the State are the *chief* concern of the party, and since it aligns "those who toil" against "those who prey," and "those who are robbed" against "those who rob," it may also be considered to be broad in its platform appeal.

through the intermediation of the State or nation; in other words, through an extension of State control over industry.[1]

What the democracy desires, however, is not government ownership for itself, but merely enough government ownership, regulation, or control as may be necessary to a true socialization of industry. The democracy's goal — the socialization of industry — is a viewing of our manifold business life from the standpoint of society and not solely from that of the present beneficiaries or directors of industry. It is such a coördination of business as will permanently give the greatest happiness and the highest development to the largest number of individuals, and to society as a whole.

Socialization is thus a point of view. It is less a definite industrial program than the animating ideal of a whole industrial policy. It is a standard by which industrial conditions and industrial developments must be adjudged.

In certain industries socialization may involve a government monopoly. In others, it may mean government operation in competition with private businesses; or a government ownership with private management; or a division of the profits of private industries. Or it may involve a thoroughgoing regulation of an industry, prescribing rates, prices, services, wages, hours, labor conditions, dividends, and the internal economy in general. Or, socialization may mean a lesser regulation; or mere publicity; or encouragement; or subsidies; or legal recognition; or simply the prescribing of a minimum capital or of a preliminary training. Again, socialization may mean a deflection of the stream of wealth which flows from an industry, a deflection accomplished by tax laws, or by laws altering the conditions

[1] The old cry, "Vote yourself a farm," represented an individualistic point of view. It was the man's share of a divisible and alienable public domain that was wanted; not his joint share in an indivisible thing, such as a public library, a public park, improved educational facilities, etc.

of conveying property. Finally, socialization may be accomplished without direct governmental regulation. How far the government shall interfere depends on the business. An insurance company, to which people who are not actuaries give money *now* that their widows may receive money fifty years hence, requires a different regulation from the business of the corner tailor, who presses your coat while you wait.

Because it is not restricted as to means, socialization may effect itself without a million minute rules. To-day each of our ninety-two million citizens is enjoined against thousands of crimes and misdemeanors and against thousands of possible violations of the property rights of each of his ninety-two million neighbors. And yet, most of us obey the law without thinking. In many industries profit seeking (with certain broad restrictions and encouragements) will result in a substantial socialization. A few hundreds of millions a year intelligently spent on agricultural and general education, on experiment stations, on public roads, etc., would do more to effect a better socialization of agriculture than a fifty-volume code of agricultural law.

Nor does socialization involve the negation of profits. The love of gain is a tough and wholesome human fiber. It is the crude motive power of industry. Socialization considers profit seeking neither as a universally beneficent regulative impulse nor as the stubborn root of all industrial evils. It regards profits and wages as contributions to a larger end, to be balanced as such against other results of the industry. If a given industry creates on the whole an excess of costs over utilities, or if it affords a smaller surplus of utilities than would the same amount of capital and labor invested otherwise, then it is within the province of society to reform, or even to abolish the industry.[1]

[1] If society, without warning, prohibits actions and business methods which it formerly encouraged or tolerated, there may be a fair question as to whether employers and workmen, suffering losses from such unantici-

Socialization considers industry as a whole. The national business is "one and indivisible"; an indissoluble union of autonomous, but linked, industries.[1]

In emphasizing this oneness of business, socialization is doing on a large scale and from the point of view of society what the trust did on a smaller scale from the point of view of the profit-taker. Like the trust, socialization subjects rival or dissimilar businesses to the sway of a single aim. Like the trust, socialization attains unity without sacrificing variety. The trust does not always end the separate existence of constituent companies. So, under a complete socialization of our national industry, we would have thousands of separate kinds of business under different forms of ownership, management, and control, but each continuing its existence and mode of life because adapted, in the opinion of society, to contribute its share to the best progress of industry as a whole.

Like the trust, also, socialization does not end competition. The trust encourages *internal* competition. The right hand is stimulated to do better than the left, and the left to excel the right. The factory manager who attains a greater output or a lest cost per unit of product than rival managers is appropriately recompensed. It is a "personally conducted" competition, which differs from the competition outside the trust (the industrial *bellum omnium contra omnes*) as the Prince Charles spaniel differs from his savage cousin, the gray wolf. Similarly, socialization relies upon competition,

pated prohibition, may not justly claim compensation. The essential point of socialization, however, is not this eventual compensation, but the right, reserved and exercised by society, of determining, in last resort, what things may be produced and how.

[1] There is a theory of business which is diametrically opposed to industrial socialization. This theory, which we may call industrial autonomy, considers the national economy as a series of largely unconnected industrial parts, each the province of the people actually engaged in it. It regards industrial enterprises as international law regards the nations, — as sovereign bodies, with the internal affairs of which no one may meddle.

which educates and steels competitors, though it opposes competition which injures the contestants or others.[1]

In actual fact socialization, in so far as it involves the actual intervention of the state, is used largely to supplement or correct competition. It is where competition is atrophied, as in the case of monopolies, or where it appears in a pathological form, as in child labor, industrial parasitism, etc., that the intervention of the state is most needed.

Especially is this true of monopolies. "Where monopoly is inevitable," says the Wisconsin Republican Platform of 1910, "we favor complete government regulation." The Illinois Democrats are in favor of an extension of the governmental policy of conservation, because they "are opposed to the gobbling up of the mines, the forests, the oil fields, and the water-power sites of the country by the greedy representatives of Big Business." All through our political literature runs the attack upon "monopolies," "the trusts and monopolies," "the corporate trusts," "certain corporations and combinations of capital." [2]

One reason for the government ownership or regulation

[1] This distinction between social and antisocial competition is emphasized by trade-union leaders in their defense of minimum conditions. They argue that the competitive battle should be fought out along the socially advantageous lines of directive genius, improved factory organization, the installation of better machinery, and not along the socially disadvantageous lines of a lowering of wages, a lengthening of hours, a worsening of conditions, or an exploitation of the labor of little children. The end of the lower competition is the sweatshop; that of the higher is that wonderful series of inventions which cannot be utilized except when labor is sufficiently intelligent and sufficiently rewarded.

[2] While it is impossible to draw an absolute distinction between competitive industries and monopolies (since there is an appreciable monopoly element in businesses usually called competitive, and an appreciable competitive element in most of our so-called monopolies), still, in the majority of cases, we can tell roughly whether the industry is preponderatingly competitive or monopolistic. On the whole, a competitive industry is one in which any person or corporation possessing a moderate capital is able to produce the product at approximately equal advantage with the majority of the persons already engaged in the industry.

of monopolies is that, unregulated, they lead to an absorption by small groups of too large a share of the social surplus. Under the old theory of competition, such a business hypertrophy was impossible, because high profits would attract new competitors and profits would fall. But to-day competition is aborted, and shares more modestly with monopoly the rule of the industrial world. We cannot trust to competition to reduce the monopoly profits of the anthracite carrying railroads, just as we cannot afford to throw ourselves upon the "enlightened selfishness" of these corporations.

Hitherto our federal government has lagged far behind the governments of western Europe in the matter of direct ownership and management of businesses. Such progress as has been made along these lines has taken the form of a gradual growth of functions already exercised. The government has enormously expanded a number of non-profit-earning businesses, in which it has long since engaged.

It is probable, however, that a considerable extension of the federal government's ownership and direction of business will take place in the future. Three factors are leading in this direction. One is the increasingly evident monopoly character of many large businesses; a second is the improvement in our civil service; a third is the progressive democratization of the government. As monopoly invades business, the choice lies between government and private monopoly, instead of between government monopoly and competition. The monopoly element in the business aligns "the many" against a few insiders. As the civil service improves, moreover, the government is enabled to conduct business both honestly and efficiently. As the state becomes increasingly democratized, the people accept it as their natural representative, as opposed to an entrenched industrial oligarchy in a monopolized business.

The logic of the situation seems to demand that where there are no advantages in the private industry from individual initiative, or where those advantages do not overweigh the advantages which the state could secure from the conduct of the industry, the business should be taken over by the state after compensation to owners, and should be conducted by the state under conditions which guarantee reasonable permanence, stability, and security to all engaged, while preserving a regulated competition within the industry with promotion for extra ability or extra effort (according to definite rules of preferment) and with suitable rewards, monetary or otherwise.

How far and how rapidly the federal government will take over private business is a question which to-day cannot yet be answered. It seems by no means improbable that the government will shortly take over the express business by embarking upon the lucrative and easily conducted parcels post. It will probably extend its banking business. It may not improbably take over the telegraph systems of the country, which have developed slowly because they have been run so exclusively for profit. The government may enormously increase its business of providing itself with supplies, with ships, and harbors, and blotting paper. It may engage more and more largely in the construction of irrigation dams and in the sale of water to a larger number of farmers. It may attain to a preëminent position in the lumber business of the country. Beyond these proximate fields lie others which may or may not come to be occupied. The government may (and if regulation fails, it will) buy, own, and operate the railroads of the country; it may own and operate the coal mines. It may in time take step after step towards an ownership of those large, easily overseen, and inherently monopolistic businesses where centralization and subordination rule, and where the choice lies between a government monopoly and a private monopoly.[1]

It is partly the fear of such a possible extension of government ownership and operation that is at the base of much of the opposition to the policy of conserving our natural resources. This policy, one of the most elementary forms of business socialization, was dictated by pressing need. Our supposedly unlimited supplies of timber were proved to be nearing exhaustion.[2] "Our coal supplies are so far from being inexhaustible that if the increasing rate of consumption shown by the figures of the last seventy-five years continues to prevail, our supplies of anthracite coal will last but fifty years and of bituminous coal less than two hundred years."[3] Yet despite this threatening dearth, public foresight is so utterly at variance with our former free-handed American practice that thousands of our conservatives were found to be bitterly antagonistic to conservation.

Intrinsically conservation is nothing but saving; it is the common lot against the looters. Though its opponents

[1] An exactly analogous development under similar circumstances and for like reasons is already taking place in our States and especially in our cities. Municipal ownership and operation of public services — the furnishing to the citizens of water, gas, electricity, traction services, etc. — seem inevitable as we progress towards a purification and democratization of municipal government. In 1908 American cities (each with a population of over 30,000) spent $275,000,000 on account of new properties, and the City of New York alone received over $18,000,000 from revenues of public service enterprises. American cities are far behind the cities of England and of the continent of Europe in everything partaking of the nature of civic prevision, and especially in the foresighted boldness which leads to an extension of civic functions. The trend, however, is in that direction.

[2] "The lowest estimate reached by the Forest Service of the timber now standing in the United States is 1400 billion feet, board measure; the highest 2500 billion. The present annual consumption is approximately 100 billion feet, while the annual growth is but a third of our consumption, or from 30 to 40 billion feet." Pinchot, Gifford, "The Fight for Conservation." New York (1910), p. 14.

[3] Pinchot, G., *op. cit.*, p. 6.

represent it as a dog-in-the-manger policy, as a plan to put our natural resources into "cold storage," in reality conservation is opposed, not to use, but to private appropriation, or at least to unfair, unequal, and wasteful appropriation. Conservation is merely a policy of protecting the public interest in our national forests, lands, mines, and water powers.

Despite its seeming innocence, however, the policy of conservation carries with it certain implications, disquieting not only to the hopeful spoilers of the public domain, but to many of their innocently eloquent coadjutors. In Alaska and elsewhere there are still some billions of dollars of national property, and it now seems probable, in the light of our recently developed "conservation sentiment," that the nation may lease this property for a valuable consideration, with the result that the people will share in the profits of exploitation. It is bad enough in the eyes of many honest citizens that the state have temporal possessions at all; that it should actually make profits (thus lowering itself to the level of mere financiers) seems to our profit seekers incongruous and almost immoral. But an issue even more dire remains in the background. If the state presumes to withhold national resources from private capital, then at some future time it may actually go farther. It may not only keep but develop its mines, forests, and water powers. It may go into the mining, lumbering, and electrical businesses. *It may compete with private business.*

The tendency of the government to go into such businesses is reënforced whenever regulation meets with failure. There are times when men feel that the nation is flouted and mocked by the trust; is only half-obeyed and is wholly blamed. Occasionally we tire of having the national government act as chaperon to the trust.[1]

[1] From the point of view of the trust (especially if exposed to censorious tongues of investors or legislators), a certain amount of public chaperonage

Where, however, regulation succeeds, where ends similar to those secured by government ownership may be obtained through the enforcement of uniform laws, it is often preferable to leave the business in private hands subject to public control. Whether a particular business, affected with a public interest, is better adapted to government operation or to private operation with government regulation depends upon a number of conditions and is a question which the advocates of industrial socialization need not decide in advance. They may proceed as does the court, which indulges in wide-ranging *obiter dicta*, but cautiously decides each case upon its merits.

What will ultimately decide in each case the question between government operation and government regulation (when one of the two is desirable) will be the relative efficiency of the two methods. There are certain definite limits set to an extension of government ownership by the necessity of preserving the highest possible industrial efficiency.[1] While the federal government is becoming yearly more efficient, and while the vast private monopolies often show the same industrial weaknesses as government does, nevertheless there remains a certain advantage with the trust, owing to the greater play of the desire for profits, the greater elasticity of its arrangements, and the wider latitude given to its directors. Industrial autonomy, however clear its drawbacks, does at least produce a hard, alert, wide-awake industrial agent. The disadvantage of the trust is that it is

is advantageous, since the presence of a duenna, however dull and deaf, covers a multitude of financial indiscretions. From the point of view of the "regulated" corporation, there should be enough regulation to give confidence, but not enough to regulate.

[1] A socialized industry must have a considerable efficiency because the socialized democracy of which it is a part will be one with a high cost of maintenance. It will be a society which will do without child labor and without excessive toil of men and momen. It will spend enormous sums on education. A high standard of living maintained by a large population means inevitably an enormous national expenditure.

too likely to sacrifice the public interest and even the interest of the investors to a series of private interests, which are excessively stimulated. The disadvantage of public ownership, on the other hand, is that it tends to develop too little that sharp private interest which leads to unobserved extra exertions and to a keener and more intelligent application.

A compromise between this public interest and the private interest is sought to be effected by government regulation. The object of government regulation is to combine the advantages of individual initiative and of public control.

Against every such exercise of government regulation the theory of industrial autonomy is opposed. This theory maintains that, on the whole, the welfare of society will best be subserved by the largest practicable autonomy of business. It presupposes the least possible limitation of a perfect freedom of contract; of the right of a man to work when and where and how he will; of the right of the manufacturer to run his business in his own way. In its crassest form the theory expresses itself in the sentence, "Business must be independent of politics."

What this engaging phrase really means is that society, politically organized (and to-day it is only politically that the whole of Society is democratically organized), should have no control over the industrial processes by which it lives. Industrial autonomy contemplates a state within a state; an industrial power dividing actual sovereignty with a political power. Industrial autonomy would subject society to business.[1]

[1] There is a modified and weakened version of industrial autonomy expressed in such phrases as "the trusteeship of wealth" and assuming that our industrial leaders are holding and directing the wealth of the community in the community's ultimate interest. Between this theory, however, and the ordinary economic and legal tenets of its adherents, there are many uncomfortable contradictions. The "trustees" seem unwilling to be held to an accounting. They seem to believe that the rare qualities

This theory, however, although once imposing, is now only a theory of shreds and patches. So many strands have been taken from the fabric that nothing but the most devoted blindness can discern the original pattern. We have ridden roughshod over the sacred privacy of business. We have drawn ledgers and daybooks and bank presidents into the profane daylight. We have compelled employers to put guards on machinery (even when no one but the factory inspector wanted them). We have forbidden landlords from letting their empty premises to men who clamored at the gates. We have declared that a railroad rate may not be charged (even though the passenger stands ready to pay it); that a service must be improved, even though the shipper demands no improvement. Surely, at first blush, it seems reasonable to allow a seller to sell cheap. Nevertheless, a railroad corporation is forbidden to sell transportation below the market rate; and a railroad president, who out of kindness gives (not sells) a pass to a friendly legislator, may for his complaisance go to jail.[1]

There was never a time when the government held entirely aloof from industry. Even in the palmiest days of American individualism, there was always a certain expression of industrial socialization, since without some subordination of private initiative to public welfare, business itself is impossible.[2] Then, as now, the penal law took cognizance of the rudiments of business socialization. There might be profit in the unrestricted sale of poison, but the disadvantages of such unregulated sales so manifestly overweighed any good arising from profits and wages that the business was either regulated or forbidden.

of trusteeship may be inherited and devised. They do not fix any time at which the ward may be expected to arrive at an age of discretion.

[1] That is, he may *theoretically* go to jail, which is the pleasantest way of going.

[2] Even the California Vigilance Committees recognized that horse stealing was a business which "interfered with business."

Certain other industries in which there is supposed to be an excess of resultant evil over good have also been legally destroyed. For over half a century Maine has prohibited the manufacture and private sale of alcoholic beverages, and recently the country has been swept by a prohibition wave which in many towns, counties, and states has closed saloons and has annihilated businesses built up on the till then tolerated drink habit. Laws against gambling have diminished the value of race tracks, pool rooms, and telegraph systems, while the prohibition of the sale of firecrackers to our patriotic youth has meant fewer fires, fewer funerals, and slimmer profits. The principle is well established that the continued existence of many businesses depends, not on the demand for their product, but on the will of the general community.

Despite the opposition, therefore, of those who believe that the state should hold "hands off," the governmental regulation of business is steadily progressing in America. To an increasing extent the federal government undertakes the control of corporations. Especially in railroad legislation, great progress has been made. The Interstate Commerce Law of 1887 gave to a Government Commission the right, among other rights, to pass upon the reasonableness of rates, while forbidding rebates and discriminations by railroads in favor of persons or localities. The law of 1906 still further strengthened the power of the federal government. The Interstate Commerce Commission was given the right to fix reasonable rates upon application of a shipper of an interested locality; in other words, was granted the enormous power of determining the price of all services rendered by railroads doing an annual business of two and one half billions of dollars. By a series of laws between 1887 and 1910, the power of the Interstate Commerce Commission has been extended to all common carriers engaged in the carriage of oil (pipe lines); to telegraph, telephone, and cable companies; while the jurisdiction of the Commission has been extended as to through rates and joint rates, freight classification, switch connections, etc. The Commission has also been granted the right to make investigations on its own motion, without awaiting the initiative of an injured shipper. By the Act of March 2, 1893, railroads were obliged to equip their cars with automatic couplers and other safety devices, and by the law of April 14, 1910, this act was supplemented by requiring railroads to equip their cars with sill steps, hand brakes, ladders, running boards, and grab irons, and the Interstate Commerce Commission was empowered to designate the number, dimensions, location, and manner of application of these appliances. The Arbitration Act of 1898 provided for government mediation between interstate railroads and their employees. The Interstate Commerce laws prescribe a uniform system of accounting for all railroad corporations, a filing of annual reports, and an inspection by the Commission of all accounts, records, and memoranda. By the law of 1910, a special commission is provided to investigate the issuance of railroad stocks and bonds. Step by step the whole business of transportation and communication is more and more subjected in all its parts and in all its relations to a strict government regulation in the public interest.

In the future we shall enormously increase the extent of regulation. Not only can we pursue an active social policy by means of the regulation of industry, but we can also so direct and restrain and guide the strong economic impulses of society as to make the product of industry not only larger, but more widely and more fairly distributed. Not only can we conserve our natural, and reserve our national, resources; not only can we retain for the people the franchises, grants, and valuable privileges which they now possess or which will come to them in the future; but we can so regulate business as to prevent or lessen waste, internal friction, inter-business friction, the excessive fluctuations of seasonal trades, the wide fluctuations between good years and bad years, the duplication of plant or product, the production of useless or deleterious articles, the use of chicanery and of false representation, the extortions of monopoly, the unfair, unequal, and uneconomical distribution of the product, etc., etc. We should aim to secure at the lowest possible cost in effort the greatest possible production of articles worth consuming, and so distributed as to give the greatest possible satisfaction in their consumption.

In the regulation of industry it is not necessary or desirable to pass laws where the personal interests involved, whether of employer or employed, of seller or buyer, of director, manager, promoter, or investor, are capable of accomplishing the same result. It is important that the democracy make use of all existing agencies for the attainment of its industrial program.

One of the most representative and powerful of such agencies is the labor organization. The trade-union is not an urbane body of abnegating workmen united for the good of the employers or for that of the general community. It is not without fear, nor without reproach. Nor, for that matter, were the mailed barons who extorted Magna Charta from King John; nor the tedious old councilors who secured the liberties of the towns; nor the purse-proud Commons who won a measure of political democracy (for their own class) by withholding their money, as the trade-unionists to-day withhold their labor. In point of fact the trade-union is a group of workingmen pursuing their joint interests in much the same spirit as each member might be supposed to pursue his individual interests. But because those interests are joint and because in general they are the interests of people who are least represented in industry, the trade-unionists in what has been called their "corporate egotism" are promoting industrial democracy. Actually, trade-unionists are far better democrats than their immediate interests necessitate, since their feeling of solidarity (except among a minority) stretches far beyond the boundaries of their trade.[1]

While, however, it is not necessary to secure for workingmen what their trade unions have already secured for them, it is desirable, in the interests of fairer-minded employers themselves, to make uniform the progress already attained, and to enormously extend the scope of factory and labor legislation, in order to lessen hours, improve sanitary conditions of factories, decrease the mortality and sickness in the trades, and generally to improve conditions which are as much a part of the workman's real wage as are the dollars which he finds in his pay envelope.[2]

[1] In America the great mass of farmers, small tradesmen, and professional men fail to sympathize with the trade-union through lack of an understanding of its fundamental aims and of the environment of the men who stand for those aims. The average outside individual objects to the trade-union, not because it insists on higher wages (which all are willing to concede — provided some one else pays them) but because it demands "the recognition of the union." Actually, however, in our more and more centralized industry this demand for recognition is the nearest possible approach to a real industrial democracy or even to a real industrial liberty for the workers. The kindly and often sympathetic opponents of the closed shop and of the recognition of the union appeal to the freedom of every individual, unionist or non-unionist, to make a fair contract with his employer. It is perhaps a pleasanter ideal than collective bargaining with striking, picketing, and a compulsory membership in a union, but it is an ideal, which, for the present, is unattainable in many trades.

[2] Whether we shall within the near future prescribe minimum wages by law, as has recently been done for several trades in the United Kingdom, will depend upon whether or not we attain the desired results by other means. It was once held that it was economically unthinkable — in fact, almost impious — to attempt to fix wages or prices by law. Within certain bounds this was true. If you make legal wages so high or legal prices so low that no incentive remains for production, then production will cease. But there is a wide margin of action between this and the establishment of definite minima of wages considerably above those in our worst-paid trades. Within that margin it is economically as possible to regulate wages as to regulate hours or sanitary conditions. It is

In some industrial situations, regulation must be plenary, detailed, and all-comprehensive. In other situations it may be more restricted. In still others, it may be limited to a mere insistence upon publicity of operations.

To an increasing extent we are putting our trust in business publicity. It is a splendid means of unchaining public resentment or of inciting public approval. Knowledge permits potent economic forces to unbind themselves. Consumers, investors, voters, and the community in general are aided in their action by the certainty which publicity brings. Where publicity fails to restrain, a more thoroughgoing regulation is necessary. Where the thoroughgoing regulation is in prospect, publicity is an excellent antecedent.

How much publicity is required depends upon the business, upon the extent to which it is invested with a public interest, upon whether there already exists a beneficent regulation by competition, upon the extent of the dangers which may flow from secrecy. Many men still claim that their particular businesses cannot be run with publicity. This is true only to the extent that a man whose business secrets are known is at a disadvantage in competition with a man whose business secrets are unknown. Publicity, doubtless, works often to the advantage of the large purse and the established firm, since those who are already strong have a relative advantage in securing, let us say, credit facilities. On the other hand, secrecy and the power to exert undue influence work to the advantage of the unscrupulous.

Complete industrial socialization does not stop short at production and sale. It does not content itself with regulating the conditions under which articles shall be produced or the prices at which they shall be sold. It requires a

as easy to forbid the manufacturers of cottons or woolens to pay less than a defined scale of wages as it is to forbid the manufacture of counterfeit coins or the distilling of untaxed whisky. All that is required is a changed point of view in ourselves and our judges.

reasonable and just distribution of the product of industry, a fair adjustment as between wages, profits, interest, rent, and the share of the state. It affects the redistribution of wealth after the ordinary distribution has taken place. It affects past accumulations, and the returns upon past accumulations.

There are several ways in which the continued growth of enormous fortunes may be hampered, if not prevented. The social wealth to be created may be deflected to the community by a governmental acquisition of natural monopolies. During the next one hundred years American railroads, American mines, American forests, and American lands are likely to increase stupendously in value. With any reasonably large growth of population, these properties should increase to an amount which is entirely beyond anything in our experience, and is almost beyond our conception. By the gradual acquisition of such properties, or of strategic elements of such properties,[1] the community could divert to itself a large part of this probable new wealth. It could accomplish this purpose by taxation, by the direct and increasing taxation of the unearned increment. The state might make a periodical valuation of all property invested with a public interest, as well as of all property to which in a marked degree a future unearned increment will adhere, and at regular intervals might take for itself a part (and a constantly increasing part) of the unearned increment which had accrued since the valuation immediately preceding.[2]

Theoretically there are no limits to state action along these lines. The sovereign state has a primordial, intrinsic, underlying right to all property, more valid in the final instance than the property right vested in the legal owner.

[1] If the nation owned the railroads and thus controlled transportation rates, it could easily determine what part of the value of mines and forests should belong to it, and what portion should belong to the legal owners. The anthracite railroads determined the value of the anthracite mines by fixing the charges for the transportation of anthracite coal.

[2] See the English procedure under the Lloyd-George Budget.

The right to tax involves the right to destroy. In no other great country of the world, moreover, would this residual claim of the nation be so capable of being enforced, since the property of American citizens is so largely invested at home. The British owner of South American gold mines may escape British taxation by removing to a foreign country, but in America the expatriation of the owner cannot effect the withdrawal of his capital. The property is here. To an overwhelming extent, the wealth of the nation is irrevocably and forever situate in this country.

Even after the wealth has passed into the hands of individuals it is not beyond the reach of the state. By progressive taxes on property, incomes, or inheritances (including taxation upon gifts *inter vivos* within a certain period prior to death), the state can do much towards preventing too insensate an accumulation of individual wealth. Theoretically there are no limits to taxation along these lines. The nation might legally make itself sole heir to each of its citizens.

Actually, no such extreme contingency is at all probable. The levying of a one hundred per cent inheritance tax would not meet with the approbation of more than an insignificant and ineffectual fraction of the people. A far more moderate tax would largely dry up the wells of enterprise; and even an entirely reasonable, and from a social point of view a very low, inheritance or income tax is evaded systematically and flagrantly. State income taxes are of practically no value in reducing inequalities of wealth, since a man can acquire an exempting citizenship in a neighboring State far more easily than he can secure a new agent to look after his property.

In the socialization of wealth by means of taxation, two inevitable tendencies are observable. The first of these is an increasing emphasis laid upon the national as distinct from the State governments, since the latter are not sufficiently formidable to cope with the gigantic private interests to which they may be opposed. The second is a change in our conception of the fundamental purposes of taxation.

The prevalent theory in America during the last century was that taxation was to be levied for the sole purpose of raising government revenues. It should therefore be as little as possible, and should be divided among the people according to their ability to pay. In other words, it should leave all citizens in the same relative position as it found them. We are now going over more completely to a conception of taxation as an instrument for the socialization of production and wealth; as a means of changing the currents and directions of distribution. In other words, the *social*, as well as the merely *fiscal*, ends of taxation are held in view.[1]

With a government ownership of some industries, with a government regulation of others, with publicity for all (to the extent that publicity is socially desirable), with an enlarged power of the community in industry, and with an increased appropriation by the community of the increasing social surplus and of the growing unearned increment, the progressive socialization of industry will take place. To accomplish these ends the democracy will rely upon the trade-union, the association of consumers, and other industrial agencies. It will, above all, rely upon the state.

[1] The protective tariff (as opposed to the tariff for revenue only) had an avowed social end. So also taxes on the liquor trade, etc.

CHAPTER XVIII

THE POLITICAL PROGRAM OF THE DEMOCRACY

THE democracy seeks a complete control over governmental machinery and processes. It seeks to break the power of a politically entrenched plutocracy, to attain to a government by the people for the people.

Without such democratic control of government there can be no permanent democratic control of industry. For, in ultimate analysis, we own our house, inherit our farm, draw our profits, or obey the factory bell by grace (or command) of the political sovereign. Bequest, inheritance, private property, free contract, are subject to law. Law is legislative enactment, executive administration, judicial interpretation. The legislature, executive, courts, are, in democratic countries, immediately or finally, actually or potentially, the creatures of politics. They are the *genii* of the ballot box.

In attempting to secure political control, the democracy proceeds along five paths. These paths are (1) the democratic control of parties and of party nominations; (2) the democratic control of elections; (3) the democratic control of representatives already elected; (4) direct legislation by the people; (5) increased efficiency of the democratized government.

Control of political parties is the very beginning of political democracy. The people are no longer content to vote for one of two candidates, collusively nominated by the allied corruption of two parties, and foisted upon the public, as a gambler "forces" a card upon a raw novice. In the interest of a popular election, a popular nomination is demanded. To choose between candidates, the people must choose the candidates.

The legal regulation of parties, which has already progressed far, has been made possible by one of those subtle changes in American political life, which, though they leave no mark upon constitutions, fundamentally alter the actual bases of government. The party, hitherto unrecognized by our constitutions and laws, was forbidden to place its nominees upon the official ballot unless the party officers certified such nominations to be genuine. "Parties of a certain size, which had been given a privileged position for their nominees upon the ballot were, in return for this privilege, subjected to special restrictions. It was an easy step from permitting the two great parties to have their candidates placed upon the ballot (when certified by the party officials) to requiring that these nominations should have been made only in accordance with such rules and regulations as might be deemed necessary—in short, to prescribing in detail regulations governing the entire procedure of party primaries. The party ceased to be a purely voluntary association, and became a recognized part of the nominating machinery." [1]

Legal control of party and primary, once initiated, was rapidly extended. It developed from a local or special regulation, optional with the party, to one which was general, State-wide, and compulsory. It led in a number of States to State-wide compulsory and universal direct primaries.

Prior to the adoption in many of our States of direct primaries, the average political partisan cast his ballot, not for the ultimate candidate, but for men who chose men who chose the candidate. The result was often a complete travesty upon popular rights. Controlling financial interests acquired what was almost an acknowledged right to nominate the candidates. With direct primaries, on the other hand, the people directly select their own candidates. Where direct nominations are reënforced by laws against corrupt

[1] Merriam (C. Edward), "Primary Elections." Chicago (University of Chicago Press), 1909, p. 30.

practices, the power of the majority over the making of nominations is correspondingly augmented.

With each year the popularity of party regulation and of direct nominations becomes more evident and new means are devised to render the system simpler and more efficacious. "The Connecticut democracy," says the 1910 State platform, "favors the direct primary form of nominations in order that the people may select their own servants," and Republicans, Prohibitionists, Socialists, and others are in full accord. "The Direct Primary Law," say the New Hampshire Republicans, "has proved an unqualified success. The choice of delegates to national conventions should be brought under its provisions." Everywhere there is a demand for an extension, simplification, and improvement of the system of direct primaries. Utah Republicans (1910) clamor for a "direct primary law, by which all general officers, including candidates for the United States Senate, may be chosen by vote by the whole people." Iowa Democrats and Minnesota Republicans ask for a lessening of the expenses attendant upon primary elections, while in other States the demand is made for the publication of the expenses of all candidates for the nomination prior to the primary. New York Republicans insist "that the same safeguards should surround primary elections as have been shown to be effective in preventing repeating and frauds at general elections."

The chief object of direct primaries and of other proposals for the democratization of the party is to break up the alliance between corrupt business and corrupt politics. The question is often raised as to whether men of wealth (because of their greater liability to taxation or for other reasons) should not be accorded a larger power in the state than an equal number of penniless citizens. So stated, however, the problem is academic, for to-day, in all countries, men of wealth possess this advantage. Democracy is faced with the problem, not of according wealth a certain extra influence over legislation, but of so limiting and moderating that influence as to permit an even partial effectuation of the will of the majority.

Much of this influence is ineradicable. Wealth gives leisure and intellectual opportunities. Money buys publicity, orators, advocates. There are always disinterested wealth worshipers, who find in the counsels of the millionaire grace, logic, and the sweetest reasonableness. We cannot legislate against the glamour of possessions.

But the influence of wealth takes a more tangible form when, in the thick of electoral campaigns, our great corporations, not unsolicited, draw near to our party managers, and thrust into their expectant hands a modest contribution to the cause of justice and liberty. If we are not to be subdued by the plutocracy, we must beware these Greeks bearing gifts. We must control the party through its purse.

Already great progress has been made. The reform of the federal Civil Service during the last thirty years has tended towards the moralization and the democratization of the party by reducing on this side the amount of blackmail which it is enabled to levy. Laws against the granting of free passes by railroads have put a stop to another form of party corruption. Finally, the prohibition of campaign contributions by corporations and the compulsory publication by the parties of the source of moneys received and of the destination of moneys expended limit the scope of an evil financial influence upon the party.

The democratization of the party and of the primary is chiefly desired because it leads to the democratization of elections. About the voting booth is fought the main battle between democracy and plutocracy.

The democratization of elections no longer takes in the main the direction of an extension of male suffrage. Fortunately the federal Constitution left to the several States the right to determine the qualifications of voters,[1] with the result that the religious and property tests of 1787, not descending to us as priceless heritages, were rapidly and successively abrogated. Forty years after the adoption of the Constitution, De Tocqueville could write "Universal suffrage has been adopted in all the States of the Union."

This "universal suffrage," debarring, as it did, women and Negroes, was an adult, male, white suffrage, and that in the main is what it is to-day. The voters, who in 1908 were qualified to vote for Taft or Bryan, would for the most part have been qualified in 1840 to vote for Harrison or Van Buren. In 1840, with few newspapers, bad roads, and a sparsely settled population, there were 14.1 voters to every thousand of the population; in 1908, there were not quite 17 voters per thousand. Although full woman suffrage has been established in six of our States, over 95 per cent of the adult women of the country are still without this full vote. The suffrage, extended after the Civil War to the Southern Negroes, has practically been withdrawn.

Nor is there much likelihood that, in the near future, there will be any diversion of the democratic activities of the majority to the securing of a wider vote for Negroes. In the matter of Negro suffrage we have witnessed a sharp reaction from the noble optimism of fifty years ago. To-day, millions of men, discouraged by the dwindling but still large residuum of Negro ignorance, discouraged by the passion which sweeps like a torrid wind over every phase of the question, seek to avoid the subject of Negro suffrage, as their grandfathers, the "finality men" of the fifties, sought to evade the subject of Negro slavery. There are sons of Northern soldiers who deplore the invidious distinction between black ignorance and white ignorance, between black

[1] Art. I, Sec. 11. While the federal government has the right of creating citizens, the State governments, subject nominally to the 14th and 15th amendments, have the right to determine who shall vote.

grandfathers and white grandfathers, but who wish to postpone the problem of Negro enfranchisement until other pressing problems of our new democracy are in process of solution. Similarly many men, who have more than a platonic affection for woman's suffrage, are too absorbed in the problem of increasing the potency of present voters to give more than a casual adherence to the cause of the women. "Let us increase our vote," these men seem to say, "but above all let us make our present vote count."

The first step in making the vote count was to see that it was counted. From the beginning ballot stuffing, the rifling (or stealing) of ballot boxes, the adding of votes by the most fantastic processes of political arithmetic, had made of voting an unmeaning, if rather an impressive, rite. Fortunately the task of remedying these evils was begun decades ago. Systems of preëlection registration resulted in an heroic purging of a phantom electorate, and stopped the worst excesses of our "plural" voters. The sweeping victories of the Australian ballot moderated the widespread intimidation of voters and enormously reduced the scope of bribery.

Even with these reforms, we are far from an absolutely democratic election. Apart from our gerrymandered electoral districts and our non-representation of large minorities — and even of majorities — we still halt behind our ideals. Progress, however, is being made. Our latter-day democrats are no longer satisfied with the husk of a meaningless vote. They do not wish to give their suffrages to candidates without knowing who they are, for a vote in ignorance is no vote. They do not wish to vote for a tail of insignificant nobodies upon the soaring kite of one conspicuous candidate. Finally, they desire no more electoral middlemen, but prefer to vote directly for their own representatives, even for United States senators, rather than to vote for men who will vote for these officials.

That the American democracy is possessed of political capacity and resourcefulness is shown by the fact that a large proportion of our United States senators are already being elected by what is practically the direct vote of the people of their State. The Constitution of the United States distinctly prescribes that the Senate "shall be composed of two senators from each State, *chosen by the Legislature thereof*." [1] An amendment to this constitutional provision has often been proposed, but the indirectly elected senators have not been precipitate in its welcome. In the meanwhile, a number of Western States have used the direct primary to attain this result indirectly. In these States any person seeking a nomination as State legislator may promise in advance that if nominated and elected he will vote for the people's candidate for United States senator *irrespective of personal preferences;* or, by declining so to pledge himself, he may commit political suicide. The result is that the *recommendation* of the people becomes binding upon all legislators irrespective of party, so that it occasionally happens that a State legislature of one party elects a United States senator of the opposing party. With respect to this one function, the State legislators become mere delegates, as automatic in their actions as are the members of the Electoral College, who choose the President. The people elect their own senators.[2]

Even though the people nominate and elect their candidate, how can they control him *after* election?

The old solution of this difficulty was to threaten the repre-

[1] Art. I, Sec. 111.

[2] Senators thus directly nominated have constituencies, but senators elected according to the old method have none. The State legislators who elect the latter are politically short-lived members of assemblies, which lapse long before the six years' term of the Senate is over. Their representative quality is exceedingly dubious, since in any modern sense of the phrase a man cannot be represented by any one over whose selection he does not exercise direct control.

sentative that if he betrayed his trust he would *never* be reëlected. This method was not efficacious. The legislator shrewdly interpreted the word "never" in a Gilbertian sense, as meaning "hardly ever." The boss was near; the "people" (to the politician the word was only a political expression) were distant. Many a roistering legislator preferred a short and a merry political life to a leaner career spread over a longer period.

The new solution is the recall. The recall is like the long arm of coincidence. It is always ready. It is always threatening. In the heyday of his political triumphs, the legislator is in the valley of the shadow of the recall. The corrupt official is not even sure of immediate gleanings, since he may be cut down in his prime by the very people who have just elected him.

The virtue of the recall, which has already been adopted by many American cities, lies in its ease of application. A certain fraction of the qualified voters (usually 25 per cent) may sign a petition for the removal of any elected officer. In the ensuing special election the official is a candidate (unless he specifically declines to run); but if he fails to receive a plurality, he is deemed removed from office as soon as the plurality candidate qualifies as his successor.

For the time being the recall is in high favor with the democracy, and the demand for its adoption appears with increasing frequency in the platforms and protestations of the political parties. It is to be noted, however, that the democracy does not everywhere proceed along identical lines, but that in different places and even in the same place it proposes alternative reforms for the same evil. It labors for the democratic control of the party, while simultaneously striving for its abolition.[1] It asks at once for the democratization of the representative system and for its displacement

[1] See the movement for nominations by petition, which is intended absolutely to circumvent the party and destroy its main use.

by a direct democracy, in which the people, rather than their representatives, will propose and enact legislation. The recall, intended to increase the control of the people over suspected representatives, is likely to have a useful life during a period of political transition, but it is hardly probable that it will be widely used if America goes over to direct democracy.[1]

There are two great complementary features of direct legislation,—the referendum and the initiative.

The referendum is the people's veto. Under the referendum, bills passed by the legislature are referred to the people, either automatically or upon the demand of a certain proportion of the voters, and are accepted or rejected by the people. On the other hand, the initiative is a device by which a certain number of electors may *propose* a measure, which, with or without the approval of the legislature, must be referred to the people. The referendum enables the people to veto undesired legislation. The initiative enables the people to enact desired legislation.

The fundamental principle of the referendum is that it is desirable that the voters have the opportunity of expressing themselves upon all problems which they consider of paramount importance. Our present system is far from this ideal. In our presidential elections, there are always a score of issues and half a dozen potentially "paramount" issues, upon each of which each of the two great parties delivers itself in emphatic ambiguities. The American voter, as confused as a child at a four-ringed circus, seeks to answer a dozen questions and decide among a hundred candidates, not by writing a three-volume book, but by putting his mark under the Republican or the Democratic emblem. To state his preference on all these problems, "to say aye or no to these

[1] In the Swiss cantons the recall (on a somewhat different basis), while it remains a possible weapon in times of emergency, is now rarely used, inasmuch as the referendum and the initiative make an appeal to it seldom necessary.

particulars," he would have to borrow Gargantua's mouth. Instead — to change the metaphor — he can only wag his tail up or down. The result is that post-election reasons for victory and defeat "are as plentiful as blackberries," and the journals of the opposed political parties are farther apart in interpreting "the plain verdict of the people" than were party platforms or party candidates before election.

The referendum gives the dumb god, Demos, a voice. The referendum, combined with the initiative, is the yes or no answer of the people to a definite question, propounded by the legislators or by the people. It is the power of the voters to propose laws and amendments to the State constitution; to enact or reject such laws and amendments, and to confirm or nullify all legislative action. It is the ultimate appeal from the people's representatives to the people.

The adoption of the referendum and initiative tends to limit the range and decision of our elected legislators. It tends to transform these legislators from representatives, possessed of personal, individual opinions (although elected because their opinions are in supposed accord with those of their constituents) into mere delegates; into mere mechanical forecasters and repeaters of popular deliverances; into parrot-like, political phonographs. The recall, by keeping the popular thumb upon the recalcitrant lawgiver, acts in the same way.

The result may not always be good. A high-spirited statesman, placed in a position where he may be checked, halted, thwarted — often, most unreasonably — where an appeal lies from his every action, where even his tenure depends upon his "giving satisfaction," is tempted to withdraw from the impotent eminence of office; or, if he remain, he may suffer in initiative, courage, and self-esteem. If we adopt direct legislation with anything like logical consistency, we shall not have a Pitt, a Burke, a Webster, a Calhoun in every State assembly and city council.

Without direct government, however, we have a plentiful lack of such notables, and we have blundered through a legislative century with lawgivers who were not always high-spirited, nor even invariably honest. If a measure of direct government does not improve our best legislators, it may accomplish something equally important. It may improve the worst.

Moreover, although men are crying that representative government is dead and that the occupation of the legislator is gone, the fundamental issue in America is in reality not between representative and direct government (both of which systems have merits, inconveniences, and perils), but between a *misrepresentative*, plutocratic government and a democratic government, whether representative, direct, or mixed. America is seeking the cure of a seeming democracy in real democracy. If universal suffrage leads to ignorant voting, the cure is not a restriction of the suffrage, but an education of the voters. If the party controls politics, then the party must be democratized or destroyed. So with our so-called representative system. It must be democratized or destroyed.

The referendum is not perfect any more than the secret ballot or the policeman's club is perfect. It is merely the best expedient in the present circumstances. With the referendum we shall doubtless enact into law a vast deal of sublimated nonsense — as we do now without the referendum. Even if the average quality of our laws were to be somewhat lowered by the referendum (which in America seems improbable), we might still accept that drawback because of the measure of insurance which the direct appeal to the people gives us against corrupt legislation and the grant of valuable franchises and concessions by men who have been paid their price.

Under our so-called representative government, bribery becomes as safe and as venial as mere perjury. Bribed men tell no tales; bribers are equally reticent. When the consideration is a fee for "professional services," or the chance to be carried on a broker's books and win "heads" or "tails"; when bribery appears under as many disguises as the good M. Lecoq, our primitive, punitive laws, while necessary, are singularly innocuous. The incarceration of a few pitiable bribe takers (whose offense is mere unskillfulness) is as little consoling to the robbed people as would be the spectacle of thieves rotting on gibbets, especially when the briber flourishes like a bay tree and the franchise (the occasion of the bribe) is gone forever.

To prevent bribery in such cases, an ounce of referendum is worth a dozen State prisons. If no franchise may be given without the special consent of the people, it wonderfully reduces the vogue and scope of financial corruption. For the briber is a frugal and a timorous man, who will not trust his argosies to unknown waves, and the vote of an alderman, councilman, assemblyman, or State Senator — to go no higher — is of less value, when what he has to sell has "a string to it," and the unbuyable people hold the string.

In their use of the referendum, the American people will be far more fortunate if they remember some of its defects and limitations. Its tendency (at least when separated from the initiative) is somewhat conservative.[1] Its result depends upon the manner in which the legislative questions are propounded. It is likely to weary the electors if too freely used. It is likely to be used by weak-kneed legislators to throw the burden of an awkward decision back upon the electors. Finally, it cannot accomplish the impossible. It cannot do alone what can only be accomplished by a com-

[1] Under the Swiss federal referendum about two thirds of all laws submitted are rejected. The Swiss, both in federal and cantonal votings, tend to reject novel proposals, although a measure rejected once or twice or oftener may ultimately be accepted. The majority against a law may be merely a bundle of minorities, one group voting against one clause, another group against a second clause, and a third group against a third clause.

bination of reforms. It cannot remake the people. If the people are a sleeping princess, waiting for the fairy prince of political saviors to awaken it, then the referendum will not avail any more than any other device of government. If the people do not want, they will not get. A referendum is no more valuable than a vote of an assembly, if the people do not vote at the referendum.

Within the limits set by these conditions, however, the referendum, united with the initiative, has vast possibilities in our present state of politics. Not only may it check much of our residual corruption, not only may it directly give to the people a larger measure of political control than they now possess, but it may have the even greater merit of being a vast school of democratic education. If our referendum votes can be made educational campaigns, free from personalities, the result may be a large and direct contribution to political morality and education.

When we analyze these changes — direct nominations, the recall, the initiative, the referendum — we find that their common characteristic is the directness of their appeal to the rule of the majority. This directness is part of a democratic tendency to make all political processes simpler. Our legal and political, like our industrial, problems are becoming daily more intricate. Despite our more diffused education, therefore, it becomes increasingly necessary that our disconcerting difficulties should not be increased by obscurities, stumbling blocks, and handicaps in our political machinery. Our governmental system must be as understandable as is compatible with efficiency and with a just representation of all classes. We must have a glass-house government; a government standardized and systematized; a government with double-entry bookkeeping; with conspicuous heads; with the line of responsibility leading straight and clear from the obscurest subofficial to the responsible chief. Obscurity works in the interest of special classes; clarity in the interest of the people. If the people are to rule, they must not be made to waste their vision, enthusiasm, or indignation in vain attempts to determine who is to blame or what it is all about.

This simplicity of political arrangements is necessary to governmental efficiency, without which no great extension of governmental functions is possible. If an oligarchic but efficient industry is opposed by a lax and inefficient government, the former will easily escape effective regulation. If factory inspectors, tax receivers, and "plain-clothes men" accept bribes; if civil servants buy their places with contributions to political parties; if the government, losing money on all its ventures, spends two dollars where only one dollar was spent before, the industrial oligarchy will be safe, because the people will prefer present evils to those which a corrupt and inefficient government might introduce into business.

Years ago our public administration was so dishonest and so incomparably inefficient that private business did not anticipate any great popularity for the governmental regulation of industry.[1] To-day things are different. Thanks largely to the incentive of business men, government is becoming quite reasonably efficient.

When the plutocracy began to organize the country's business, it found that it was also necessary to improve certain phases of government. To compete with British and German manufacturers, we needed a better consular service. For the sake of business, we needed better fire and police protection, better sanitation, better administration of the wharves, a better service generally. Efficiency, however, is a contagious virtue, and inefficiency, which lives comfortably by itself in pleasant dark places, cannot co-exist with efficiency. One branch after another of the civil service of nation, State, and city improved. Red tape,

[1] Thirty years ago we did not know how corrupt *private* business was, nor from what respectable sources official corruption came.

goose quills, and a bewigged and pompous ceremonial gave way to counting machines, public automobiles, and an easy and rapid dispatch of public business. Intolerable conditions became in some governmental places tolerable; in some places, fairly good; in some, excellent.

To-day the administrative efficiency of our federal government is as much superior to what it was a generation ago, as is the efficiency of the locomotive of 1911 to that of the locomotive of 1876. The superlatively efficient Standard Oil Company probably does not conduct its business with truer economy and efficiency than have been manifested by the federal government in the construction of the Panama Canal. We are carrying out our great irrigation works, and conducting (in connection with them) a manifold series of auxiliary businesses with a reasonable degree of success. Our post office service, though somewhat hobbled by holdovers (both men and methods), compares nevertheless in net efficiency with the great express companies.[1] Our national forests are admirably run; our federal Department of Agriculture (which is a great nonprofit-earning business) is conducted as well as the average University, or private philanthropic institution. The same is true of many branches of our State and local governments.

The improvement in our civil service alone marks a great step forward. A quarter of a century ago, one of the most convincing arguments against a proposed government operation of railroads was that the admission of half a million railroad employees would still further demoralize our corrupt civil service. In 1911, with almost two million

[1] Comparisons between the rival efficiency of government, and private businesses cannot be made solely on the basis of profits. The government willingly pays higher wages than it is compelled to pay. It willingly gives a better service than it is compelled to give. It gladly conducts a large part of its business at a fiscal loss, but at a social gain. On the whole, the people of the United States can better pay high wages to government employees than allow exorbitant profits to promoters of express companies.

steam railroad employees, this particular difficulty seems less formidable. There are everywhere signs of an increasing recognition by our more democratic governments that to fulfill their functions they must be efficient. The last twenty years have witnessed an enormous advance in the sheer efficiency of our local governments. Bureaus of Municipal Research point out improvements in municipal administration; annual congresses of municipal officials enable comparative studies to be made of municipal methods.[1] In many localities we have efficient government of cities by small commissions, democratically elected, invested with great power and with clear responsibility, and subject to immediate recall by an adverse majority.

All this efficiency is important, but a still greater efficiency on a far higher plane is necessary if we are to democratize our industrial and political life. Our political machinery — national, State, and local; legislative, executive, administrative, and judicial; constitutional and extraconstitutional — our whole political machinery in all its parts must be adapted to all the changing purposes of government. It is of small advantage that our legislators are democratically nominated, elected, and controlled; it is of small advantage that each separate government wheel turns with a noiseless ease, if the system *as a whole* is ill-geared. If in a government there is a lack of proper coördination among parts; if certain parts are weak which should be strong, and certain

[1] It is important that efficiency be not identified with lessened governmental expenditures, with a cheeseparing and a special care for the preservation of the governmental lead pencils and the soap and towels in the public offices. In these days of rapidly expanding governmental functions the bark of "the watchdog of the treasury" is not the epitome of political wisdom. The true policy is fairly well stated in the (1910) Platform of the New York State Independence League: "While emphasizing the importance of a business-like and economical administration, we believe that the State should unhesitatingly expend whatever is necessary for the complete performance of its functions."

parts are strong which might be weak; if between State and nation there are jurisdictional disputes; and if there are jurisdictional disputes between legislative and judiciary; if there is fluctuation where there should be stability, and a stiff unchangeability where there should be elasticity and change, — if there are these or any of these, then no true efficiency can be maintained.

Of all these elements of national inefficiency the delimitation of powers between the federal and the State governments is the most patent. Democratic reforms are often far more difficult to effect than in England or in France because in the United States there may be a conflict of authority between State and federal jurisdictions. Labor laws which in England or France would be passed by the national legislature and become law for the whole country must here be enacted, not by the federal government, but by each State for its own residents, and a law passed in any such State may be declared unconstitutional because in violation of the federal Constitution.

We are increasingly perceiving that many of our problems are national problems and cannot be solved by any governmental unity less than the nation. Regulation of interstate railroads has long since passed beyond effective State action, and the regulation of our great industrial corporations is similarly beyond the scope of State action. In the matter of the conservation of our natural resources, in the matter of the taxation of incomes and of inheritances, even in the problem of education and of certain forms of labor and factory legislation, we should be far better off for an extension of our federal powers.

By this it is not meant that we should surrender our federal system of "an indissoluble union of indestructible States," or that we should reduce those States to the status of counties or *départements*. There are many advantages to our present system. It permits the more progressive

States to go forward without waiting for the consent of the less advanced States.[1] It permits us to maintain political experiment stations, where new ideas may be tried out quickly and on a small scale. It enables us to make our mistakes cheaply. But it is also used to halt progress and to maintain reactionary districts from the impact of democratic forces. It is used as an obstacle to progress, when men who want *no* conservation plead for State as against national conservation. It is used to prevent national action and to thwart State action, and to delay each in the supposed interest of the other.

To an extent, our government already answers to the needs of the people, but it does so ineffectually, like a clumsy, ancient engine which utilizes only one or two per cent of the power applied to it. More or less we can obviate the evils of our present imperfect federal system by creating new extra-legal agencies, such as the house of governors, or other means of creating a unanimous action by a large number of States. Progress towards a really effective and specialized democratic government can be made in other ways. We can establish a larger measure of municipal home rule; we can reform our legislative methods in the House of Representatives[2] and elsewhere; we can more completely separate local from national politics, and we can increase our independent voting both in municipal and in

[1] Under a system of uniform, contemporaneous legislation by a group of progressive States, a more rapid advance can probably be made than could be made by waiting for the larger political body — the nation — to move.

[2] The attempt to reform the rules of the House of Representatives led, in 1910, to a severe conflict between house insurgents and house "standpatters." It is interesting to reflect that the rules of the House of Representatives, which can be changed at any moment by a vote of a majority of the House (without the concurrence of Senate or of President) have probably done more within later decades to obstruct democratic progress than has the unequal distribution among the States of senators, although the latter cannot (theoretically) be changed against the will of any State *even by the process of constitutional amendment.*

national elections. Finally, within the States we can secure proportional representation.[1]

Much of our progress towards a complete majority government might be made without any change in the federal Constitution. Sooner or later, however, the growing political democracy will be aborted and halted by the inelasticity of that document, and in the time to come a demand will be made for fundamental constitutional transformations and adjustments.

Upon the manner in which this demand is made and met will depend much of the future political history of the United States. If the Constitution will permit itself to be changed to meet the changing needs of the nation, it will grow in dignity and prestige. If, on the other hand, it does not change, or if it changes too slowly to permit political transformations to be made with a minimum of friction, then it will be broken, violently distorted, or swept aside.

It would be a mistake on the part of those who wish the Constitution to remain forever as it is to count too much upon its popularity as an obstacle to change. That the document is stupendously popular is evident. But the Constitution will remain popular only so long as it permits the progressive attainment by the people of the things which they desire. The veneration in which the Constitution has so long been held, has largely been due to our prosperity

[1] So completely are we wedded to the idea of a political representation of geographical districts instead of a representation of classes, and of like-minded groups of men generally, that we do not, as a rule, even consider the advisability of adopting proportional representation. Under that system, if there are one hundred legislators to be elected by one million voters, then any ten thousand voters, no matter where situate, would be qualified to elect their candidate. The advantage of proportional representation is that it gives representation, not only to the minority, but also, and even more effectually, to the majority. It puts a stop to gerrymandering, and by making legislators more truly representative of like-minded constituents, it allows men of conviction to take the places of our present eclectic and shrinking representatives.

during the constitutional period, just as the late Queen Victoria owed much of her popularity to a similar cause. Like the Republican Party the Constitution has profited by good crops and a boundless continent. If, however, it comes to be believed that whatever the plutocracy wants is constitutional and whatever we want is unconstitutional, — there will follow an astounding deliquescence of the wisdom of our ancestors.

For the time being, the Constitution will probably change, as it has changed during the last century, by process of interpretation. Nine men, seated in the Supreme Court at Washington, hearing more or less distinctly the clamor of a hundred million people outside, judging more or less wisely of the constitutional needs of these hundred millions of people, will continue under the fiction of interpretation to adapt our century-old Constitution to our present needs. Upon these nine politically irresponsible men will rest a tremendous moral reponsibility. It is possible for them by a few progressive judicial decisions to democratize the Constitution. It is equally possible to evoke a dangerous constitutional conflict by a few reactionary decisions.

It is to be hoped that as the years roll on the nine Supreme Court judges, making and remaking a Constitution for a hundred million people, will more and more feel the impact, the psychological attraction, of all these millions. It is to be hoped that the stamp of the popular will may be stamped on these nine minds as it is stamped upon the minds of our presidential electors, upon our western legislators assembled to elect a United States senator, and to a less degree upon the minds of our Congressmen and of the President of the United States. We can reach to the Supreme Court only through a series of channels. But already it is evident that Presidents are becoming increasingly anxious to appoint justices who will meet with the approval of the nation, and that the senators, who confirm the appointments are not entirely unsusceptible to similar influences. Direct election of senators should mean more democratic senators; more democratic senators should mean more democratic Supreme Court justices; more democratic justices should mean a more democratic Constitution.

All this is progress, but it is the progress of the child, not of the adult nation. The Constitution should be revised by the people. A radical revision of the Constitution by a special constitutional convention, such as was contemplated by the document itself, would be one of the greatest single steps towards establishing a political democracy in the United States.

An alternative step, perhaps even wiser, would be, not a complete transformation of the document, but a mere change in the method of amendment, a change which would make future amendment easier and would give the power of proposing and of adopting amendments to the people, rather than to legislatures, State and federal.

Herein lies the scope of the constitutional initiative and referendum, which transcends the scope of the legislative initiative and referendum as the Constitution transcends a law. In changing our federal Constitution we should adopt a system similar to that adopted by the far more democratic federal republic of Switzerland. A given number of qualified voters, let us say one or two millions, should be allowed to propose any constitutional amendment, which should then be voted upon (on a single day) by all the qualified voters of the nation, and should be considered carried and should be made a part of the Constitution of the United States if accepted by a majority of all the voters, as well as by a majority in a majority of all the States.

Even with a constitution sensitive to the popular will, even with the referendum, initiative, and all the instruments and weapons of a pure political democracy, it would not follow that legislation would be in the interest of the people.

The referendum enables the people to decide. It does not make them decide wisely.

Under a political democracy the people may vote in their own despite. They may be jingoistic, imperialistic, reactionary. They may vote themselves a king, with or without a title. They may break into warring factions, and, in the absense of unity, allow real sovereignty to slip through their fingers. A nation in breechcloths, but without a king, is not a democracy. Neither is a nation with a twentieth century political democracy, but without the mind and the will to rule itself.

The end goal of the democracy is thus a social goal. It is the improvement, physical, intellectual, and moral, of the millions who make up the democracy. It is such an advancement and increase of the progressive masses that the gains made on the political and industrial fields may be increased, retained, and wisely utilized.

CHAPTER XIX

THE SOCIAL PROGRAM OF THE DEMOCRACY

THE social goal of the democracy is the advancement and improvement of the people through a democratization of the advantages and opportunities of life. This goal is to be attained through a conservation of life and health, a democratization of education, a socialization of consumption, a raising of the lowest elements of the population to the level of the mass.

The most elemental phase of this social policy is conservation. The phrase "the conservation of human resources" has attained a considerable popularity because of the vogue of the analogous policy of the conservation of natural resources. But the word "conservation" is too narrow, for the democratic ideal is not only to maintain, but vastly to increase and improve, the life, health, intellect, character, and social qualities of the citizenry.

This policy does not consider life solely from a quantitative standpoint. The demand for large populations is not democratic in origin. It is the despot who wants soldiers; the business prince who wants cheap labor; the jingo who believes in a swaggering, fighting nation. In democratic countries, on the other hand, a decrease in the birth rate has accompanied an improved education, a more diffused comfort, and a rise in the general standard of living. The more advanced the country, the section, or the social class, the more marked in general has been the tendency away from the old blind propagation of the species. The democracy does not desire that life be given to so many that the gift becomes of no value. It does not wish to see a swarming population pressing upon the means of subsistence. It desires a full life for all who are born, but it does not measure national success by the numbers who are born.

This distinction between the number and the value of lives explains one of the most curious anomalies of modern democratic policy. Although the democracy is beginning to desire rather a lessened than an increased birth rate, it demands absolutely that every child born shall have a chance to live. The basis of democratic strivings toward human conservation is an ethical belief in the sanctity of human life, and the desire for an equality in this universal possession. Life is the one thing which all have in common; and while the expectation of life is by no means equal as between social classes, it is far more equal than is property, education, political power, or economic opportunities.

How far we still are from any real equality even in the probable years of our lives is seen in our statistics of accidents and of preventable diseases, which reveal our social recklessness toward our very poor. It is the poor who die young. It is the poor who die of preventable diseases, or are killed by accidents and by dangerous occupations and poisonous foods. When society fails in its duties, the poor die. And the more the poor die, the more poor there remain.

To save life involves a social intelligence and a social conscience. Our ideas of protecting life are as yet rudimentary. We do not permit a man to put arsenic in his neighbor's coffee nor a stiletto in his neighbor's side, but we have only begun to prevent the selling of "embalmed beef" and other deadly foods, and we still permit the killing of workmen and workwomen by means of lead, phosphorus, and unfended machinery. We do not allow a man to contract to commit suicide, but we not only permit, we actually *presuppose*, a contract by which the workman in a dangerous occupation assumes the "ordinary risks" of the trade. As for the tens of thousands of infants who annually die of bad milk and bad houses, we do not even know that they die needlessly.

A large part of our unprevented mortality is due to our fearful national heedlessness. Just as for years we have sacrificed thousands of lives to our Fourth of July barbarities, so we have annually sacrificed other thousands to our desire to cross railway tracks, and to our general willingness "to take a chance." But behind this recklessness, individual and social, there remains the desire of individuals to profit at the expense of the people, whether the price is paid in life, or in health, comfort, and money. The railroad runs its locomotives through the heart of a metropolis, and only accepts automatic couplers after years of obstruction. The manufacturer insists upon leaving his machinery unguarded; the great mining company upholds its right to neglect the most elementary and least costly of safety devices. In our mines, railroads, and factories we kill two, three, and five times as many workmen per thousand as do other nations; and in many industries and in many States we do not even trouble to count the slain. We are still unwilling to pay for the complete sanitation of a city, for the uprooting of tuberculosis, for the distribution of proper milk to infants, or for a civilized housing policy which would lessen the disgraceful mortality of certain districts of our large cities.

Everywhere we are halted in our progress towards the conservation of the lives and health of all the people by the obstruction of interested persons and by considerations of cost. We save pennies to individuals and cause society to lose pounds by our petty savings of money at the expense of life and health. On a mere calculation of dollars and cents, it is a foolish extravagance to allow a baby to die for lack of a few dollars' worth of pure milk, or to allow an expensively bred workman to die for lack of a few hundred dollars spent in protection and prevention.[1] But we do not yet realize

[1] Every preventable death is a reflection upon the good will or the in-

that it is we as a community who pay for these deaths, although we only too clearly realize that it is we who pay for their prevention.

In contrast with our old attitude of tolerance for social assassination, however, we are now beginning an energetic campaign of human conservation. We are instituting excellent and, in many places, free hospital and dispensary service. We are making nurse and doctor public servants, and are introducing them into the public schools. We are fighting typhoid fever with uncontaminated water supplies, and tuberculosis not only by a direct attack but with improved housing and factory conditions. We are improving city and State Boards of Health and are striving for a National Board of Health, which shall supervise the general health conditions of the nation. In our cities we are providing public parks, public recreation centers, public baths. Our city and State authorities are doubling the protection of the milk, meat, and other foods of the people. Our factory legislation and our laws regulating dangerous occupations have resulted in a considerable saving of life, while our laws against child labor have had an enormously beneficial effect. All of which changes, together with a rapid advance in sanitary science and a vast improvement in the standards of living of the people, have resulted in a rapid decline in the death rate, especially in the cities.

After all this progress, however, we are still only in the beginning of our democratic campaign of life-saving. To conserve life and health, society must enormously increase its efforts along present lines and must open up new routes of progress. We must organize the campaign on State (and national) lines. Sooner or later we must insure our popu-

telligence of the community which suffers it. Society should regard every death below the age of sixty as a subject of serious thought. There should be a coroner's inquest when a man dies of typhoid fever or lead poisoning. Dying young should be forbidden by law.

lations against sickness, accident, and invalidity, and must devote enormous sums to the prevention of these calamities. The advantage of an obligatory, universal state insurance is not only that it changes one's unknown individual liability for a known social liability, but also that it compels society to recognize that it itself is the loser from each preventable death and each preventable sickness. When the State of New York makes itself *financially* responsible for the health and lives of ten or twenty millions of citizens, it will be willing to spend money to prevent sickness and death.

To secure the health and lives of the people we must socialize the business of health-keeping. It would pay us in the higher efficiency and better tone of the community to spend annually hundreds of millions of dollars of public money upon the prevention and cure of disease. Once we regard the health of the population as a social instead of merely as an individual asset, when we come to consider the maintenance of the citizen's health as a social duty rather than as a personal prerogative, we shall have enormously advanced towards a healthy and prosperous community.[1]

The lessening of the infantile death rate (combined with a lessening of the birth rate) is a sign that we are already making progress in the conservation of life. The birth of babies who die in infancy is a pitiable social waste. If a high death rate of babies meant a selection of the socially fittest, if it were a subtle eugenic plan of nature, it might be worth all it costs in misery. In present circumstances, however, the death of babies is as arbitrary as decimation.

[1] Our poverty, while a cause of illness, is largely a consequence of illness and of early (preventable) death. Much of the misery of the great cities affects the widows and orphaned children of men who died young, the wives and children of sick men, and people of both sexes and all ages who have become permanently debilitated as a result of illnesses which need never have been contracted.

The economic position of the baby, not its inherited qualities, constitutes its chief danger or immunity.

Like the newborn infant, so the growing child is accorded an ever widening protection. Instruction becomes compulsory and universal. The free school, through the kindergarten, reaches out towards babyhood and, through the high school, to adolescence. The state, as guardian, increases its authority, as the paternal authority weakens. Wide programs of child welfare work are proposed and progressively executed. The greatest revolution of the last half century is the revolution in the status of the child.

Similarly, in the interest of human conservation we must rectify or totally destroy our parasitic trades. There are two more or less distinct classes of parasitic industries; those which prey upon other industries, and those which prey upon human life. An industry is parasitic in this latter sense in proportion as it directly or indirectly increases sickness, produces deterioration, or shortens life.

It is in the sweated trades that the labor of women and children (especially of immigrant women and children) is most harshly exploited. In the making of artificial flowers, in the sorting of rags, in the fabrication of many articles of clothing, the work is carried on under the worst possible hygienic conditions for a derisory wage, in the interest of a cheap product.

From the point of view of society this cheapness is dearness and sheer wastefulness. It would be wiser to pay a few cents a gross more for our artificial flowers. It would be cheaper to pay our bounty in dollars than in the life and health of the workers.

To cure the evils of parasitic trades we must have recourse to legislation. We cannot trust that the exploiters (themselves for the most part exploited) will desist from their profits. A parasite which had compunctions about inconveniencing its host would be likely to succumb.

What is necessary is a wide extension both in the application and in the principles of our factory laws. We must extend the signification of the word "parasitic." We must come to regard as parasitic, not only those industries which destroy women and little children, but also those which, though paying high wages, have an unnecessarily high mortality or morbidity rate, and also those which, because of long hours, excessive strain, or for other causes, do not permit a reasonable development of the personality of the workers. We must regulate factory conditions for men, women, and children, and we must so change our legal traditions as to permit the state to establish, not only maximum hours of labor of men, but also, in the worst-paid trades, minimum wages.

The conservation of human resources is a step towards the equalization of the chances of life and health of the citizens. The democratization of education is a step towards the equalization of the chances of intellectual development.

A progressively diffused education is necessary to the maintenance of the democracy. A political democracy may be reactionary in its industrial and social policies, and the people may secure control both of the state and of industry without knowing enough to turn such control to their advantage. To maintain itself, the democracy must use its powers to still further educate and strengthen itself.

There was a time, in the optimistic days preceding the French Revolution, when men believed that no long training would be necessary to teach men to rule. The people would attain their full intellectual and moral stature as soon as political tyranny was destroyed. Democracy was in its youth. It was violent, hopeful, moody. It saw visions. It had a touching faith in many beatitudes. It believed that all men were by nature good; that all ills were due to civilization—to law, government, titles of nobility, small clothes, and small talk. Civilization, being but an excrescence upon nature, might be excised. The bitter, million-year-old world would become young and sweet again. The masses of the oppressed would become wise and temperate men ruling themselves by the light of reason.

Unfortunately the hopes of the eighteenth-century philosophers were not entirely realized. Skulls are desperately obstinate things, and unreasonable convictions have a woeful longevity. Ignorance, superstition, reaction, crushed to earth, rose again — and again. The peasants, after emancipation, did not become philosophers.

Our more sober democracy of to-day has a less absolute faith in the immediate perfectibility of man. It realizes that men's minds change slowly, and that much education and much time are required. We realize, to-day, that just as the people have not all the vices, so also they have not all the virtues, ascribed to them. They are not so arbitrary, undisciplined, ignorant as was predicted. Nor are they so public-spirited. The average man does not cheerfully give up his holiday to serve on a jury, and the average housewife is more anxious to secure a good servant than to have the Panama Canal finished. The people are often too patient or too passionate. They are often too belligerent.

The most diverse classes are united upon the policy of educating the whole people because upon that education depends the safety of the various groups which constitute the nation. The very possibility of misrule by a passionate, accidental majority is the *saving menace* of a democracy. It is this menace which crumbles our intellectual snobbery and abases our intellectual pride. For, if we are to have universities, and the universities are to receive public funds, not only must the learned come from their cloisters (as to so large an extent they have already done), but they must appeal to a population sufficiently intelligent and cultured to appreciate learning and culture. In a democracy, wherein a real political power (including a real control over industry) extends downwards to the masses of the people, it is manifestly impossible to give a monopoly of any of the benefits of life to any one class. For the sake of the cultured, the masses must have the opportunities of culture.

Not only is an extension of education indispensable to the maintenance of a socialized democracy, but it is precisely in a democracy that education is most necessary to a high national efficiency. Education reacts powerfully upon the production, distribution, and consumption of wealth. There is no private industry in the United States which pays as high dividends as does the business of furnishing the proper education to the proper persons. If the government were annually to give free agricultural and industrial instruction to hundreds of thousands of youths (and were actually to pay them to attend school), the increase in the productiveness of the farms and factories would more than pay for the expenditure.

We have already taken many steps towards the socialization of education, but we are still far from the ideal of a society in which all forms of education are entirely accessible to all qualified citizens. We should have free education from kindergarten to university for all children and youths who are willing and able to follow the courses, and we should have scholarships and scholars' pensions for all capable scholars who have not the means to abstain from gainful work. All this would of course cost money, especially if we not only increased the quantity, but raised the quality, of our education, but there is no better way in which the increased wealth of the country could be invested.[1]

[1] Many pressing educational reforms, such as the increase in the number of teachers, the raising of the standards of teachers, improvements in methods and equipment, are chiefly held back by considerations of cost. Whether or not the federal government, with its far greater resources, should aid in the extending of school facilities in poor districts is a question which deserves far more consideration than it has received. It is un-

The higher education of the multitude, the granting to men who will become farmers, carpenters, typesetters, perhaps even hodcarriers, of what would be an equivalent of a high school (or even of a modern college) education, would create a revolutionary force in the community of astounding power and magnitude. It would be a force which would act increasingly until our society had become entirely different from any in the history of the world. Not only would such an absolute democratization of all forms of education enormously hasten economic and political control by the masses, but it would render that control permanent and beneficent.

The future education of the masses, however, should not be the traditional, Procrustean, unrelated, and undifferentiated education of yesterday, but an education which fully equips the child for his industrial, political, and social life. For too long the school has been half asylum, half penitentiary. For too long it has stood alone in irrelevant isolation, knowing neither factory nor farm, neither kitchen nor voting booth. For much too long it has been a place where ignorance has taught ignorance, where individuality has been weeded and crushed out.

The progress already made towards a differentiated, modernized education, bearing upon all essential phases of humanity and nurturing all socially valuable individualities, must be indefinitely continued. Our future education must exalt social obligations above mere competitive egoisms. Our new education must expand beyond our expanding schools. It must flow over into the library, the newspaper, the club, the factory. It must be an education which will aid society in the conservation of the life and the health of the citizens and in their progressive development. It must

doubtedly true that the intellectual progress of the nation is hampered by the arrested educational development of the poorer of our Southern States.

aid men in their industrial pursuits, in their political activities, and in their private life outside of industry and politics. It must guide society and individuals in the wise consumption of wealth.

To socialize production we must also socialize consumption. We are entering into an age where men will suffer more from an injudicious, than from an insufficient, consumption of wealth. Food, clothes, books, tools, utensils, amusements, are already pouring in on us at an unprecedentedly rapid rate; and we are consuming without judgment, without moderation, without regard to our individual interests or to the interests of society. Much of this consumption is absolutely noxious. To-day more Americans are seriously injured by an unwise consumption of wealth and by an inept use of leisure than by overwork or by evil conditions of work, although the latter, to a considerable extent, induce the former.

The importance of socializing consumption becomes quite evident when we reflect upon the enormous revenues which under a socialized production would come to the people. A billion dollars saved from banal and pleasure-destroying consumption is a billion dollars — and more — saved. We do not often realize the extent of this waste. What has been called the anarchy of production is order superlative in comparison with the prevailing *anarchy of consumption.* Competition has been carried over from the making of goods to the using of them. Much of our expenditure is a pure competition of display. Fashion, conspicuous waste, absurd extravagance, even among the poor, destroy an astonishing proportion of the national product. The pleasure of Americans consists largely in the breaking of expensive toys.

Much of this unwise and antisocial consumption of wealth is due to ultra-individualism. In consumption, men lack the discipline and coördination which they have learned in production. Moreover, there is manifested in consumption a certain instinctive conservatism, which lies deep in all of us. The man who follows every craze and fad, buying when the crowd buys and forgetting when the crowd forgets, is a timorously conservative consumer of wealth. There are women who are heterodox in religion, politics, and cooking, who nevertheless dare not wear a small hat when other women wear their hats large.

To a considerable extent, mere economic pressure and stimulus may be relied upon to break this conservatism of consumption. The "flat" displaces the house when rents and housemaid's wages rise, and apartment hotels become patronized (and liked) by people who a few years earlier could not have been induced to enter them. The number of persons sleeping out of doors increases far more slowly than does the knowledge that this habit is beneficial; but the multitudes who use safety razors, phonographs, telephones, cameras, and other advertised wares grow with astounding rapidity. The advertisements in magazines and newspapers are thus a better index of the contemporaneous civilization than are the articles and editorials. Unfortunately, however, business cannot always be relied upon to socialize production. It acts equally in the opposite direction by producing articles which are deleterious and absurd, and with no other merit than that of being a link in an endless chain of tasteless ostentation.

To socialize our consumption we must therefore depend upon the direct or indirect action of the state and upon the gradual education of the consumers. We cannot of course revert to sumptuary laws, for nothing would so increase the demand for ostrich feathers as a law forbidding their use to persons "of low degree." We can, however, forbid the unregulated sale of such articles as opium and cocaine, and we may somewhat reduce the consumption of alcohol[1] and

[1] The extreme difficulty of the problem of socializing our consumption is illustrated in the history of our liquor traffic. For too long we have

tobacco by levying a tax upon their manufacture or sale. The renting (and therefore the using) of insufficient or insanitary housing accommodation may be rigorously forbidden by law, and a definite irreducible minimum of quality may be established for all foods bought by the people.

The state can also socialize consumption by furnishing a larger number of common goods. By "common goods" is here meant those commodities and services which are furnished to the citizens in their individual capacity freely, though the citizens pay for them in their collective capacity. To an ever increasing extent the state (national, State, and municipal) is spending for all of us. It is far better that the people of a city enjoy a large park than that a hundred citizens have private parks and a hundred thousand have none. Much of this governmental expenditure (notably that for army, navy, etc.) is still unwise and primitive, but gradually the socially useful expenditure increases. Expenditure by government has the advantage of being non-competitive as between individuals. It has the advantage of buying for the community things which the individuals cannot buy for themselves. It is better regulated. It is on the whole more economical. It gives a greater pleasure per unit of cost, because it is so largely a rendering of satisfactions wholesale instead of retail.

The influence of education upon national consumption is potent and pervasive. Through education we may some-

followed a purely instinctive policy. Prohibition laws are passed and left unenforced, so that "the women have their law and 'the boys' have their whiskey." We incarcerate inebriates for a day or two and discharge them with a thirst, or we send them from court with a three-dollar fine or a semi-humorous reprimand. We have only begun as a nation to learn the interactions between alcoholism, on the one hand, and insanity, feeble-mindedness, child mortality, tuberculosis, and other diseases, prostitution, suicide, unemployment, poverty, and national inefficiency. We are only beginning to trace much of our alcoholism to poverty and much to a starved intellectual life. After decades of striving, we are still at the beginnings of a solution.

what discourage the elephantiasis of consumption to which our present taste runs.[1] Through education we may throw the emphasis upon those economic satisfactions which may be had jointly as opposed to other satisfactions which are personal and exclusive. In educating society to socialize its consumption, moreover, we shall in turn socialize our production, some of the worst evils of which result from our undisciplined consumption.

The article of consumption most often neglected is leisure. Leisure is an indispensable element to all enjoyment. It is the thing in which the American, despite his overflowing wealth, is the poorest.

Americans have never taken time and still do not take time for leisure. We seek to telescope our pleasures, to enjoy much in little time. As a nation we are like the instantaneous American traveler who does the Louvre in an hour and the Vatican in half a morning. We are obsessed by the doctrine of a strenuous life, of a life of effort and labor, without leisure or quiet development.

The American conception of leisure has always been one of mild disapprobation. There was rather a feeling that we should live to labor, not labor to live. This conception, which was more or less explicable during the days of the conquest of the continent, is not a little ludicrous to-day when advanced by the financier who is benefiting by our accumulating surplus. An austere disapprobation of holidays is also given expression by many of our newspapers, and when, to please the Italian vote, a State legislature made Columbus Day a holiday, some of our journals preached eloquent sermons against idle workmen, supine legislators, and reckless Genoese sailors. In the eyes of

[1] We may perhaps also expect a certain approach to a sanity of taste with a more assured income enjoyed for some time. Our present society runs to excess — not only because it is so obstinately competitive, but because we are still *nouveaux riches*.

these journals and of many well-meaning manufacturers and professional men, the workman should prefer to work twelve hours instead of eight, if by working four hours more he earns more.[1]

What is, however, more needed in America than almost anything else is a wider leisure and a better knowledge of how to use it. We need shorter hours for workman, merchant, banker, lawyer, doctor, engineer. The American who has made his money and now dies of *ennui* represents the situation at one end of the line; the Polish workman in a steel mill who labors all day and every day, Sunday, weekday, and holiday, represents it at the other. Between the two we have the "ambitious," "self-respecting" hard-working man, with no idea but labor. What does he earn, this tame, virtuous, self-driven, over-ambitious drudge? More dollars in the bank, fewer years of life, and fewer pleasures while he lives. Better a "sturdy beggar" or a vermin-infested tramp than a desiccated toiler who works twelve hours a day, seven days in the week, fifty-two weeks in the year.

The democratic policies of conservation, education, and the socialization of consumption have one element in common, a tendency to promote equality of opportunity. The same element appears in the fourth social policy of the democracy; in the policy of extending the advantages of progress and democratization to all groups in society.

We may secure the life and health of the people. We may educate them and promote a wise and beneficent consumption of the fruits of the nation's labor. One question, however, remains. Who are to be the ultimate beneficiaries of all this progress? Who are to be admitted to,

[1] Professional men, not on salary, rarely care for fixed holidays, because to so large an extent they are masters of their own time and choose their own holidays. Workmen may not miss a day (without leave) and may not be late a minute.

and who are to be debarred from, the new civilization which is preparing?

It would be an easy problem for democracy if, as standards rose, the whole of the people would rise with them. Under such conditions progress would be uninterrupted, equal, easy. Unfortunately, however, society bears with it always the burden of the submerged. The ignorant, incompetent, vicious, weak, the feeble-minded and feeble-willed we have always with us. We drag behind us the chain and ball of the ruthlessness of the past. The democracy, even when successful against the pretensions of privilege, finds itself opposed to the obstruction and dead weight of the nether world.

There is a current theory that this nether world, left to itself, will destroy itself, and that in this destruction lies the salvation of the democracy. This theory, which is based on an assumed analogy between biological and social phenomena, asserts that progress, even under a democracy, can come only through a perpetual, rigorous weeding out of the unfit. Those who fall into crime, prostitution, and misery, those who fail to meet the standards set by the democratic majority, must die as the unfit have died for tens of thousands of centuries. Workhouses, jails, slums, hunger, disease, must be allowed to do their work.

If all the unfitness in society were due to heredity and none of it were due to social arrangements, if it were possible painlessly to remove at each generation all who were *indubitably* unfit to survive and all who were *indubitably* unfit to propagate, we might perhaps resign ourselves to this recurring excision of the submerged. But all this is not possible. We are not sure even of our own standards of fitness. As we look over history, we see that men with certain instincts and capacities are regarded as noxious in one generation and as social saviors in a second. There are, it is true, extreme cases in which we may act. We need not suffer the indiscriminate breeding of our hundreds of thousands of feeble-minded, nor of others with assured and ineradicable hereditary taints. But with our present knowledge we cannot go far in this direction. We can no more trust ourselves with any absolute dominion over life and death than we could trust the medieval scribes with the preservation of classical literature. That way lies too dead a uniformity, too brutal a tyranny of the present over the future. We dare not be overrash in the extermination of human types which deviate from an approved norm. We must preserve our hereditary heretics.

No such annihilation of the dwellers of the nether world ever really takes place. The submerged social classes do not die, but merely become sick. And in their sickness they avenge themselves upon society, much as certain Orientals are supposed to do, by committing suicide on their oppressor's doorstep. The girl forced into prostitution through society's carelessness is not without her revenge upon society. The boy who becomes a criminal, when with a little social wisdom he might have been a useful citizen, does not bear his burden alone. From the nether world spreads the virus of physical and moral contagion; and every immorality, bred of weakness, finds its ultimate victims both above and below the poverty line.

The nether world does not die of mere social neglect, but, on the contrary, grows upon it. Although the mortality of the submerged is excessive, the nether world reacts violently with a birth rate so high and desperate as to fill the gutters with hopeless children. Moreover the nether world grows by accretion. Democracy rests upon a multitude of restraints and inhibitions. The slum attacks these restraints and inhibitions. It furnishes company to those who are tempted to fall. The sight of the slum, the example of it, the direct teaching of it, draw ever new recruits. The slum becomes a rallying ground and an alternative to those who are hesitating on the verge of democratic duties.

As the tolerated nether world grows through immigration from above, so also it grows through a continual shifting of the social boundary between it and the classes above. The attitude of mind which concurs in a division of human kind into the terrestrially saved and the terrestrially damned cannot but permit a similar division among the men above the slum. New sections of the community are left to themselves to work out their own destruction. The slum, increasing in size, increases its power of mischief. In a democracy in which it does not share, as in a plutocracy, the slum remains cynically corrupt. In the divisions which will arise in the differentiated democracy of to-morrow, the venal slum — if it survives — may well hold the balance of power. As to-day, so to-morrow, the slum may share in ruling.

The problems and possibilities of the democracy in its relation to the nether world are not unlike the problems and possibilities of the trade-union in its relation to men incapable of earning union wages. As the labor organization raises the standard of remuneration of its members, the pressure upon workingmen unable to secure employment at these wages increases, with a resulting deep embitterment. So long as the labor organization includes a majority of the more efficient men in the trade, it is able to profit by its victories. If, however, there grows up outside too large or too strong a body of non-unionists; if the union, instead of striving to become a majority, is content to remain a minority, a mere closed corporation resisting infiltration from below,—then the balance of power is likely to change. The rejected non-unionists may overrun the trade. The standards, so hardly won, may be abandoned. The union, defeated and brushed aside, may crumble and disintegrate.

Like the union, the democracy must combat, with all the forces in its control, the growth of a disaffected group below its level. It must struggle, not only against the oligarchical few at the top, but against the creation of an anti-democratic helotry at the bottom. Like the union, it cannot afford to increase its numbers by lowering its standards, but through education, through social betterment, and through an active and persistent propaganda it must raise so many (if not all) of the submerged to its level as to render its own destruction impossible. Like the trade-union, the democracy must always be open at the bottom.

The democracy is thus compelled to cure the slum to prevent its own destruction by the slum. Its instinct to live as well as its justice and clemency impel the democracy to this course. No democracy can be achieved, and no democracy, once achieved, can be maintained, except as the dead weight of the masses below the democratic levels is progressively lightened.

The policy of the democracy towards the submerged divides itself into three parts: first, the redemption of men who have fallen below the democratic levels; second, the utmost possible prevention of social failures, not by ending social contests, but by improving the contestants; third, the provision of a reasonably satisfactory situation for incorrigibles, and their effective isolation from the rest of society.

This program of the democracy, which is the old program of human conservation upon a new level, is so wide-reaching that it is impossible to give within a small scope even the vaguest outlines of its main features. What we are chiefly seeking to do is to shut off all the channels which lead to the under world, to cure the slum at its hundreds of sources.

Everywhere progress along these lines, though obstructed, is evident. Although the first juvenile court in the United

States was not established until 1899, the whole attitude of the nation towards the delinquent child has already been revolutionized, and the young boy who formerly would have been transformed into a criminal is now treated in many courts with tender solicitude and a far-seeing social wisdom. Our whole social attitude towards children, towards child labor, truancy, the neglect of children, is being changed. We are beginning to see that bad teeth in children, neglected adenoids, or starved little bodies may result in hundreds of thousands of social wrecks, and we are slowly bringing ourselves to face the stupendous problem involved in the neglected presence in our midst of blind, crippled, feeble-minded, and defective children. The democracy is reaching out into the home, and the parental tyranny of former days is giving way to an enforced parental responsibility, based upon the inalienable and indestructible rights of the child. A hundred years ago, a father might with impunity beat, starve, or slowly kill his child, for a man could do what he wished with his own. To-day not only do we protect the child from the cruder forms of physical violence, but we enter into degraded homes to save the child from underfeeding, physical or moral infection, and exposure to evil influences of all kinds. Where parents are too ignorant, too drunken, too immoral, or too dispirited to prevent their children from becoming a prey of the criminal slum, the State intervenes. A California law goes so far as to provide "that the expense of maintaining their own children may be allowed to parents out of the public funds at the discretion of the court, within the limits fixed by the law.[1]

As the child is being saved from contamination, so on another plane the young girl is being protected from the

[1] Breckinridge (Sophonisba P.), "The Community and the Child," *The Survey*, February 4, 1911, referring to the McCartney juvenile court law, Section 21.

most debasing influences of our modern life. Gradually, though far too slowly, laws are being passed regulating the hours of labor of women,[1] forbidding night work and prohibiting the employment of women in certain dangerous and noxious trades. The magnificent upbuilding work of the Women's Trade Union League, which seeks to represent all the interests of all women employed in industry, is a force of tremendous moment in our struggle for democracy, and the analogous work of protecting and guiding immigrant girls tends in the same direction. Numerous institutions and societies arise for the purveying of amusement and recreation both to children and young folks, on the principle that all work and no play makes Jack not only a dull, but a vicious boy.

The full brunt of the democratic campaign against the growth of an under world thus lies, not so much in the uplift of those who have fallen, as in the provision of conditions which prevent falling. "The new penology," says Dr. Edward T. Devine, "concerns itself less with what is done in penal and reformatory institutions and in courts — radical as are the changes which it would introduce there — than with agencies for prevention. Crime in the last analysis is not to be overcome after arrest, but before. Schools, churches, playgrounds, settlements, trade-unions, and charitable societies — agencies of social progress and of social reform, public and private — are the handmaidens of the new penology. We shall transform police, courts, and prisons when we have further transformed society, and the forces which help to raise and give stability and vitality to our standards of living and our standards of action are the forces to which in the end the bad features and the obsolete features of the existing penal system will yield. The environment is transformed by child labor laws

[1] See the laws of Massachusetts, New Jersey, Wisconsin, Illinois, Missouri, and other States.

and the protection of children, by housing laws and improved sanitation, by the prevention of tuberculosis and other diseases, by health-giving recreational facilities, by security of employment, by insurance against the fatalities of industry and the financial burdens of death and disease, by suitable vocational training, by all that adds to the content of human life and gives us higher and keener motives to self-control, strenuous exertion, and thrift. The stronghold of crime is social misery. The cure for misery is better adjustment of social elements to one another and to the infinite possibilities of the environment." [1]

The mere existence of a phrase like the "new penology" shows the changed spirit with which the rising democracy faces the submerged masses. We are still shamed by bad prisons, evil laws, and an absurdly inadequate criminal procedure. But we are slowly passing out of the old retaliatory attitude towards offenders. We are laying emphasis upon sane discipline, physical exercise, and the instruction and healthy employment of prisoners. We are attacking fixed sentences, solitary confinement, and inefficient inspection of jails, and we are beginning to look upon the prison almost as an adjunct to the school. "The new penology," to quote Dr. Devine once more, "is not sentimental. . . . At least in its present transitional stage, the average term of restraint which it imposes is considerably longer than in the penal system which it displaces. It sentences, however, to a hospital by preference rather than to a dungeon. It sentences to cleanliness, good food, and wholesome discipline, and not to infection and degradation." [2] In the same way the clean, sanitary municipal lodging house of today, with its decent food and its enforced compensatory work, begins to take the place of the vermin-infected tramp lockup, in the congenial vileness of which hardened crim-

[1] "The Correction and Prevention of Crime," *The Survey*, January 21, 1911. [2] *Op. cit.*

inals instruct the ingenuous, occasionally unemployed, boy.

Fundamentally the new attitude of the democracy towards the criminal and potentially criminal classes is one which is dictated by wisdom and a growing sense of social responsibility. To make outcasts of those who have once broken the law is to increase the number of society's enemies. Individual responsibility, it is true, cannot be done away with, but in the time to come the culpable individual will be allowed to plead the contributory negligence of society. For every wayward man and woman, society must be called to the bar. In other words, society must prevent crime by promoting education and happiness, or must accept the underlying responsibility for its default. It must not "punish" the criminal or hunt him forever within society, but must offer to him a life which, though dependent and below that of the rest of the population, is at least secure, reasonably eligible, and with as little constraint as is consistent with the safety of society and the education of the criminal. The democracy must not raise up enemies within its ranks.

What applies to the incapables and the criminals, applies with even greater force to special groups who are separated from the rest of the population and are hated or despised. In America we have a racial problem of more fearful portent than that of any of the nations of Europe. We are still paying the endless price of slavery. The South is psychologically cramped. The North is bewildered. The Negro problem is the mortal spot of the new democracy.

At the moment we are beset by the problem of Negro suffrage. It is being urged by a dominant school of thought that the immediate salvation of the Negro is less political than economic, and that his possession of money and education (above all of technical and industrial education) will eventually compel the grant to him of full political rights at a time when he can best avail himself of them. This non-resistant attitude is hotly repelled by another group, who declare that Negro acquiescence in Negro disenfranchisement is a denial of democracy, a surrender to race prejudice, and an obstacle in the path of the accumulation of money and education, which is the very alternative proposed to political rights. "If we have not the vote," they say, "we shall have neither education nor justice; if we have not the vote, our schools will be starved and our farms and our jobs will be lost."

Whatever the merits of this controversy as a matter of ethics or practical politics, it seems probable that the present democratic movement, uneasily recognizing this danger in its rear, will move forward, leaving the problem of Negro suffrage to one side. It is a sign of disillusionment. We look at the Negro vote in Philadelphia and Cincinnati, and wonder whether it is worth while to lay aside other problems to secure a Negro vote in Atlanta and Charleston. Thus it happens that men, animated by a spirit analogous to that which freed the slaves, are seeking to ignore the problem of Negro disenfranchisement. Even the Socialist party, which is a defender of desperate causes, seems to avoid the problem.

It is perhaps possible to evade this issue of Negro suffrage if we can satisfy ourselves that the vote is not immediately essential to Negro civilization; if we can honestly believe that the denial to the Negro of the vote is advantageous, not only to us, but to him.[1] We may not, however, presume to make the negro an "underman," to offer him a subhuman or a subcivilized life. For as he grows, the Negro, if he be not given, will take. Even as we advance,

[1] If, as is claimed, the ballot is, at present, really disadvantageous to the Negro, we need not give it to him merely to be logical. But we shall do well to beware of sophistries intended merely to give a justification to our disinclination or fear of raising the issue. The mouse can find many reasons, philanthropic and other, for not belling the cat.

hoping perhaps that the democracy won and wrought by the whites will descend as an easy heritage to the reënfranchised Negroes, we are oppressed by the dread of what may occur. There may arise a Negro consciousness, a dark sense of outraged racial dignity. There may come a stirring of a rebellious spirit among ten, or, as it soon will be, of twenty or thirty, million black folk. We cannot hope forever to sit quietly at the feast of life and let the black man serve. We cannot build upon an assumed superiority over these black men, who are humble to-day, but who to-morrow may be imperious, exigent, and proudly race-conscious.

Moreover, a grave (though perhaps not a near) danger lies in a failure to grapple with the race problem. The time may come when the plutocracy, hard driven by the rising tide of the new democracy, may attempt to save itself by raising anew the question of the Negro's position in industry and politics. The best antidote to democracy is jingoism and race hatred.[1] It is an appeal from higher and newer to lower and older instincts. It is an appeal which in America would open the dikes and let in the dark waters. The plutocracy, which has much to fear from a democratization of politics and industry, would have nothing to fear from any Negro suffrage which it itself champions; and it might have much to gain both from the votes and the labor of the grateful black men.

If it be attempted to repress the Negroes, to show them their place, we may encounter the possibility of an inconceivably savage race war. If white men and black men were ever to fight on the old plantations of the South we should have an awakening of brutalities such as no war of

[1] The ally of the reactionary is the "hereditary enemy." Once you can stir up race or national hatred, you have postponed your social development. If you can but hate a Spaniard or a Boer, you will for the time being cease to hate all public iniquity, however flaunting.

modern times has evoked. Even so trivial a thing as a prize fight between a Negro and a white man led recently to a disgusting subemotional debauch of tens of millions of us, and to a violent recrudescence of the lynching spirit. If there were ever a reign of terror throughout the Black Belt, if a few thousand white men and women were to be slaughtered by hordes of enraged Negroes, there would be a backwash of civilization, a recurrence of barbarism, which would reach to the furthermost hamlets of Maine and Oregon.

And yet, if the democracy in America is to be a white democracy, and the civilization in America is to be a white civilization; if it is proposed to make of the Negro a thing without rights, a permanent semiemancipated slave, a headless, strong-armed worker, then let the white civilization beware. We may sunder the races if we can; we may preserve a race integrity if we can; we may temporarily limit the Negro's suffrage. If, however, we abate the ultimate rights, prerogatives, and privileges of either race, if we seek permanently to set up lower standards for one race, we shall plant the seeds of our own undoing. Our self-protection, as much as our sense of justice, must impel us towards the increase in the Negro's ability, *morale*, and opportunity. Just as a diphtheritic Negro will infect a white man, just as the tubercle bacillus, oblivious of the color line, will go from the black man's home to the Aryan's, so weakness, immorality, ignorance, and recklessness will spread from one race to the other as a prairie fire spreads from farm to farm. Whether we love the Negro or hate him, we are, and shall continue to be, tied to him.

If to-day our ten million American Negroes resided, not in the United States, but in a contiguous territory, asking for admission into the Union, it is extremely improbable that the mass of white men would permit the annexation. We might very well feel that, however engaging many of the qualities of the Negroes are, and however much the present bitter racial antagonism may be allayed, it would be the part of folly to lay aside our own problems to take up new problems of racial adjustment. For the Negro's sake as well as for our own, we should prefer to stay apart.

A somewhat analogous problem is presented by our increasing immigration. Here it is not a problem of racial hatred so much as it is one of economic and social adjustment. We need not claim a superiority over the people who throng in at Ellis Island. We may concede their splendid qualities, and still advance proposals for the stemming of this human flood.

The policy of a restriction of immigration does not involve a disbelief in America's future. It does not base itself on the belief that the country is "full up." Under proper economic and social conditions, we could easily take care of two hundred, or even more, millions of people. The crux of the difficulty, however, is that a too speedy and unregulated immigration tends to prevent the very adjustments which would make the prosperity of the greater millions possible.

For many decades Americans have hesitated to lay an embargo upon this inspiring westward movement. It was our proudest boast — our highest ideal — that America was to be the haven of the world's oppressed. So long as we had free lands in the West, so long as each new immigrant added inevitably to the wealth of his neighbors, this ideal was rooted in the economic conditions. But in the course of time we deeded away the continent which was to have been the home of the oppressed, and, year by year, we found it more and more impossible to deflect the broader stream of immigration from the congested districts of our cities. To-day the ideal is in conflict with our economic and political conditions. Failing its economic root, the ideal has degenerated into a tradition.

In the next decade or two our intensifying struggle for democracy will render a further restriction of immigration imperative. The change will not be too violent, for our present residents will somehow smuggle in their nearest relatives, and there will always be openings in the gate. But when we illogically and brutally, though wisely, forbade the immigration of the Chinese, we made an unhealable breach in the rule of hospitality, and gave a precedent and a colorable pretext for future restrictions.

It is significant, to-day, that many of the people who are opposed to a practically unregulated immigration are the very ones who are seeking to promote the welfare of those immigrants who are already in. The policy of the democracy towards immigration is coming to be one of a checking of the rapidity of the flow, a selection of the best candidates for admission, and the quickest and most thorough possible preparation of the accepted immigrants for the duties of American citizenship. The danger to the American experiment in democracy of too near a contact with European poverty can hardly be overestimated. If, during the next fifty years, we receive thirty or even fifty millions of unsifted newcomers from Europe, we may find ourselves but little further advanced in democracy after that period than before. If, on the other hand, we so limit immigration that but five or ten millions enter — and if these five or ten millions be people especially selected for their adjustability to American conditions, we may so far advance in the task of improving the economic, political, and psychological development of the masses as to render inevitable the progressive attainment of the social goal of the democracy.

CHAPTER XX

CAN A DEMOCRACY ENDURE?

WHEN we review American history from the Declaration of Independence to these days, we find that we neither possess a socialized democracy, nor have we lost one. Neither in 1776 nor in 1789 did we have institutions, conditions, or habits of mind upon which such a socialized democracy could have been built. Our conquest of the Continent, though essential to national expansion, and even to national survival, did not aid such a democracy, except in so far as it provided for it an eventual material basis. On the contrary, the economic, political, and psychological developments inseparably connected with the struggle with the wilderness worked against the immediate attainment of a socialized democracy, and led to wild excesses of individualism, which in turn culminated in the growth of a powerful and intrenched plutocracy.

We are now beginning to realize that our present acute social unrest is not due to an attempt to return to the conditions and principles of the eighteenth century, but is merely a symptom of a painfully evolving democracy, at once industrial, political, and social. We are beginning to realize that our stumbling progress towards this democracy of to-morrow results from the efforts, not of a single class, but of the general community; that the movement is not primarily a class war, but, because it has behind it forces potentially so overwhelming, has rather the character of a national adjustment; that the movement does not proceed from an impoverished people, nor from the most impoverished among the people, nor from a people growing, or doomed to grow, continually poorer, but proceeds, on the contrary, from a population growing in wealth, intelligence, political power, and solidarity. We are awakening to the fact that this movement, because of the heterogeneous character of those who further it, is tentative, conciliatory, compromising, evolutionary, and legal, proceeding with a minimum of friction through a series of partial victories; that the movement is influenced and colored by American conditions and traditions, proceeding, with but few violent breaks, out of our previous industrial, political, and intellectual development and out of our material and moral accumulations, and utilizing, even while reforming and reconstituting, our economic and legal machinery. It is a movement dependent upon a large social surplus; a movement which grows in vigor, loses in bitterness, and otherwise takes its character from the growing fund of our national wealth, which gives it its motive and impetus. Finally, it is a movement which in the very course of its fulfillment develops broad and ever broadening industrial, political, and social programs, which aim at the ultimate maintenance of its results.

The question, however, remains, Can such a democracy endure? Are there in society forces making for the permanency of such a high democratic civilization, once attained?

We may well walk warily in this problem, since its consideration involves matters of which we cannot surely know. The telling of society's fortune — what one may call social astrology — results in a prophecy which is in part a reflex of the prophet's personality and is in part determined by what the credulous patron likes to hear. Even if we substitute for pure prophecy a reasoned social projection, —a mental carrying out of forces already at work, — we advance but little along the path of authority. Our data are too few. We are all — pessimists and optimists alike — but clamorous spectators before a curtain which is just rising. We see the feet, not the faces, of the actors, and we can guess only rudely at the play which is going on. What consideration we give to the problem must be accompanied by an admission that from any real knowledge of the future workings of democratic principles we are as far removed as are they whose opinions we repel.

There are many men, expurgated democrats, who, while they desire a certain extension of democracy, fear its complete rule more than they fear the rule of tyrant or dictator. They look into the face of the new monarch and are afraid. They listen to the prophetic flatteries of popular courtiers, who appeal to the most brutish instincts of the Demos. They call the rule of the millions, not a democracy, but an "ochlocracy." They expect from this rule, not civilization, but decivilization.

This fundamental dread of democracy lies in the supposed incurability of its errors. In every other form of government there is some sort of quasi-appeal from the minority to the residual right of revolution of the majority. But in a democracy there is no appeal from the majority. Only under a democracy can a nation commit suicide.

There is a certain lack of robustness in all these fears; a certain oversophistication of men who forget of what tough, resistant fiber our million-year-old race is made. We have survived worse evils than the worst with which we are now threatened, and we shall doubtless evade the "logically inevitable" results of democracy, as we have evaded the logically inevitable results of every other system of government and society. A democracy threatened with war, hunger, or national extermination would instinctively change under the stress. It would evolve vigilance committees, committees of public safety, temporary dictators, who, if the conditions demanded it, would become permanent. Democracy is not perpetual except in so far as it promotes race survival. It is an experiment, as fire and clothes and science and religion are experiments. It is our present hope that democracy has many centuries in which to develop, and that nothing but a dissipation of our material natural resources can produce the threatened decivilization. If, however, for any reason democracy becomes incompatible with progress and happiness, it will simply cease.

The supposed incompatibility of democracy with progress rests on the assumption that democracy means an intolerable "tyranny of the majority" over the minority, of the ignorant over the wise, of the careless over the prudent, of the mediocre over the men of genius and spirituality. It is feared that democracy would perpetuate ignorance, would worship an unnatural equality, would despise liberty and the development of individuality. This accusation has its basis in several concepts; firstly, that the ruling mass of society is and would continue to be ignorant, besotted with a sense of its knowledge, jealously hating men of larger intelligence, and hating to hear Aristides called the Just; secondly, that this mass holding the reins of power and ruling by its own ignorance, would have no reason to educate itself or to permit or reward education in others. In other words, having no intellectual class to act upon it, it would remain intellectually inert, an undrained, dismal bog of human ignorance.

These assumptions prove on analysis to be arbitrary. The sullen jealousy against intelligence found in certain sections of all populations seems due, in part at least, to an ignorance born of evil social conditions, and directed against men who have had better intellectual, because they have had better economic, opportunities. But the mass of Americans cannot by the wildest exaggeration be placed in this mental state, and the eyes of America, as of the world, are set towards a greater and more diffused education. The very lessening of pecuniary differences would inevitably set up competitions upon other planes, notably upon the plane of intellectual development. The more (though not necessarily the most) intelligent would inevitably exercise a dominating influence over the less intelligent. Then, as now, a relatively high degree of intelligence among millions of people would be necessary to the welfare, even to the very existence, of the community, and then, as now, even the ignorant voter would know when things went ill with him. Both the opportunities and the desires of men would spur them to greater efforts, so that a general intelligence of the whole community on a level with that of the more intelligent tenth of society to-day would be well within the range of possibility. The more intelligent could not rule except through the great mass, but the incentive and, above all, the opportunities of the mass would be greatly increased.

To-day a part of our educational initiative is due to social capillarity, to a desire to rise from one social or economic class to another. But such desires and such opportunities would also exist under a socialized democracy. No social organization has the remotest chance of establishment which is not based on the fullest recognition of the inherent inequalities of men, and of the infinitely wide range of human tastes, capacities, and aptitudes. What a socialized democracy demands is an equalization, not of men, but of opportunities, although by raising the status of the lowest, it reduces by comparison the material rewards of the successful. Its effect, however, should on the whole be an increase rather than a decrease in the competition for the superior positions. To-day, to employ a certain exaggeration, the son of a banker becomes a banker much as the Prince of Wales becomes king of England. The chance of a banker's son becoming a hodcarrier is only a little less than the chance of the hodcarrier's son becoming a banker. The competition for the superior position and the competition for the education which will qualify for the superior position are very much less in our wealth-stratified society of to-day than they would be in a socialized democracy, in which the fullest conceivable opportunities would be accorded to all. To use a loose illustration, the establishment of a socialized, differentiated democracy should have the same influence upon education and the struggle for a favored position as has the establishment of competitive civil service examinations for positions which formerly went by favor.

The fear of a destruction of human liberty seems equally unfounded. It is true that a democracy which did not have its basis in economic and social needs might possibly restrict liberty, for essentially unstable governments can only maintain themselves — and that only temporarily — by encroachments upon the rights of the citizens. If, however, we assume that a socialized democracy is the best form for attaining the material welfare of the majority, and if by liberty we mean the right to do things which one should have the right to do, then there is no reason why a socialized democracy should not mean an increase, rather than a decrease, in the sum total of liberty.

Much of our complaint about the restriction of liberty is an echo from the forest, a belated cry from the old pioneer period. It is true that many absurd laws restrictive of liberty are annually enacted. But a real need of restrictive legislation results from the greater density of our population and the increasing number of social liens and contacts. On the frontier addiction to a phonograph is a habit which may well be left to the individual and his conscience. In a membranous New York apartment house a man's unregulated right to indulge his musical tastes may run counter to his neighbor's equal right to sleep soundly of nights. The city, the factory, the trust, the huge fortune have given birth to a host of possible offenses which did not before exist. Moreover, as has already been pointed out, economic freedoms can often only be attained by legal prohibitions, and what is often interpreted as a limitation of freedom is in effect an increase of liberty, through the protection of some individuals from the hitherto permitted aggressions of others. Unfortunately, there are only two means of preserving the citizens' liberty — education and the policeman's club. The prohibition of employing children in factories, while it may in individual cases adversely affect a child or its parents, is so protective of the rights of children as a whole that it is as much an increase in the liberties of the citizens as is the prohibition of counterfeiting, wife beating, and highway robbery. Under a socialized democracy, we shall have an increase in the amount of education, in the number of legal inhibitions, and in the sum total of the liberties of the citizens.

All these arguments are adduced against democracy on the ground that it is too evil to survive. An equally inveterate argument is advanced that it is "too good to be true."

Seemingly illogical as is this argument, there is, nevertheless, a certain basis for it in our past experience. We have never had a Utopia, though we have often dreamed that we were on the verge of one. Mankind "never is, but always to be, blest." A perfect state of terrestrial bliss, a lying down together of the human lion and the human lamb, is as remote from our racial experience as is the collision of sun and moon.

The mortal defect of Utopias is that they are too static. The kingdom of heaven on earth is always a permanent, unchanging, perfect, and unutterably stupid place, than which our present society, with all its imperfections, is vastly superior. Utopias break down because they represent attainment, fulfillment. But society does not strive towards fulfillment, but only towards striving. It seeks not a goal, but a higher starting point from which to seek a goal.

Opposed to such Utopias our present ideal of a socialized democratic civilization is dynamic. It is not an idyllic state in which all men are good and wise and insufferably contented. It is not a state at all, but a mere direction.

Were we to move into a democratic, socialized civilization, where misery had become as unknown as witchcraft to-day; where the people, educated and in process of education, ruled in their own interest both in industry and politics; where the common wisdom of a nation was united to solve common problems and work out a common destiny, we should still be faced by problems new and old. We should carry into the new civilization the tenacious appetites of to-day. We should struggle along with human frailties, with a residual ignorance, perverseness, meanness of outlook, exaggerated egotism. With the raising of the standard of life we should awaken new appetites and stimulate present ones. Our racial hatreds, our inveterate race animosities, would give way but slowly, so that even in a society advanced in civilization, lynchings and other horrible reversions to barbarism might occasionally occur. We may not hug the illusion of an instantaneous change in the old clinging evils. Drunkenness, prostitution, and a whole series of vices which are but pathological social forms of normal human instincts will but slowly give way. "Virtue cannot so inoculate our old stock but we shall relish of it."

With all these evils we need not now concern ourselves. It will be a wonderful advance in society when our crimes and vices will be crimes and vices of prosperity instead of those of poverty. We may confidently face the new, unknown dangers of prosperity with the powers and knowledge which that prosperity will bring. For this century we need but take this century's forward step. If we can extirpate misery, that will be progress enough.

By the rigorous Malthusians, we are told that even this more moderate program is now and forevermore impossible. We are warned that a democracy which gives an assured income to all will stimulate our lax and thoughtless millions to so rash a procreation as to cause society to expand beyond the food supply necessary for its support.

Forty years ago this dreadful threat of human fecundity still lay like an incubus upon the souls of all social reformers. Malthus was the prophet. We saw the nations growing daily in population. France and Ireland were exceptions, but France was alleged to be decadent, and distressful Ireland was admittedly bleeding through emigration. But since the eighties the birth rate in one nation after another, England, Scotland, Wales, Germany, France, Italy, Belgium, Sweden, etc., has declined, and to-day we are spectators of a world-wide decrease in natality in almost all nations and in almost all sections of all nations. The more democratic and advanced nations seem on the whole those whose birth rate has most rapidly fallen. If the birth rate continues to decline (even though the decline in the death rate also continue), the danger of decivilization through overpopulation will be completely dissipated.

According to others the menace to democracy lies less in the fear of overpopulation than in that of depopulation. Numbers are an element (although only one element) of national power. Democracy, with its high national productiveness, may mean a capacity for sustaining larger populations, but the individual ambitions and the higher standards of living among a democratic population may result in an excessive and debilitating slackening of the rate of increase and in a lessened fighting capacity, which, until world-wide changes have worked themselves out, must remain the ultimate determinant between rival civilizations. It is conceivable that frugal, prolific, and undemocratic civilizations will become the most formidable. There may possibly come a time when a hundred million highly cultivated Americans may be threatened by half a billion well-armed, well-organized, prolific, and abstemious Celestials, as Gaul was threatened and at last overrun by the Franks, and Britain by the Saxons and Danes.

That this problem, like others, may some day arise to tax the resources and the wisdom of an American democracy cannot to-day be gainsaid. If democracy means a lessened population, and that in turn means a lessened capacity for defense, then in future generations we may well be forced to accommodate our further progress in democratic evolution to that which is made to other formidable nations. For the time being, however, the danger is too shadowy and hypothetical to justify any slackening of our progress towards a socialized democracy. We need not put on our armor for battles which our children must fight.

INDEX

T

U

V

W

www.ingramcontent.com/pod-product-compliance
Ingram Content Group UK Ltd.
Pitfield, Milton Keynes, MK11 3LW, UK
UKHW040856180926
475701UK00001B/18

* 9 7 8 0 7 6 5 8 0 8 3 5 6 *